Embedded Firmware Solutions

Development Best Practices for the Internet of Things

Jiming Sun
Marc Jones
Stefan Reinauer
Vincent Zimmer

Embedded Firmware Solutions: Development Best Practices for the Internet of Things

Jiming Sun, Marc Jones, Stefan Reinauer, and Vincent Zimmer

Copyright © 2015 by Apress Media, LLC, all rights reserved

ISBN-13 (pbk): 978-1-4842-0071-1

ISBN-13 (electronic): 978-1-4842-0070-4

Trademarked names, logos, and images may appear in this book. Rather than use a trademark symbol with every occurrence of a trademarked name, logo, or image we use the names, logos, and images only in an editorial fashion and to the benefit of the trademark owner, with no intention of infringement of the trademark.

The use in this publication of trade names, trademarks, service marks, and similar terms, even if they are not identified as such, is not to be taken as an expression of opinion as to whether or not they are subject to proprietary rights.

While the advice and information in this book are believed to be true and accurate at the date of publication, neither the authors nor the editors nor the publisher can accept any legal responsibility for any errors or omissions that may be made. The publisher makes no warranty, express or implied, with respect to the material contained herein.

Managing Director: Welmoed Spahr
Lead Editors: Steve Weiss (Apress); Stuart Douglas (Intel)
Coordinating Editor: Melissa Maldonado
Cover Designer: Anna Ishchenko

Distributed to the book trade worldwide by Springer Science+Business Media New York, 233 Spring Street, 6th Floor, New York, NY 10013. Phone 1-800-SPRINGER, fax (201) 348-4505, e-mail orders-ny@springer-sbm.com, or visit www.springeronline.com.

For information on translations, please e-mail rights@apress.com, or visit www.apress.com.

About ApressOpen

What Is ApressOpen?

- ApressOpen is an open access book program that publishes high-quality technical and business information.

- ApressOpen eBooks are available for global, free, noncommercial use.

- ApressOpen eBooks are available in PDF, ePub, and Mobi formats.

- The user-friendly ApressOpen free eBook license is presented on the copyright page of this book.

Contents at a Glance

Contents

About the Authors

Jiming Sun is a firmware and BIOS industry veteran who started to write RTOS kernel code (pSOS) for Bell Labs in 1986. After changing career paths from telecom to PC, he was involved in the early laptop PC evolution, and was among the first batch of firmware engineers to implement System Management Mode (SMM) code for 386SL in the early 1990s. After joining Intel in 1993, Jiming did early APM (Advanced Power Management) and ACPI (Advanced Configuration and Power Interface) implementation. Jiming is one of the creators of Tiano, which turned into UEFI, at Intel, and he is the major contributor of AMD's AGESA (AMD Generic and Encapsulated Software Architecture). Besides his experience with Intel, Bell Labs, and AMD, Jiming has also worked for Zenith Data Systems, HP (Compaq), Insyde Software, Dell, and Apple. Jiming recently grandfathered Intel Firmware Support Package (Intel FSP) and was instrumental in launching the product in October of 2010. Jiming has master's degrees in Electrical Engineering and Management of Science and Technology, and he has 19 granted and one pending US patents. He currently lives in the Bay Area of California with his wife and two sons.

Vincent Zimmer is a senior principal engineer in the Software and Services Group at Intel Corporation. With over 23 years' experience in embedded software development and design, Vincent holds more than 310 US patents and was awarded two Intel Achievement Awards for his development of firmware architecture and security. He has a Bachelor of Science in Electrical Engineering degree from Cornell University, Ithaca, New York, and a Master of Science in Computer Science degree from the University of Washington, Seattle.

Marc Jones is an accomplished firmware developer with over 18 years' experience in x86 embedded systems development. Marc has been a vital, active member of the coreboot community since 2007. As a lead firmware developer at Sage Electronic Engineering, his most recent focus has been on Intel FSP coreboot integration, Google Chromebook development, and AMD embedded APU solutions. Marc got started with coreboot as the lead developer and coreboot project liaison at AMD. As a senior software engineer, he developed coreboot source code for the AMD Barcelona Family10 processor, AMD Geode processor, and AMD CS5536 chipset. In addition, he contributed to the development of support for the AMD RS690 and SB600 chipsets along with reference mainboards. Prior to coreboot, Marc was one of the primary architects of the AMD GeodeROM BIOS, the basis of most Geode systems. He has also developed firmware and BIOS for Cyrix and National Semiconductor. Marc has been a proponent of open source development for years and has written papers and blog posts that spotlight its merits. He has presented coreboot at the Southern California Linux Expo (SCaLE) 2013, 2012, 2010, the Free Software Foundation (FSF) Libre Planet 2009, the 2008 High Performance Computer Science Week Conference, and the 2007 Ottawa Linux Symposium. For the past five years, Marc has been the coreboot administrator and a mentor for Google Summer of Code, which provides students summer internships with open source software projects.

Stefan Reinauer is a staff engineer/manager in the Chrome OS Group at Google Inc. He has been working on open source firmware solutions ever since he started the OpenBIOS project in 1997. Stefan joined the LinuxBIOS project in 1999, and worked on the first x64 port for LinuxBIOS back in 2003. In 2005, Stefan founded coresystems GmbH, the first company to ever provide commercial support and development around the coreboot project, working on ports to new chipsets and mainboards. In 2008, Stefan took over maintainership of the LinuxBIOS project and renamed it "coreboot". He was the original implementer of the project's ACPI and SMM implementations. Since 2010, Stefan is leading the coreboot efforts at Google and contributed significantly to what is the largest coreboot deployment in the history of the project. Stefan currently lives in the San Francisco Bay Area.

About the Technical Reviewers

Xiang (Maurice) Ma is an Intel software architect on IA firmware, BIOS, and bootloader. He has more than 15 years' extensive experience in the legacy BIOS, UEFI firmware, bootloader, and embedded OS development for various Intel IA platforms, including embedded systems and workstation/servers, focusing on the core architecture, silicon reference code design and prototyping, as well as platform enabling and porting. Xiang Ma now works in the Intel IOTG group on the Intel firmware and bootloader initiatives. He is the primary architect who defined the Intel FSP design specification and prototyped the initial Intel FSP solution on Intel Haswell and Bay Trail platforms. He holds a master's degree in Control Theory and Control Engineering from Huazhong University of Science & Technology in China.

Ravi Rangarajan is a firmware architect with 15 years' experience in a range of areas, from embedded systems to server firmware development. He has a bachelor's degree in electronics and a master's degree in computer applications. He is currently working for the Intel Corporation. Ravi's interests include computer architecture, firmware, and operating systems.

Ravi was one of the original authors of the FSP Architecture Specification and was part of the team that prototyped, designed, and developed the Intel Firmware Support Package. His involvement continues in the evolution of the Intel FSP.

Edward Roache graduated from Dublin City University in 1993 with a B. Eng in Electronic Engineering. He has been working with BIOS for 15 years. He joined Stratus Technologies, Inc. in 1999 and worked on BIOS for their ftServer Fault-Tolerant servers. From 2006, he worked for Ircona providing BIOS services for companies such as Fujitsu-Siemens and NettApp. He joined Intel in 2011 as the BIOS technical lead for Quark X1000. He lives with his wife, Ann, and their son, Darragh. He's a keen GAA follower and helps coaching of the underage teams in Ratoath, Co. Meath where he lives.

Kangkang Shen is the chief architect for BIOS in Huawei. As a BIOS industry veteran, he has experienced the development of the PC industry since its early days. After joining Award software in 1993, he became one of the key developers for BIOS boot manager, PCI BIOS, and many other key BIOS features. In 1998, he joined Phoenix Technologies as engineering manager and director responsible for Phoenix and Award BIOS kernels. In 2003, he was assigned to lead the Phoenix R&D center in China. In 2006, he cofounded Nanjing Byosoft, an Intel-authorized BIOS vendor. In addition to his industry experience, he worked in Nanjing University of Technology as a professor from 2008-2011. He has a Bachelor's of Science in Optical Engineering from Zhejiang University, China and a Ph. D. from Georgia Institute of Technology, Atlanta.

Acknowledgments

We thank our families first for their support of us in writing this book. Since all of us have a demanding job to focus on during the day, we frequently spent our precious family time, evenings, weekends, and holidays, writing this book. Without our families' support, this book would not be possible.

We accepted the challenge of a tight publishing schedule because, like everything else in the high-tech world, the contents are actually "perishable". We had just about enough time to catch up with the latest development in the space; as soon as we thought we were done, we found areas that needed to be updated. This book is useful only if we can make it accurate and up-to-date so that developers can benefit from the information in this book. Thankfully, we have many high-caliber reviewers and alpha book readers to help us to correct the information in the book.

Without a particular order and with no implication of the importance of their contributions to the book, these people include:

- Aaron Durbin

- Edward Roache

- Maurice Ma

- Ravi P Rangarajan

- Martin Roth

- Kangkang Shen

- Bob Hart

- Ron Minnich

We thank you for your efforts in making this book useful to many more people like you.

Foreword

By Ron Minnich
Creator of LinuxBIOS (later renamed coreboot)
Software Engineer at Google, Inc.

I started the coreboot project at Los Alamos National Lab in 1999. At the time, it was seen by hardware vendors as an impractical idea that would soon vanish. Now, 15 years later, it is mainstream: millions of x86- and ARM-based Chromebooks and Chromeboxes run coreboot, as its speed and reliability are an essential part of the Chrome OS user experience. coreboot is now a key component of the fastest-growing consumer laptop segment.

It might come as a surprise to embedded programmers that the initial goal of coreboot was to make very large supercomputing clusters manageable. We had a 128-node VA Linux cluster at Los Alamos in 1999 that had no keyboards or displays. BIOS upgrades required that we wheel around a "crash cart" with a keyboard and monitor; boot DOS on a floppy, which in turn started an autoexec.bat script; and wait 5 to 10 minutes for the process to complete for each node. If anything went wrong, it got more fun: we had to crack open the case, move a jumper, and do the recovery with no working graphics. As if this were not bad enough, the vendor BIOS had a habit of coming up displaying "No keyboard present—hit F1 to continue" on a nonexistent monitor, asking us to hit F1 on a keyboard that it had already discovered was not there!

Could this possibly get any worse? It could, and did, on the Thunderbird cluster at Sandia National Labs: 4400 nodes, none having a keyboard or a monitor, came up one day with that same vendor BIOS message. The fix? Dispatch 20 people with 20 keyboards to 220 machines each; they had to plug in the keyboard, hit F1, and hope it all went well.

By 2002, we had a 1024-node Linux cluster using coreboot. The reflash process for all 1024 nodes took 30 seconds total, not five days. If something went wrong, coreboot would figure it out on the next boot, switch to a backup BIOS image, and boot up: the nodes could not be put into an unrecoverable state. There was no longer a need to open the nodes and move a jumper. coreboot represented a huge jump in the manageability of cluster nodes.

coreboot has had many uses since its inception: everything from the smallest systems (Apache Military Modem II) to some of the largest supercomputers. While there is wide adoption in Chrome OS systems, coreboot's earliest and continuing use is in embedded systems such as televisions, network switches, and robotic systems. In fact, about the same time we deployed a supercomputer using coreboot, iRobot had ported coreboot to its Packbot robot.

Embedded systems used to be very simple: a low-power CPU connected to low-performance memory and peripherals, used in low-performance and limited applications such as digital clocks and automobile computers. But in the last ten years, we can see low-power embedded CPUs used in unexpected places. The highest-end systems—such as IBM Blue Gene supercomputers, which were the fastest in the world for many years—used 65,536 embedded PowerPC CPUs with 18 cores each. We now see higher-power CPUs used in small embedded systems such as Chromebox videoconferencing systems—an inexpensive system with a very powerful Intel CPU.

These embedded Intel CPUs have memory bandwidth much higher than classic Cray vector supercomputers and hence are fiendishly complex to design. Once designed, this high-performance hardware is quite difficult to initialize, and even should we wish to write the code to manage the initialization, the programming information is not public.

This has led to a dilemma: How can we enable coreboot on complex systems that are not fully open?

This book shows one path. Intel has released in binary form a basic set of functions to initialize the messiest—and hardest to program—bits of the Intel chipset. The calling conventions and behavior of the binary are completely and clearly documented. The developer is freed from having to deal with very difficult chipset setup. Upgrades of this software are simple: just replace the old binary with a new one. This code is called the Firmware Support Package, a.k.a. FSP.

The result is that high-performance Intel chipsets can be used with coreboot in all kinds of systems, including embedded ones, with a binary supplied by Intel that removes much of the porting difficulty.

Wearable embedded systems are a growing area right now, and many use the CPU described in this book. This book is an ideal companion for those wishing to be current with current and future embedded technology.

coreboot has succeeded because of the efforts of the many talented people involved in the project for the last 15 years. The reader is fortunate that this book is written by four of the best minds in the business. There is a lot to learn here and it will stand you in good stead if you continue to work in embedded systems.

I'd like to thank Jiming Sun and the team for conceiving FSP and bringing it to fruition. Without their tireless efforts and diplomacy, we would not have FSP or this book.

Introduction

We consider ourselves lucky enough to live in an era when new things and new ideas seem to come out every few years, if not every few days. We are not only experiencing an explosion of new ideas, but also witnessing some existing technologies being completely maxed out in our lifetime, including the semiconductor technology. Since Brattain and H. R. Moore made a demonstration of the first transistor at Bell Labs on December 23, 1947, the semiconductor, as we know it today, is reaching its physical limit, even though we are still trying very hard to shrink it below 10 nanometers. For the sake of argument, even if we can still shrink a couple of nanometers below 10 nanometers, how much further can we really go without changing the fundamental theory the technology is based on?

In the meantime, there are many other technologies that are approaching the limits of our sense and sensibility. Do we need more than 12 bits of color depth that shows more than billions of colors? Do we need a frame rate that is beyond what our eyes and brain can process? Do we need cars that go faster than our own response time? We now have display devices, media playback technologies, and transportation vehicles that achieve the best that they need to be.

Even though that is the case, there are still unlimited opportunities to make devices smarter and more connected to make our lives easier and safer. People are calling these devices the Internet of Things, or IoT for short. The explosive cycle of the IoT has just begun: cars will be talking to cars in the near future, thermostats and sprinkler systems can adjust themselves based on current weather forecast, buildings can manage lighting and air circulation based on where people are, and the list goes on and on.

Yes, this book is related to the explosion of the Internet of Things. We are addressing a technical area that is rarely talked about—the firmware inside of the Internet of Things. Firmware is the first piece of software that runs after silicon, coming out from the power-on reset state. Sometimes it is mysterious to people why building a firmware stack is hard and why firmware can be problematic. Considering the fact that the time it takes to run a piece of firmware is only between subseconds to a few minutes at most, why are we writing a book about it? After all, there are already books that talk about BIOS, UEFI (beyond BIOS), and techniques to optimize the firmware to boot faster. Why do we need yet another book to talk about firmware for the Internet of Things and the embedded system in general? There is one important reason: the firmware for IoT is different from the firmware running on a PC (BIOS or UEFI-based firmware), and there are many unique requirements for IoT firmware, and we will talk about them in the second chapter of this book.

This is what this book is about. We are going to examine the uniqueness of firmware requirements in embedded systems and IoT devices, and then we are going to introduce the technique Intel introduced to help IoT system firmware developers overcome the steep learning curve in developing a firmware stack for their versatile IoT products.

In this book, we are going to use two open source firmware stacks—coreboot and UEFI—to demonstrate the concept and show the steps to develop a workable firmware stack using widely available platforms from Intel. We are also going to show how the firmware works in a Chromebook, and what it does in a Chromebook, and we will also discuss the firmware for Intel® Quark family.

The targeted audience for this book are firmware engineers, hardware engineers, software engineers, and other professionals curious about IoT firmware. This is a good book for students who are learning about firmware, because we are going to give step-by-step instructions about how to build a workable firmware stack using commercially available platforms. For developers who have been involved in PC firmware, this can be a good reference book to understand the differences between PC and IoT, and the alternative solutions available. For people who have been struggling with Intel® Architecture (IA) and its firmware stack due to a lack of technical information from Intel in the past, this book reveals an opportunity for you to quickly get over the silicon initialization hump, and you will be able to quickly develop an effective firmware stack using the techniques learned from this book.

This book uses a lot of pages to describe the Intel® Firmware Support Package (Intel FSP) because it is a way to encapsulate the complexity of silicon initialization to make firmware development work easier. Since its launch in October, 2012, many developers and designers of alternative architectures have benefited from this product.

Why Should You Read this Book?

There are not many books out there talking about firmware because it is not a standard discipline that can be talked about generically. Every subject in the realm of firmware can be a book of its own, and there have been books about UEFI, BIOS, Fast Boot, RTOS, assembly languages, and so forth. There are also many system requirements and constraints that can dictate how a firmware is chosen and written; therefore, it is a topic that cannot be easily addressed holistically without an objective. Our objective is to show you how you can take advantage of Intel Architecture, and how to prepare a firmware stack for Intel microprocessors regardless of the firmware stack that you choose. There will be areas that are not covered in this book, such as power management and secure boot features, but readers can certainly find in-depth discussion of those topics in other technical books in the market. This book is written to help you build a workable firmware stack for Intel Architecture.

What Chapters Should You Read?

Since there are many interesting but distinctly different topics surrounding IoT device firmware, busy readers can pick and choose the chapters to read and skip if needed.

If you are just curious about what firmware options you may have for IoT devices, you may read Chapters 1 and 2 before diving too deeply into actual implementations.

If you are interested in developing a coreboot-based firmware solution for Intel Architecture, you can get a complete picture of the process by reading Chapters 1, 3, and 4.

If you are more interested in developing an EDK II–based firmware solution for Intel Architecture, you can get a complete picture of the process by reading Chapters 1, 3, and 6.

If you are more curious about what Chromebook is about and how the firmware for Chromebook works, you can read Chapters 1, 3, 4, and 5.

If you have heard about Quark and you are interested in building firmware for Quark, you can read Chapters 1, 2, 3, 4, 6, and 7. Why do you need to read more chapters for Quark? It is not because it is complicated, it is because it can be used in many varieties of applications using different firmware stacks. If you want a complete picture about firmware solutions for embedded applications and IoT devices, you should take your time and read all of the chapters in this book. After all, this is the purpose of the book: to give you a complete picture of the firmware solutions for IoT devices.

Hobbyists should be able to obtain a platform mentioned in the chapters, follow the instructions to download the source trees and tools, build a firmware image to try on a real platform, and enjoy the accomplishments.

Every firmware stack has its advantages and disadvantages; there will be situations when a developer needs to pick a different and unfamiliar firmware stack for the applications at hand. From time to time throughout the book, you might find some unfamiliar terminologies. We will list them here for reference. If you are still puzzled by a specific terminology, Wikipedia is probably the best resource to check. Internet search engines may be the second best source, but careful filtering of information is needed.

- *Bootloader*: This term might be confusing from time to time. In coreboot, bootloader is identified as the payload, which loads the OS, but in some cases, bootloader is used to represent the code from the reset vector to the hand-off point to an OS. The definition changes based on context. Also, this term is mostly used outside of the Intel Architecture (x86) world, where hardware initialization is not as complicated. In this book, we will not use bootloader to represent the complete firmware stack. When you see this term in this book or outside this book, you need to read the context to see which part of the firmware stack it is referring to.

- *Firmware stack*: In this book, we use the term to represent all the components in a firmware solution; there might be phases in the boot process of a firmware solution, but the term firmware stack will cover them all. We will also refer the firmware stack used to integrate Intel FSP as the "host firmware".

- *PI and UEFI*: Platform Initialization and Unified Extensible Firmware Interface. These are two major standards governed by the UEFI Forum. People are frequently using UEFI to represent the modern firmware stack that boots 64-bit OS in a PC. "UEFI BIOS" is frequently used to represent the firmware stack developed based on UEFI and PI specifications. PI specifications is a set of specifications that focuses on platform and silicon initialization.

- *BIOS*: Basic Input/Output Systems. This is a term that is used "conveniently" to represent the firmware stack of a PC, even though it is no longer the same 16-bit hardware abstraction layer to interface with a 16-bit OS. Today, as a habit, people are still using this term to call the firmware stack of a PC, even though the firmware stack has become more powerful, more dynamic, and has more features. You will see "legacy BIOS" and "UEFI BIOS" terms in the book when we describe the implementations of PC firmware stacks today. Some companies might still use "BIOS" in the names of their products, but the purpose is to associate their products to a more familiar terminology so that PC developers understand the products better.

- *FSP*: Firmware Support Package. Intel FSP is the silicon initialization module that Intel produces to encapsulate basic silicon initialization code.

- *Microprocessors, CPU (Central Processing Unit), chips*: These three terminologies are used interchangeably to represent the silicon that does more of the general computing and control tasks.

- *I/O*: Input and output.

- *SoC, SOC, SIP*: Silicon-on-Chip, Silicon-in-Package. This represents silicon designed to include more than one component on a die or in a package; typically these components are CPU cores, northbridge(s), I/O components, and other glue logic. From the outside, they function as an integral unit.

- *Southbridge, northbridge, and companion chips*: Today's SoC still contains components that we used to call *northbridge* and *southbridge* for two distinct functions that used be on different sides of a front-side bus (or a high-speed point-to-point bus) that connects all the components internal to the chip. Even though internal buses have evolved in modern SoC designs, the names northbridge and southbridge remain in many code bases to represent the functions that used to be there: northbridge deals with CPU, memory controllers, and other related features, and southbridge deals with I/O–related features.

Obviously, this book cannot cover all of the peripheral knowledge that you might be interested in. Here are online resources and links for further reading and research:

- http://www.intel.com/fsp

- http://www.tianocore.org

- http://www.uefi.org

- http://www.coreboot.org

CHAPTER 1

Introduction

If you can fix a hardware bug in firmware, it's not a bug but a documentation issue.

—An anonymous hardware manager

What Is Embedded Firmware?

Since you are reading this book, you must have some understanding of what the words *embedded* and *firmware* mean in the context of computer technology. There are quite a few interesting discussions on the Web about the difference between firmware engineers and embedded engineers. Some say that an embedded engineer is a software engineer turning into a hardware engineer, and a firmware engineer is a hardware engineer turning into a software engineer. There is some truth to this because most firmware engineers learned how to design circuits in school, but there are definitely a lot of smart firmware engineers out there with a computer science or nonhardware degree. Regardless, writing firmware is a unique skill that deals with both hardware and software at the same time. You need to know something about signal strength, timing, voltage, and at the same time, data structure, algorithm, and modularity.

For the purposes covered in this book, let's define *firmware* as the layer of software between the hardware and the operating system (OS), with the main purpose to initialize and abstract enough hardware so that the operating systems and their drivers can further configure the hardware to its full functionality. To make embedded systems run faster and be more robust, the relationship between the firmware and the OS is transitioning from isolating themselves from each other to cooperating with each other. In the past, you might have seen the same hardware initialized by the firmware first, and then initialized again by a driver in the OSas shown in Figure 1-1; but in modern systems, you see more effort in trying to eliminate redundancy between the firmware and the OS.

1

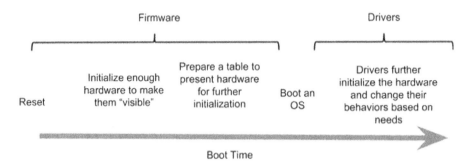

Figure 1-1. *The roles of firmware and device drivers during the boot process*

Hardware design is also moving toward being more "software friendly" so that hardware takes less effort to program. Self-initializing chips and a built-in boot ROM are just two examples currently available in System-on-Chip (SoC). Due to the evolution toward software friendliness, the heavy-duty hardware initialization responsibility has been gradually shifted from the firmware to the drivers of the operating systems, and the operating systems are relying less and less on firmware to carry out the hardware initialization work. Some real-time operating systems (RTOS) and specialized operating systems, such as Android and Chrome OS, are carrying out a lot of hardware initialization functions with help from the hardware vendors. This is especially true when system designers compartmentalize their design to a set of standardized hardware components and constrain the hardware selection pool; in some cases, hardware configuration can be achieved with a GUI (graphical user interface) -based configuration tool instead of relying on rewriting programs in firmware or software.

The line between firmware and specialized operating systems is definitely blurring, if not disappearing completely. The very minimum things that firmware has to do in a well-coordinated environment are presenting a data structure of features that can be further processed by OS drivers, such as an ACPI (Advanced Configuration and Power Interface) table, and carrying out the tasks that can only be done more effectively by firmware, such as memory controller initialization. When a seamless cooperation between the firmware and the OS cannot be guaranteed, firmware still plays a significant role in the system to make sure all system features are utilized properly. Therefore, no matter what the design trend is, firmware remains a critical component in a system.

Let's face it: firmware does have a troublesome reputation in the x86 world. In the dawn of laptop computers, System Management Mode (SMM) was created to do many things behind the back of the OS. System Management Interrupt (SMI) was not only nonmaskable, but was also not controllable by the OS. Firmware would take its own initiative to blank the display to save power, put the system to sleep when no user activity was detected, slow down the clock when running on the battery, take care of battery warnings when they happened, and react to Fn hot keys when they are pressed. These functions were not coordinated with the OS, and they just happened, seemingly at random. Obviously, none of these are bad features, but the amount of time it took to go through the process, and the adverse effects (missing timer ticks, long latency in interrupt delivery, etc.) on the OS were too much for the OS to ignore. Therefore, ACPI was created to allow the OS and firmware to coordinate and cooperate on these features. The utilization of SMM has been gradually reduced over the years. In addition to some SMM firmware dealing with actions requested by ACPI and security features, chip vendors are the only entities still using SMM to work around chip issues when necessary.

Where Is Firmware?

Firmware is generally considered part of the hardware (rather than part of the software) because it resides inside a hardware component, which is typically a Flash storage device or ROM. However, when it comes to the programming language, the tools, and the methodology a firmware engineer follows, firmware is clearly a type of software, even though it is tightly coupled with hardware in most cases.

What Do Firmware Engineers Do?

Regardless of whether firmware engineers are hardware engineers turning into software engineers, or the other way around, firmware engineers have a lot of interesting work to do. One of the most important and challenging jobs that a firmware engineer does is to make a new circuit board work when it is first manufactured, especially when most components on the new board are also new. It is not a unique case to have many new components on a brand-new circuit board because most hardware evolves in similar cycles. In chip manufacturing companies, some firmware engineers' only job is to bring up and test a new chip on a new board. The combination of a new chip, new components, and a new board not only makes debugging work much more complicated, but also makes the preparation work much more challenging.

When a firmware engineer prepares for the bring-up of a new board, he or she does not just wait for the hardware to show up, and then write the code; he or she needs to read a lot of early specifications, such as datasheets, a couple of months before the new board shows up. Since these specifications are mostly evolving, the information may not be 100 percent correct. Firmware engineers need to help correct the information in datasheets and write programming guides as they go through the debug process. In a typical hardware-oriented company, firmware needs to be ready when the first circuit board shows up. It is not acceptable for hardware to wait for firmware because hardware is usually more difficult and more expensive to alter than firmware. Manufacturers want hardware bugs to be discovered and fixed as early as possible. In the beginning, firmware only needs to have enough functions to test the circuit board to determine if the new components can be manufactured, but it is a lot of hard work to do it right the first time.

Firmware Preparation for New Hardware

During the preparation, firmware engineers need to figure out what to program, how to program, and the sequence in programming the new components after they study the materials available to them. The obvious challenge after writing the program for the new components is to figure out how to test the new code before the new hardware shows up at the door of their lab. Many manufacturers have simulators designed to test early firmware and software, such as Intel's Simics and AMD's SimNow, but the usefulness of a simulator depends on the behavioral models written to simulate the hardware. The accuracy and fidelity of the models in the simulation tool decide whether or not you can find bugs and programming errors in your early firmware.

Besides simulators, FPGA-based emulators are also frequently used to test early firmware and the circuitry inside a new chip. Compared to simulators, FPGA-based emulators are much more accurate in representing the final hardware, but since they are running in a much slower clock speed, timing-related issues may not be discovered easily, and firmware is sometimes modified to accommodate the slower clock speed; therefore, some parts of firmware are not well tested. In most cases, based on our experience, these simulators and emulators actually deliver pretty solid results, and the simulated and emulated firmware usually works when it is put on the real hardware for the first time they integrate. Even with the help of simulators, it typically takes a couple of days, weeks, or even months of effort to iron out all the hardware issues.

The Mystery of Bits

In the process of preparing a bring-up firmware, a firmware engineer spends a lot of time figuring out what needs to be programmed into the microprocessor and chipset by studying datasheets and specifications. In this case, literally, every bit matters. Even though many bits will work in their default states, a single mistake in misinterpreting the definition of a bit in a chip can turn the circuit board into a brick, and there are many bits to be programmed from their default states in order to work properly.

A datasheet is like the Bible for firmware engineers (see Figure 1-2); it has almost everything a firmware developer needs to know about the chip. Using a published datasheet from Intel as an example, the datasheet for Intel® Communications Chipset 89xx Series, published in October 2012, contains 1,682 pages of useful register data. The list of tables that are used to describe the registers span across 30 pages, with about 60 entries on each page.

Description:					
View: IA I	Win:Idx: APIC_WDW:APIC_IDX		Bus:Device:Function: B0:D31 :F0	Offset Start: 10h Offset End: 11h	
Size: 64 bits	Default: Bit 16 = 1. All other bits undefined			Power Well:	

Bit Range	Bit Acronym	Bit Description	Sticky	Bit Reset Value	Bit Access
63:56	DEST	Destination — If bit 11 of this entry is 0 (Physical), then bits 59:56 specifies an APIC ID. In this case, bits 63:59 should be programmed by software to 0. If bit 11 of this entry is 1 (Logical), then bits 63:56 specify the logical destination address of a set of processors.			RW
55:48	EDID	Extended Destination ID — These bits are sent to a local APIC only when in Processor System Bus mode. They become bits 11:4 of the address.			RO
47:17	Reserved	Reserved			
16	MASK	Mask: 0 = Not masked: An edge or level on this interrupt pin results in the delivery of the interrupt to the destination. 1 = Masked: Interrupts are not delivered nor held pending. Setting this bit after the interrupt is accepted by a local APIC has no effect on that interrupt. This behavior is identical to the device withdrawing the interrupt before it is posted to the processor. It is software's responsibility to deal with the case where the mask bit is set after the interrupt message has been accepted by a local APIC unit but before the interrupt is dispensed to the processor.			RW
15	TRIGMOD	Trigger Mode — This field indicates the type of signal on the interrupt pin that triggers an interrupt. 0 = Edge triggered. 1 = Level triggered.			RW
14		Remote IRR — This bit is used for level triggered interrupts; its meaning is undefined for edge triggered interrupts. 0 = Reset when an EOI message is received from a local APIC. 1 = Set when Local APIC/s accept the level interrupt sent by the I/O APIC.			RO
13	INTPOL	Interrupt Input Pin Polarity — This bit specifies the polarity of each interrupt signal connected to the interrupt pins. 0 =Active high. 1 = Active low.			RW
12	DELIVS	Delivery Status — This field contains the current status of the delivery of this interrupt. Writes to this bit have no effect. 0 = Idle. No activity for this interrupt. 1 = Pending. Interrupt has been injected, but delivery is not complete.			RO

Figure 1-2. *An example of a datasheet page*

Learning and understanding what each bit does and does not do is as tedious as sorting sand on a beach, especially when some of the data documented in the datasheet does not provide as much detailed information as needed to understand how to use it. Sometimes, it takes a lot of trial and error in the process. There are also many undocumented bits that are there either for internal testing or for tuning purposes; these bits are usually not documented inside a datasheet. Therefore, missing critical information could be another challenge for firmware developers.

From time to time, a mysterious problem can stall the debug and development effort for a long time, and the final solution is sometimes a mysterious bit that was somehow discovered after scrubbing the design data. With a stabilizing feature set and better tools, these kinds of problems are not happening as frequently in modern chips.

It is the purpose of early-stage firmware to find the problems of a newly designed chip. Even though there are chip bugs that cannot be resolved without fixing the chip itself, more often than not, a chip problem can be resolved with fixes in firmware; chip vendors frequently call these kinds of fixes "work-arounds." If there is a work-around for a chip bug, it usually involves a bit or a set of bits that need to be programmed or changed. Or, there will be an algorithm developed to work around a problem only when certain conditions are met. To apply a work-around with as little impact as possible to the existing software, designers frequently suggest the fixes to be implemented in the SMM. Since SMM code takes away operating cycles and time, these kinds of fixes are sometimes intrusive and problematic. It is ultimately up to the designers to reveal the fixes after studying the original design of the chip. Most of the time, the fixes are not obvious; the designers need to analyze and figure out if there exists a setting of bits that could fix the problem, or check if they should turn off certain new features that are not working properly. Even though a firmware engineer may accidentally find a fix to resolve an issue through a trial-and-error process, this is very rare these days—especially when the work-around involves an undocumented bit or bits. Designers ultimately hold the key to resolving a chip issue.

How do undocumented bits exist? As stated earlier, when designers design a chip, they put many configurable bits in a chip to help tune the chip or control features that are supposed to be hidden from the programmers. They keep some of these bits undocumented and locked so that no one can accidentally program them to cause unintentional damage or adverse effects. There is a nickname for these bits, called "chicken bits." The origin of this phrase is unknown, but it may have something to do with the fact that these bits are scattered everywhere in the chip like the food for chickens; or it may imply that the designers were too "chicken" to show these bits to others, therefore hiding them.

There could be as many as 60,000 chicken bits in a chip, depending upon the complexity, the functionality, and the size of the chip. This also explains why a chip vendor cannot possibly document every programmable bit of a chip in a datasheet or a programming guide, even if they wanted to try. As a matter of fact, most of these chicken bits will never be documented, and a small portion of the chicken bits will be documented only when they are needed to work around a chip problem. Many of you may have heard of or even read an errata sheet from chip vendors; this errata sheet frequently contains information for bits that were not documented before.

Programming Guides

When designers design a new chip, they will compile of a list of registers to support various chip features. During the chip design phase, hardware engineers and firmware engineers work with designers to design, simulate, and validate the chip. By doing this together, the function of bits and bytes in registers are defined, refined, and documented so that a comprehensive programming guide can be available at the same time that the first chip shows up at a customer's door, typically a manufacturer of a product using the chip. In Intel, this programming resource is named the *BIOS Writer's Guide* (BWG) because it is designed to help BIOS developers write a BIOS for a PC to begin with. For a modern chip like Quark, the name of the document has been changed to the *UEFI Firmware Writer's Guide* to distant itself from the term *BIOS*. Regardless, this programming guide has all the information a firmware engineer needs to know beyond programming a PC and for every embedded system as well.

In 1996, the BWG for the Pentium Pro was 73 pages long; but today, the BWG for the BayTrail SoC is 440 pages divided in two volumes; it grew more than six times in 18 years. Not only the amount of information, but the complexity has increased as well.

For example, the Pentium Pro BWG describes very basic programming information that most people can probably figure out themselves after reading a few standard specifications from Intel, like SMM, BIOS INT functions, and how to handle multiprocessor initialization and so forth. In comparison, besides basic SMM multiprocessor topics, BayTrail BWG uses 34 pages just to talk about MSR (model-specific register); other information includes CPUID handling, the Microcode Update, SpeedStep, C-State Control, thermal management, and more. This list is just the information contained in volume one. In volume two, almost all the subjects require a domain expertise to understand, such as HD audio, graphics, the HPET timer, xHCI, EHCI, DDR3, ISP, P-Unit, SIO, PCIe, PCU, TCO, and so forth. (If you don't recognize any of these acronyms, you get the point: modern-day BWGs have become very specialized repositories of information.)

The programming guide not only specifies the features that can be customized by the customer via programming the bits and bytes, it also methodically covers the many bits and bytes that must be programmed with particular values in a fixed order to support certain features.

Even if you have not been involved in debugging a new circuit board, you can imagine that finding a bit-setting error in an ocean of bits is pretty painful. Does a chip vendor need to put firmware engineers through a painful experience every time it produces a new chip? If the programming guide is done right, firmware engineers should not have to read through 440 pages of BWG to study what needs to be programmed just to get the chip up to the point of providing its features. Firmware engineers have better things to do than look at the programming guide to figure out which bits to flip and which bytes to write; they should spend their valuable time developing value-added features to help deliver a product with differentiating features.

The Intel® Firmware Support Package

Intel has taken the initiative to provide a way to encapsulate tedious chip initialization code into a package: the Intel® Firmware Support Package (Intel® FSP, for short; we will use *Intel FSP* and *FSP* interchangeably in this book). Obviously, there is more than one way to ease the programming pain associated with chip initialization. For example, releasing the full source code to allow people to view how it is done, or putting all the chip initialization code in one binary to hide the complexity, or anything in between. Intel has decided to go with the option to put all the chip initialization code in one place with the hope that, once it is used in the firmware stack of your choice, the developers will be able to quickly get over the chip initialization hump and move on to value-added features development work.

Why would Intel produce Intel FSP for the embedded designs and the Internet of Things (discussed shortly) in the first place? After all, Intel is already providing a comprehensive reference code for each reference platform, and there is also an open source EDK II codebase under Tianocore.org that allows people to study the UEFI implementation. The problem is not about having reference code out there or not; it is portability, scalability, and flexibility that developers are looking for, especially in the embedded and IoT space where UEFI and PC architecture are not playing a major role as things stand today.

Intel recognizes that many developers have a hard time extracting chip initialization code out of an EDK II codebase or from a BIOS to port to a different firmware stack or to a different platform design. Going to IBV (Independent BIOS Vendors) to ask for help is not always an option for some customers. Intel believes that there are a lot of smart firmware engineers out there, and once these engineers get hold of a technical specification, an industry standard, or reference code, they can produce a firmware implementation without too much difficulty. The only thing that is missing for them is the chip programming information.

That said, it does not matter how smart the firmware engineer is: he or she cannot and will not be able to figure out how to program a new chip without help from chip vendors. Over the years, some smart developers have tried to reverse-engineer what has been done in an existing platform, but the process is long, hard, and error-prone.

In this book, we talk about Intel's FSP solution; other chip vendors have also provided similar packages or mechanisms to reduce the programming burden for initializing basic chip functions, such as AMD's AGESA (AMD Generic and Encapsulated Software Architecture), and ARM's boot ROM concept. This book will not discuss these implementations, but they are efforts that chip vendors put out to ease the programming challenges.

Since its launch in October of 2012, Intel FSP has been widely used in many customers' embedded designs, including customers who chose to convert from a competing architecture to Intel Architecture. As you will discover in later chapters of this book, Intel FSP can be easily integrated into an existing firmware stack to save you time and energy in figuring out the information needed to program an Intel chip.

■ **Note** Keep in mind that Intel FSP is not a stand-alone firmware stack. It does not have all the ingredients to boot to an OS on its own; therefore, it must be integrated with a firmware stack, such as BIOS, coreboot, RTOS, or other proprietary bootloader solutions.

The Uniqueness of Embedded Firmware

It is one thing to develop firmware for a general-purpose and open system such as a PC; it is quite another thing to develop a firmware stack for a closed system with dedicated functions. Over the last three decades, firmware engineers have almost perfected BIOS (including UEFI) for the PC. The PC BIOS has the ability to deal with devices that come and go anytime (plug-and-play) and to boot to any general-purpose OS (Linux, Windows), and it is smart enough to learn about its environment (ambient light, battery status, and user inactivity) to adjust itself to save energy. Arguably, it could be the most intelligent firmware stack ever created. Over the last three decades, we have definitely seen the evolution of BIOS, and we have witnessed a great improvement of quality in the BIOS realm.

Can the experience learned from the PC BIOS be applied to an embedded firmware design? The answer is "yes" because there are many useful industry standards created and implemented in the code.

Can we use a PC BIOS stack on an embedded firmware design? The answer is "yes, but..." because it depends on the purpose of the design. Many embedded designs leverage PC architecture for cost and ecosystem support reasons. Since the designs inherit all the characteristics of a PC, the PC BIOS and similar technologies could still be the best choice for an open and general-purpose system if boot speed and the size of the firmware stack are not issues of concern. There are also a lot of embedded designs that are not based on PC architecture. In these cases, the PC BIOS and similar technologies can be used, but will need a lot of effort to fit into the design; there are better firmware solutions out there to choose from. In some cases, a PC BIOS just won't work because the special need for boot speed, a small footprint, real-time performance, and so forth, are required.

Many mission-critical and time-sensitive designs require the system (hardware, firmware, and software) to be deterministic and predictable among other special constraints; many intelligent and dynamic configuration capabilities of a PC BIOS can be prohibitors for those deterministic and predictable considerations. Some closed devices designed without any upgradability do not need the flexibility of plug-and-play, heuristic training algorithm, and bus enumeration techniques that are typical in a PC BIOS; therefore, embedded firmware can sometimes be dramatically simplified. Finally, there are more embedded designs asking for faster boot time and quicker response time, which a typical PC BIOS cannot achieve. The rear-view camera in a vehicle, for example, needs to be turned on within 2 seconds after the car engine is ignited; this is for safety concerns and also a regulation requirement in many countries. Even though it is not impossible for a PC BIOS to achieve faster boot time, the hardware and firmware stack used in an IVI (in-vehicle infotainment) system is heavily customized to achieve this stringent boot-time requirement. All of these unique requirements make a PC BIOS harder to fit into embedded applications.

The Choice of Firmware Stacks

There are quite a few firmware options in the market, such as PC BIOS (including various UEFI implementations), RTOS, open source stacks, and proprietary solutions. Each of these firmware stacks has a specific purpose to fulfill, and we will discuss their special usage models later in the book. We'll also discuss how to work with different firmware stacks using a common chip initialization module (in the next chapter, we'll take a look at a few of the options), and we will also talk about their pros and cons and how to make a choice based on your needs.

Welcome to the Era of the Internet of Things

Due to the fast evolution of microprocessors, embedded systems are not only becoming more intelligent, but also becoming more ubiquitous. Some of the devices we use today will start to make decisions for us and even protect us from danger someday. There are refrigerators that can order food for us when they are empty. There are thermostats that can call the police when they detect an intruder in our house. There are cars that can steer themselves out of danger when they are about to collide with another car. There are a lot of more new ideas and new devices in the works to make you safer and make your life more convenient. The next wave of the technology revolution has arrived, and it comes in the form of built-in connectivity and intelligence. People are calling these intelligent and connected devices the "Internet of Things" or IoT. It takes a lot of creative minds to conceive, develop, and refine such an IoT, and no doubt much of the work needs to be done at the firmware and software level. The demand for the skill sets covered in this book will increase in the foreseeable future.

Technical Coverage in This Book

This book covers topics related to embedded firmware stacks and an important ingredient that enables them—Intel FSP. Since this book uses Intel Architecture as the centerpiece, we focus on how Intel FSP works and demonstrate how it can be integrated into popular firmware stacks; coreboot and EDK II examples are used in this book. We cover detailed information about each of these two firmware stacks, including the internals and how to work with them. The reader can pick and choose a particular subject and do a deep dive, or the reader can choose to learn both of the firmware stacks in a holistic way. If you are among the readers who are not using either the coreboot or the EDK II codebase, the same principles and practices also apply to your own firmware stack once you have a basic understanding.

This book does not cover the details of implementing specific features, such as power management, device enumeration, graphics, audio/video, and other non-chip related features. However, this book will touch upon the new Intel Quark family products and talk about their firmware stack and detailed firmware architecture. Even though the firmware strategies of some Intel products are not yet using FSP as the building block, you can compare and understand the differences and the rationale behind the decisions.

There are not many books out there talking about firmware because it is not a standard discipline that can be talked about generically. Every subject in the realm of firmware can be a book on its own, and there have been books about UEFI, BIOS, Fast Boot, and so forth, and many system requirements and constraints can dictate how a firmware is chosen and written; therefore, it is a topic that cannot be easily addressed holistically without an objective. Our objective is to show you how you can take advantage of Intel Architecture, and prepare a firmware stack for it regardless which firmware stack you choose. There might be areas that are not covered in great detail in this book, such as integrating Intel FSP into a RTOS codebase, but hopefully the same practices still apply.

The Future of Firmware

We have been witnessing an interesting phenomenon since the beginning of this century: open source projects are gaining momentum, led by companies such as Google and Facebook. Many legacy and proprietary software solutions are either disappearing or losing steam very quickly; open source solutions are becoming a primary interest of technologists at an amazing speed.

Even though this century is still young, we are riding on a fascinating wave that will make the 21st century a distinctly different century than any other. The phrase "open source" clearly connotes sharing and collaboration, in contrast to the waning business philosophy of protecting intellectual properties so that "we can win as an individual company." What has emerged is a new concept to tie business success to a collaborative ecosystem effort. Under this new model, everyone has a chance to thrive in the ecosystem because innovation is multiplied with the participation of many intelligent scientists, hobbyists, and engineers.

Will embedded firmware solutions be moving toward the same model that operating systems and computing systems are currently going through? Yes, we can tell that the open source model is impacting the firmware world in equal force in the last few years. Even some of the traditionally closed solutions are adapting themselves to the open source model as we write this book. For example, even though Tianocore was created as an open source project by Intel years ago, the community did not thrive due to lack of crucial components in the source tree. Until recently, many ARM developers have tapped into the Tianocore source code to make it workable with ARM designs. Intel has also ramped up its effort to provide an FSP component so that it can be successfully built for a platform in distribution.

However, due to its many unique characteristics, firmware is a source of intense debate because it is so tightly coupled with the hardware underneath, and hardware still has IP that companies want to protect. The questions for chip vendors will always be how much firmware can be benefited by the collaborative model, and how much firmware is so chip-specific that there is nothing that needs to be collaborated on? For example, if some of the chip code is fragile enough that only the designers can program it right, does it make a difference if the code is open or not? If it is open, does it do more harm than good? How about the code inside a boot ROM that is masked? Should that code be open as well? What about the firmware that is currently outside an SoC? Where is the boundary? What makes sense to be open and what does not? These questions may be rhetorical, but the binary distribution format will gradually move away from being a mechanism to hide features, and instead be a way to simplify its integration.

Putting these rhetorical questions aside for the moment, the open source model is a trend that all chip vendors, BIOS vendors, and software vendors will continue to adapt to. In the spirit of open source communities, the best of the best will emerge after all the debates, arguments, and brainstorming. This book was written with the aim to enable the open source community to thrive on its own and alongside proprietary solutions. It will undoubtedly fall short of some readers' expectations, and it may disappoint a few hard-core open source enthusiasts. However, it is still a step toward the right direction to make chip initialization a non-issue (or less of an issue) for open source communities.

We are all aware that the state of the art in chip engineering will continue to rapidly evolve. New methodologies will emerge to make firmware development easier and faster for the developers trying to bring innovative IoT devices to the world, and perhaps subsequent editions of this book will cover those developments. In the meantime, we welcome you to this discussion. Please read on.

CHAPTER 2

■ ■ ■

Firmware Stacks for Embedded Systems

> Computers themselves, and software yet to be developed, will revolutionize the way we learn.
>
> —Steve Jobs

If you have been doing BIOS work or read a book about it, you probably have an idea about what firmware is doing for a PC. Firmware needs to do the following:

- It needs to discover devices that are connected to a system bus

- It needs to deal with devices disappearing and appearing anytime during runtime

- It needs to be prepared to boot any operating systems that are written for the PC

- It needs to wake up if an external stimulus occurs

- It needs to adjust its backlight, clocks, and speed based on the temperature, the power source, and the status of the user (inactive or active)

However, embedded systems and IoT devices have some unique firmware requirements from PC BIOS:

- *Timeliness in responding to external stimuli (real-time behavior).* The examples are industrial precision machines. These machines cannot tolerate any deviation from their specified error margins during operation.

- *Determinism during execution.* The examples are missiles and rockets. You probably don't want to see these things taking different software paths every time they fly out of their launch pad; who knows what will happen if they act differently every time they execute their software after launch? Results might be deadly if the software is nondeterministic.

- *Predictability of the outcome.* The examples are industrial machines and manufacturing robots. They need to deliver the same result repeatedly without deviating from its programmed behavior; otherwise, the produced items may not be usable.

- *Closed system with fixed function.* The examples are the set-top box and GPS. The software running inside these things are doing one function (or a few functions) very well without errors.

- *Closed system with limited expansion.* The examples are the Mars Rover and home appliances. Once these things are delivered (departed Earth or sent home), the software inside should not need to deal with components coming and going in the systems, because a closed system can safely assume no expansion after certain points.

- *Fast boot time.* The examples are rearview cameras of cars, mobile phones, and home appliances. These things need to boot fast for either safety reasons or for a better user experience. It was very annoying when some early Blu-ray DVD players took a long time to be ready to play DVDs, because no consumer electronic devices should take more than a few seconds to be ready (at least this is not what consumers are used to).

- *Small footprint.* The examples are wearable devices, sensors, and software that needs to be certified. Big software frequently needs bigger storage devices, and they tend to be error-prone and difficult to certify.

- *Security and reliability.* The examples are point-of-sale (POS) terminals and in-vehicle-infotainment systems (IVI). In IVI, you probably don't want a software crash in the DVD player of the system to bring down the GPS, radio, and phone connection, and you do not want your credit card information stolen during checkout at a store; isolation of mission-critical and nonessential elements are, therefore, very important for some applications.

- *Fixed boot target.* The examples are Chromebook and IVI. These devices only have one boot target in mind (ChromeOS or embedded Linux); therefore, the firmware does not need to worry about having a general-purpose boot loader interface ready to boot any OS. A direct-boot interface can not only save code space, but also boots faster because shortcuts can be taken.

These are just the common requirements for embedded firmware. As you can see, they are very different from PC firmware. Still, each embedded system design can have its own requirements that may or may not come from the preceding list, or it may have multiples of these characteristics.

In addition to these requirements, embedded systems tend to have a longer life cycle than PCs; therefore, the cost of extensive and deep customization can be justified. Why is this important? Because a highly customized solution can deliberately violate some commonly known design principles to achieve the best and optimized outcome—a perfect product for the very niche market. The reusability and the ability to leverage a horizontal technology may suffer, and the sustaining effort may be expensive, but some products are never meant for service after being sold in the market. Therefore, a lot of firmware stacks, especially commercial off-the-shelf (COTS) products, focus more on ease of customization than anything else. Some software companies even have products designed for specialized markets with special certification requirements, such as avionics and military applications where safety and security are the main concerns.

When we examine the list of unique firmware requirements for embedded systems, we know some of these requirements can be achieved by specialized OS or RTOS. These specialized systems sometimes consist of a well-designed microkernel instead of a monolithic kernel; they also may have a customized firmware stack that is designed for ease of adding and subtracting components. Some of the requirements need the involvement of a virtual machine monitor (VMM); therefore, picking, integrating, customizing, and designing components in these firmware stacks can be an art sometimes.

Despite all of these unique requirements, there are still embedded designs that can be based on a familiar and ubiquitous PC architecture, such as industrial controllers, vending machines, POS, switches, and routers. Not necessarily because PC architecture is the best for these applications, but because the advantages of using a well-established and well-tested architecture sometimes outweigh the cost and disadvantages.

This is particularly true when developers want to reduce the design cost: they can simply buy off-the-shelf PC motherboards. It is easier to get ecosystem support, and may shorten the development cycle as well. The developers who have decided to leverage PC motherboards can still decide on whether or not to use PC BIOS. If the developers want to boot nothing but Linux and would like to replace the existing BIOS on the motherboard, they can certainly do that. There are many pros and cons to consider when picking the right firmware stack for your product.

Is a One-Size-Fits-All Solution Possible?

Ever since computer science emerged as a popular subject in the academic world, people have been trying to invent solutions that are as flexible as possible and to cover as much ground as possible. It is a challenge to come up with a smart design that works in all scenarios and meets all the requirements in the world. Unfortunately, no matter how hard we try, we have not succeeded in creating something that can deal with extreme requirements effectively. For example:

- Can we have a firmware stack that is optimized for a closed system while keeping the capability to boot a general-purpose OS and run general-purpose applications in an open system?

- Can we have a firmware stack that is not only optimized for a dedicated function, but also to support a computing environment that is capable of expanding into other functions?

- Can we have a firmware stack that is optimized for speed while maintaining the capability for exhaustive device discovery mechanisms and heuristic self-adjustment capability?

- Can we have a firmware stack that is optimized for size with the smartness to resolve device dependencies on the fly?

- Can a firmware stack be smart and intelligent, but at the same time deterministic and predictable?

Although it is not impossible, it is extremely hard to support extreme requirements using the same firmware stack. And even if this difficult design goal was achieved, the source code would probably be too complicated to read, or the build process would be too convoluted to comprehend. Regardless, a few people are trying to make a one-size-fits-all solution; one of the attempts is the UEFI firmware stack. Supported by Intel, HP, AMD, Dell, and other partners, there is still much research and development needed in making the UEFI firmware stack fit into fast and small applications beyond the PC paradigm. We shall see the results in a few years.

The motivation of promoting a one-size-fits-all solution could be based on the desire to reduce the support cost, but there are many alternatives available to customers. The following are some firmware solutions that typical customers of embedded systems are looking for.

Microkernel

Microkernel is frequently associated with RTOS, but it can be designed without real-time elements. The difference between a microkernel and a monolithic kernel is the responsibilities carried out inside the kernel. A monolithic kernel typically handles all the privileged tasks and system services in the kernel (such as file systems, interprocess communication, I/O, and a scheduler), while a microkernel does only basic process communication and I/O control, leaving the user space applications to provide services such as a pager, file systems, a virtual machine monitor, and so forth. Linux and Windows have monolithic kernels, and microkernel is frequently used in the operating systems designed for embedded applications in a closed system. The advantage of a microkernel is its size, flexibility, and the ability to handle mission-critical tasks in a tightly controlled manner. The main drawback of a microkernel is its lack of common features, and the fact that adding extra features can be costly and time-consuming.

Real-Time Operating System (RTOS)

For our daily computing needs, we seldom need RTOS because the tasks we typically carry out on a computer are either *transformational* or *interactive*.

Transformational tasks are the tasks we submit to a computer, and then the computer executes the task and gives us the result. When there is no task, there is no result. For example, if you calculate 2 + 3 on a soft calculator on the computer, a result of 5 is generated after you submit the task for calculation. When you submit a software source code for compilation, the software source code is the input, and compiled results (binaries, symbols, and executables) are the output after transformation.

Interactive tasks are those that occur when your computer responds to your requests, and vice versa; when there is no request, there is no action. When you type a character in a Word document or play a game on a computer, it is considered to be an interactive task between you and the computer. Every key you type on the keyboard becomes a task that the computer needs to handle, and then displays the text or image on the screen to give you the feedback you are looking for. The computer will also request that you take actions when dialog boxes are displayed, and keyboard commands are sometimes needed during games and with other interactive software.

The only time you will need to consider using RTOS is when you have a *reactive* system, which needs to respond to external stimuli in a timely manner. Although with many tasks the device handles could still be transformational, the actions are secondary to the main requirement. It is most important to respond to the stimuli and finish the tasks associated with the stimuli in a timely manner. Therefore, the major design goal is not about how fast or how many tasks the device can handle, but the ability to deal with a peak load when many stimuli are happening at the same time and to complete all the tasks invoked by the stimuli within the time specified by the design requirement.

The design of the kernel of a RTOS is mostly based on a preemptive scheduler, which responds to interrupts according to preset priority, and won't let go of the task until it is finished. In comparison, a GPOS (general-purpose operating system) typically uses a time-based, round-robin scheduler to ensure fairness. There are exceptions to both camps, but scheduler design is the main difference between the two categories.

There are many RTOS vendors owning a great deal of embedded markets, such as Wind Rivers, Green Hills, QNX, and so forth. There are also many open source and proprietary RTOS projects, such as FreeRTOS, eCos, and so forth. At the time this book is written, there are more than 160 RTOS offered for various platforms and usage cases under different licensing terms. Among them, at least 120 of them are still active. This means that the needs are so diversified and so customized that any niche market can spawn a RTOS of its kind. For this very reason, many big RTOS vendors also offer a few RTOS products for the specialized markets that they serve, most notably, avionics and military.

Legacy BIOS

Even though legacy BIOS is becoming less and less popular, it has transformed itself into a "payload" or a "compatibility module" for a very specific reason: to boot and run legacy software. There are still designs offered by many companies that require legacy BIOS to boot DOS, Linux, and 32-bit Windows (such as Vista, XP, and Windows 7). A legacy BIOS can be a stand-alone BIOS, or it can piggyback on a host firmware stack as a payload, such as SeaBIOS for coreboot, or it can be a module in a firmware stack to perform the compatibility boot, like compatibility support module (CSM) for UEFI firmware stack. Legacy BIOS is not necessarily old or obsolete, because some of the BIOS vendors and developers are still updating their code base to support newer hardware and CPUs. Most users of legacy BIOS are self-sufficient because updates are rare and support is scarce; a few IBV (independent BIOS vendors) are still doing business with legacy BIOS, but the revenue stream from legacy BIOS is quickly dwindling to a minuscule level compared to its mainstream business—UEFI-compatible products.

Implementations of the UEFI Framework

A firmware implementation of UEFI Framework is a firmware stack primarily for booting a 64-bit OS. It is modular at every stage of the boot process; therefore, supporting a new device can be added individually with flexibility. During the debug phase, a new device driver can be loaded and tested separately without reprogramming the whole flash device. There is also a Dependency Expression Grammar in the core to allow modules to be loaded in the order decided by a dependency expression, instead of an order that is statically programmed. There are many other clever designs in the UEFI firmware stack.

This UEFI firmware stack has been widely adopted by BIOS vendors, OEMs, and ODMs. It has become a de facto code base for booting 64-bit OS from the Microsoft and the Linux communities. The ARM community has also started to use the open source tianocore.org for 64-bit ARM support.

Open Source Firmware Stacks

Even though various Linux communities have been in existence for a long time, and they have established a very healthy and prosperous ecosystem, open source communities for firmware projects had not been as successful in terms of participants, number of platforms, and ecosystem support. It is changing because more and more silicon, hardware, and software companies, such as AMD, Google, Sage Electronic Engineering, and Intel, are getting involved.

The major difference between the communities for Linux and the communities for firmware is their dependency on hardware vendors and silicon vendors, and this factor also contributed to their progress in recent years. Most of the Linux development and collaboration work can be done without thinking too much of the hardware or firmware. The exception is the drivers, but even with drivers, they rely less on firmware, and more on direct hardware manipulation. In the past, the abstraction of hardware was mostly provided by a layer of firmware using tables and runtime services, but this model is changing to minimize the dependency on firmware beyond basic hardware abstraction tables. Thanks to the involvement of more hardware companies that are willing to contribute directly to the Linux development communities and are committed to write device drivers for their own devices, the overall performance and reliability of the systems has improved over the years. As a result, the user experience of Linux has also improved, and Linux has gained a lot of popularity from developers who did not treat Linux seriously in the past; like an upward spiral, when Linux gains popularity, more hardware companies are willing to be involved in contributing to the Linux source code. Even if there is a lag in the contribution from a key hardware vendor, it will not stall a Linux development project completely; missing a device driver may cause inconvenience when the corresponding device is not functioning correctly or is not accessible, but the other parts of the system will remain functional, and development work associated with the kernel or applications will not be completely blocked by the missing device support.

In contrast, lacking support from a key hardware or silicon vendor could be a death sentence for an open source firmware project. Even if a hardware initialization sequence can be reverse engineered, it may take a long time for developers to come up with an implementation to satisfy the needs of a community. The dependency on hardware vendors can determine the health of an open source firmware community; for example, U-Boot developers are having more success than coreboot because ARM and PowerPC architectures are considered more "friendly" and easier to program from the firmware perspective, and they have less dependencies on hardware vendors. That is also why board-level projects based on Intel Architecture are lagging: it has been hard to get support from Intel in the past, since Intel has not been very active in open source firmware until recently. With the introduction of Intel FSP and Google's usage of coreboot in the Chromebook products, the situation is quickly changing, and Intel has become actively involved in contributing silicon code to these communities. Although Intel FSP is distributed in binary format as the book is written, Intel has also been releasing complete source code for Quark families. The debate on whether or not a binary solution is acceptable to an open source community remains, but for the purpose of helping these communities to quickly get the key components they need, regardless of which format the support code is distributed, it is a good starting point.

▓ **Note**   A quote from http://www.coreboot.org/pipermail/coreboot/2014-November/078930.html: "My personal take on this is that I would rather see coreboot run 75% free on a billion machines out there than 100% free on 1000 machines. Because that will ultimately leave the project in a better place of negotiating future ports and leaves the whole ecosystem with a higher percentage of free software total." —by Stefan Rainaure in answering the debate of binary modules in coreboot.

As mentioned in the previous paragraph, the two better-known open source firmware communities are coreboot and U-Boot; tianocore or EDK II open source communities are also getting more attention due to ARM's 64-bit movement. Among these open source firmware communities, coreboot, tianocore, and EDK II have been traditionally focusing on x86 platforms, and U-Boot has been used widely in the ARM and PowerPC designs. In later chapters, we will dive deeper into the coreboot and EDK II sides of development and practices.

This book will not discuss the different licensing agreements and terms offered by open source communities, but it is nonetheless a very important topic to study before you are fully committed to an open source project. Licensing agreement topics can usually be found in the open source community web sites.

Proprietary Firmware Stacks

Per the survey done by *EE Times* in 2013, about 24% of the companies surveyed are using in-house or homegrown software and firmware stacks for their embedded designs. We won't be able to show an example of these firmware stacks in this book, but this is certainly a viable option, and the same principles and examples shown in this book will apply to these in-house designs, especially when industry standards, specifications, and sample code are easily obtainable for the designs that require them. Regardless what choice a company makes, the design principles and methodologies for developing a robust firmware stack to meet design requirements are common to all. You can go for an extremely customized proprietary solution, or an open source solution with reusability in mind, or even something in between. Hopefully, silicon companies such as Intel are no longer a roadblock for your development work. Read on and learn how you can take advantage of Intel FSP and Intel's full source code releases for Intel products for the IoT markets.

Make or Buy

Even though a PC ecosystem and an embedded ecosystem will not overlap in most cases, many Independent BIOS Vendors (IBVs) and Independent Software Vendors (ISVs) provide solutions and services to customers in both ecosystems. However, the business models in the two ecosystems are quite different: some IBVs and ISVs need to take a different approach when facing customers from different segments. Customers have a choice to buy the service from these IBVs and ISVs, or to develop a firmware stack on their own, and the decision to make or buy a firmware stack/solution can be complicated, and it depends on many questions, such as:

- *Do we have ongoing products that we need a firmware stack for?* If the products are ongoing and last for many years, either building a long-term relationship with a vendor, or working in-house with dedicated resource should work better. Buying a short-term service contract or changing vendors along the way could be problematic because the switching costs could be higher.

- *Is there a turnkey solution out there?* If the product has become a commodity and there are turnkey solutions available in the market, it might make sense to take advantage of an existing solution to save time and cost. In this case, it might make more sense to put as few resources as possible on the firmware creation, or pay someone to customize an existing solution.

- *Do we need source code to modify after the project is done?* If there is no engineering resource in the company, source code availability is not too much of an issue. But, some companies with a low-touch development model may have one or two engineers helping resolve customers' issues, and then they need to have access to the source code in order to do some modifications. If this is the case, the company can decide on hiring a vendor for everything from cradle-to-grave, including support, or pay for a contract that allows them to own the source code after it is done with all the features. Some vendors may not be willing to give the source code as part of the deal. Be aware.

- *Who can do it faster with the domain knowledge?* Many vendors will try to convince you that they can do it faster with lower cost, but you might want to check their domain knowledge in the field you intend them to work in. Sometimes a blocking issue is not necessarily a technical or programming issue, but rather that the domain knowledge is not easily obtainable. If you know a domain inside out, you might want to assess the risk involved in teaching your vendor to learn everything from you. After you teach the vendors to obtain the domain knowledge, they may use it to serve other customers, and these customers of theirs might happen to be your competitors.

- *Who needs to maintain the code after it is done?* Anyone who has developed or implemented firmware can attest that shipping a product is just the beginning of a headache, no matter how good your quality control process is. Who has the source code and who can provide support are the issues to think about early in the decision-making process. If you don't like going back to your vendors after the contract is over, you might want to pay for a long-term contract, or maintaining the code in-house from the beginning.

- *Are there special intellectual properties (IP) and differentiators in the firmware?* This is an important question to ask because any noncommodity product may have a few areas that you can differentiate on; once the differentiators are in place, they may be considered as IP. Do you feel comfortable sharing this knowledge with a vendor? We have seen a lot of cases where the vendors have become the main competitors, who turned around and outsold the original owner of the IP.

- *Related to the previous question, do we need to control our own destiny (to protect IP and differentiators)?* One way to protect IP and differentiators is to not share the code with anyone, but keep it to yourself; however, this does not mean that vendors cannot protect your secrets for you. In most cases, carefully designed non-disclosure agreements, once in place, can adequately protect your IP. But, you cannot protect IPs forever. The intangible experience the vendors accumulate during the projects cannot only serve you better over time, but could also potentially be used to serve others.

- *Can we get the attention from our vendors when we need their help during emergencies?* Most vendors are very reliable in dealing with emergencies, but if your company is small in size, or the volume of your product shipment is smaller than that of other customers of your vendor, you might want to make sure that you have a plan to deal with emergencies if you don't plan to do in-house design.

- *Which way is more cost effective: NRE (Non-recurring engineering), royalty, or internal resource?* This is a pure financial assessment that you have to make to determine whether you prefer to pay for a one-time contract or to save upfront costs by sharing your future profit. In-house engineering is an investment that you can make if it makes financial sense after comparing different business models.

The Advantages of Outsourcing

The following are the obvious advantages of outsourcing:

- IBVs and ISVs usually have early access to programming information and silicon samples before most customers do. Silicon vendors treat ecosystem vendors with a higher priority to give them more privileges so that they can help enable the industry.

- IBVs and ISVs have more experience because they frequently deal with many customers at once; if there is a tough blocking issue facing you, mostly likely they have dealt with it or are working on it— unless you are the first customer to discover it. You may be able to leverage what they have learned before you do.

- IBVs and ISVs have built their business model around services; therefore, there will be fewer surprises when issues arise. For example, they know how to get help and where to get help when encountering issues, and it could be hard for you to do the same effectively if you haven't dealt with issues regularly.

- Why do it in-house if the product is already a commodity? Outsourcing is a better option when there is no differentiation to be done for the product. Examples are tablets and phones: they have become such commodities that the hardware selection is limited and turnkey solutions are widely available. One cannot say that there is no innovation left, but the hardware and firmware are pretty much set in most cases.

The Disadvantages of Outsourcing

The following are the disadvantages of outsourcing:

- Lack of knowledge of what is implemented. If you are curious about what has been done for you by a third-party vendor, be prepared to get lost unless you also invest your own resources to monitor the design.

- Lack of capability to sustain a product. If you plan to sustain a product after a release done by a vendor, you may not have the knowledge and experience to carry it out effectively.

- Sometimes vendors don't share the source code or the knowledge they learned from making the product work. In this case, the next project is going to look new to you even if it shares common components.

- Sometimes vendors charge money for additional support, even though they picked up the knowledge while working on your product.

In-House Development

After analyzing the pros and cons of the outsourcing model, let's take a look at the following advantages of developing in-house:

- Despite many tedious technical challenges, the knowledge belongs to the company after the project is done.

- It is easier to maintain and sustain a product if you own the resulting source code and technology. Some vendors provide the source code to you after the project is done, but you will still need to understand the codebase if you are not familiar with it.

- It is easier to add differentiating features if the product is not yet a commodity. Although it is also possible through vendors, it is more reliable if it is done by internal resources, and it is easier to protect the IP in the product.

In recent years, the reason for not doing in-house development has been cost concerns. At the beginning of the twenty-first century, it was trendy for companies to eliminate their internal resources to rely on external vendors. Initially, it seemed to provide a cost advantage, but those who blindly followed this model were hurt not only financially, but also from a technology leadership perspective. Many "sold the farm" (gave away their know-how) just for the sake of doing outsourcing.

Whether or not to leverage an external vendor is sometimes a complicated decision, but not always; many companies have tried different models in their practices. Sometimes the short-term cost benefits of using external vendors bring long-term disadvantages; sometimes internal resources investment is wasted when insurmountable obstacles cannot be overcome in a reasonable time.

It is hard to tell if you can save money in the long run if you outsource, and it is also hard to tell if you will be better off financially if you do things in-house, because the trade-offs can go either way. You, being an expert of firmware in your company, need to make the recommendation carefully.

Summary

There is a lot of common-sense discussion related to "choices" in this chapter. The purpose is to help readers gain a general understanding of the choices they can make when facing a decision that has short-term and long-term implications on a product. In the following chapters, there are in-depth examples and programming steps and results that will equip you with practical knowledge to make intelligent design decisions for your products.

CHAPTER 3

■ ■ ■

Intel® Firmware Support Package (Intel® FSP)

"Simple can be harder than complex: you have to work hard to get your thinking clean to make it simple. But it's worth it in the end because once you get there, you can move mountains."

—Steve Jobs

Over the years, Intel has made several firmware products to support the embedded industry; most of them are either BIOS, UEFI Firmware, or something with the flavor of these two.

Intel enables its customers to design products around its chips by (like every other silicon vendor) making a Customer Reference Board (CRB) to showcase its new chips and its features. Intel, like other silicon vendors, expects customers to either copy or leverage what Intel has done with hardware, firmware, and software on the board, so that their designs can quickly go to the market for sale.

After three decades of perfecting the PC ecosystem and supply chain, the PC system development process for planning and designing chip and board features has become extremely efficient. The efficiency covers every link from top to bottom in terms of parts selection, vendor roadmap, software development, technology interception, distribution channels, marketing practices, to final sales online or in the brick-and-mortar shops. Everything is done in a well-tuned rhythm, and very few companies would miss a beat or have a hiccup in the process.

The efficiency of the PC industry can be a blessing as well as a curse. Due to the maturity of the ecosystem, the selection-choices of hardware components, software, and peripherals are gravitating toward a standard set of choices. These choices become more and more limited, and products are becoming more and more homogeneous even though the number of vendors is increasing. At the same time, the hardware, firmware, and software interfaces and architectures are also gravitating toward a few comprehensive standards, such as Wi-Fi, PCI, ACPI, UEFI, USB, Display Port, HDMI, Bluetooth, and so forth. Innovation and breakthroughs can still happen in these confined areas, but it is harder and harder for innovators to stand out in the crowd. Consumers may have a preference on brands, but there is hardly any reason to be loyal to a brand. The "cool" factor of Apple Mac products is one of the few remaining examples of strong product differentiation in an increasingly homogenized market.

25

Compared to the PC industry, the embedded market and the emerging IoT industry are more vibrant and versatile. They are not as mature as the PC industry, and are not as well-regulated by standards and specifications. However, the embedded market does not live in chaos. Each vertical segment of the embedded market still has its own regulations, standards, supply chain, and practices; they are just not as organized or homogeneous as the PC industry.

Therefore, trying to provide a horizontal solution across all segments and verticals is harder to achieve in the embedded market. Since the embedded market is about customization and diversification, and the life cycle of the devices is typically longer than a typical PC device, solutions for the industry need to be tailored to the needs of the designs for the vertical segments instead of the other way around.

This was the challenge that Intel was facing with firmware enablement strategies before Intel FSP was introduced. Since not all embedded market customers are leveraging PC architecture, they struggled with the firmware choices—or the lack of choices.

In 2010, Intel produced the Intel Boot Loader Development Kit (BLDK) to help developers customize an existing CRB and its BIOS. Intel BLDK was a good idea, but fell short of expectations, because even though it provided most of the source code for customers to customize, it was not very useful when customers wanted to alter their designs or use a completely different firmware stack for their boards.

After a few years of gathering feedback and prototyping, Intel announced the Intel Firmware Support Package in October 2012. It was not an answer to all the challenges, but it was a simple solution to support versatile needs of designs and choices. Intel FSP contains only the silicon initialization code that can be integrated into any firmware stack. Once integrated, developers can design the rest of the firmware stack for value-added features.

If you are confused by BIOS, BLDK, and FSP, let's compare these three offerings using automobile metaphors. The reference BIOS on a CRB is like an 8-cylinder, fully loaded SUV: powerful, impressive, and with all the features you can dream of. BLDK, on the other hand, is like a customizable VW Beetle with a lot of accessories and parts to alter the design and to customize its look. But, the Beetle is still a car in a fixed frame. If you plan to build a different kind of car, whether it is a race car, a sand buggy, or a military tank, it is not impossible, but it is hard to pick the parts you need from an SUV or a Beetle to build the car you want.

Using the same analogy, metaphorically, Intel FSP is like an engine, which is needed by every car. Obviously, in reality, cars of different models use different engines, but in the firmware case, the engine for initializing a silicon is identical whether you are building a server, a desktop, a laptop, a set-top box, or a wearable device. If a silicon vendor does it right, it is very possible to share the same silicon code for all market segments.

Intel FSP is the engine that provides the silicon initialization code for Intel chips. Each Intel silicon and its companion chip will have their own Intel FSP. There is no super FSP that encapsulates multiple silicon families, simply because it is not necessary. The goal is to keep FSP small enough that it can be utilized in the most compact and size-constrained environment. In Intel's case, the programming information is mostly documented in a BIOS Writer's Guide (BWG) or UEFI Firmware Writer's Guide, which are confidential documents that only privileged customers can obtain (after signing a non-disclosure agreement with Intel). If you are a developer who does not want to understand or debug Intel's code, and you have no interest in reading hundreds of pages of a BWG, you can simply take the Intel FSP, integrate it into your firmware stack, and let the magic of Intel FSP work for you.

Once executed, Intel FSP initializes the memory, programs the system address space, and initializes the input/output (I/O) controllers of the microprocessor and its companion chip. You will be able to run the next stage firmware stack to do whatever you like to do from this point on. Obviously, you still have a lot of work to do to initialize the rest of the platform, but the good news is that the rest of the system depends less on silicon vendors, but more on industry standards, publicly available specifications, and your own design recipes. There is even reference code and sample code to help you finish the features that are commonly available in a system.

The Intel FSP Philosophy

As discussed in Chapter 1, Intel believes that there are a lot of smart firmware engineers out there in the embedded industry. Intel knows that some of them are looking for turnkey solutions, with which they don't have to do anything besides turning knobs on a GUI-based tool. Intel also knows that some of them are looking for completely open source solutions that bring total freedom in creating customer-specific firmware stacks. Besides the 100% GUI-tool users and 100% open source users, there are many engineers who need to work with hybrid solutions because their code bases are either proprietary or have a lot of customized features to be added beyond standard features offered by the reference designs.

No doubt in people's mind, silicon vendors know their chips inside out because they design them; therefore, providing Intel FSP to encapsulate the chip initialization code that Intel knows the best makes sense. Developers who choose to leverage Intel FSP will have a better starting point with a new Intel chip than relying on a self-learning process from reading programming manuals.

Intel FSP does not have features that are typically available in reference BIOS from Intel (such as secure boot, PCI Bus enumeration, power management, etc.). The reason why these features are not included is because Intel does not want to burden everyone with code they may not need. Intel wants to keep the FSP footprint as small as possible. For this reason, a developer may feel lost if he or she has been depending upon Intel to deliver the additional features in the reference BIOS, but the good news is that these features have publicly available specifications, standards, and even sample code to follow or copy. Obviously, the bad news is that the developer will have to somehow implement these features in the firmware stack if they need the features. If the developer is implementing them from scratch, it could be hard, but this is the price the developer has to pay when switching away from the reference BIOS model. Whichever way the developer chooses to acquire the features (do it himself/herself or pay someone to do it), the developer has a better starting point with Intel FSP than with a reference BIOS because of the additional freedom provided by FSP. Hopefully, as the ecosystem for supporting Intel FSP grows, there will be more and more ISVs involved to provide firmware solutions different than BIOS. Additionally, once the code for these peripheral features is done, most of the code is reusable and can last for a long time. For example, PCI bus enumeration code, even though is complicated, does not change between generations of chips. Most of the power management and secure boot features do not need an overhaul once the foundation is built.

It is really all about additional freedom provided by Intel FSP; it is not an answer to all the firmware needs associated with Intel Architecture. If you have a design that heavily leverages Intel CRB and standard features, you are probably better off with a standard BIOS solution; it does not likely make sense to start a new firmware stack to replace your existing BIOS. However, if you are starting from scratch, or if your design is significantly different from a traditional PC, you might want to consider the options involving Intel FSP. Intel FSP addresses a niche market where the developer doesn't use PC architecture or when the developer does not plan to use BIOS. Therefore, don't jump onto the Intel FSP bandwagon until you know your ultimate goal.

What Is in Intel FSP?

Later in this book, we will show you where to download Intel FSP. At the FSP download site on the Web, you will find self-extracting executable packages (in .exe format for Windows or in .tgz files if you are exploring Linux options).

After you download the file in .exe or .tgz format for your favorite OS, you can extract the contents from the file by executing the .exe file or by using your favorite Linux unpacking utility. And, you can find a couple of items in your expanded folder:

- A subfolder called Documentation, which contains an integration guide and release notes.

- A subfolder called FSP, which contains an FSP binary file (with an .fd file extension), a Boot Setting File (BSF, with a .bsf file extension), and two subfolders with sample header files and source code.

- A subfolder called Graphics. This folder is optional. When it exists, it contains graphics components that you might need, such as a VGA BIOS image.

- A subfolder called Microcode, which contains the microcode patches available at the time of the release of FSP. The microcode patches can be updated independently of FSP, as well as when you must download the latest ones to make sure that they match with the microprocessor used on your board.

There are additional files, such as the licensing agreement, a ReadMe (describing the contents of FSP), and so forth. These are not important to the discussion of this book. There is an important tool available—the Binary Configuration Tool—on the same download page, but it is a separate download file. We will discuss this tool later in the book.

We will explain each item in more detail, but a hard-core open source software engineer may already have a question about why Intel ships only a binary file, not the source code. Currently, there are a couple of reasons. Intel may change the design and deliverables in the future.

- Intel FSP still has some IP-protected code inside; therefore, until this code can be properly protected or cleared for protection, Intel does not have a near-term plan to release it in an open source repository. However, you may have discovered that Intel has already released 100% of the source code for the Intel® Quark™ SoC X1000 Series; therefore, Intel is gradually removing the barrier of IP protection. It may take a few years to see Intel completely open all the source code at this level.

- Intel wants to eventually move basic silicon initialization code inside the silicon one day; therefore, a binary file is isolated enough that it can pave the road for future silicon inclusion. Many silicon vendors have already included a Boot ROM inside their SoC. Since the code inside the Boot ROM is for the purpose of initializing the SoC, it should not be a concern if silicon initialization code is isolated and protected somehow. Intel FSP does offer a way to customize its internal configuration with the BCT tool; thus it further eliminates the need to change what is inside Intel FSP.

- Many vendors release binary files to abstract silicon and hardware code. This practice has been in existence for many decades; for example, the Option ROM on plug-in cards contains a binary code that initializes the hardware on the card. VGA BIOS still exists in the form of Option ROM, even though there is no longer a plug-in card. This abstraction has been working out nicely in the PC industry because it provides a simple interface and isolation so that the cards can be sold separately from the motherboards.

- Being a binary, it can be interfaced with a firmware stack without being dynamically or statically linked into the host firmware. In this way, it can help eliminate the concerns of open source codebase using General Public License (GPL) when integrating. Because this book does not provide legal advice and there are a few different versions of GPL, you need to double-check with your legal department to decide what is OK and what is not OK.

That said, Intel does realize that many hardware and firmware engineers need source code to bring up or power-on a brand-new board in order to debug a problem when the board is not functioning after the power is applied. Intel offers source code to customers under a special software license agreement (SLA). It is beyond the scope of this book to discuss how to obtain source code from Intel; therefore, you should contact Intel's sales or field engineers to ask for details.

As previously discussed, even though Intel FSP is a binary file, it needs a provision to customize its internal states and features; therefore, it has reserved a data region inside the binary for customization. The data area also contains a couple of platform-specific parameters that Intel FSP would otherwise have no knowledge about, or would initialize the board with default values. The Boot Setting File (BSF) plays an important role for this purpose. It is basically a text file that contains firmware internal settings associated with the board; for example, the SMBUS (System Management Bus) address of a SPD (Serial Presence Detect) ROM on a DIMM (Dual Inline Memory Module) is one of the data in the BSF.

```
$gPlatformFspPkgTokenSpaceGuid_PcdMrcInitSPDAddr1  1 byte $_DEFAULT_ = 0xA0
$gPlatformFspPkgTokenSpaceGuid_PcdMrcInitSPDAddr2  1 byte $_DEFAULT_ = 0xA2
```

A sample BSF can be found in Appendix A.

The data in BSF is represented in a GUI-based tool, which allows developers to visualize the meaning of each component in BSF. With the GUI and BSF, it is collectively called a Binary Configuration Tool (BCT). There are three versions of BCT: one runs under Windows, one runs under Linux, and the third is a command-line option under Linux. Figure 3-1 shows a BCT tool for Windows.

Figure 3-1. *Binary Configuration Tool (BCT) GUI*

The last part of Intel FSP is the header files and sample code. These files are for developers to include in their firmware stack to develop the interface code with Intel FSP; therefore, developers can include these files in the firmware stack or re-create the files based on these files. For example, fsp.h under the include directory, looks like this:

```
#include <stdint.h>
#include "fsptypes.h"
#include "fspfv.h"
#include "fspffs.h"
#include "fsphob.h"
#include "fspapi.h"
#include "fspplatform.h"
#include "fspinfoheader.h"
#include "fspvpd.h"


#define FSP_HOB_RESOURCE_OWNER_FSP_GUID \
{ 0x69a79759, 0x1373, 0x4367, { 0xa6, 0xc4, 0xc7, 0xf5, 0x9e, 0xfd, 0x98, 0x6e } }
#define FSP_NON_VOLATILE_STORAGE_HOB_GUID \
{ 0x721acf02, 0x4d77, 0x4c2a, { 0xb3, 0xdc, 0x27, 0xb, 0x7b, 0xa9, 0xe4, 0xb0 } }
#define FSP_HOB_RESOURCE_OWNER_TSEG_GUID \
{ 0xd038747c, 0xd00c, 0x4980, { 0xb3, 0x19, 0x49, 0x01, 0x99, 0xa4, 0x7d, 0x55 } }
#define FSP_HOB_RESOURCE_OWNER_GRAPHICS_GUID \
{ 0x9c7c3aa7, 0x5332, 0x4917, { 0x82, 0xb9, 0x56, 0xa5, 0xf3, 0xe6, 0x2a, 0x07 } }
#define FSP_BOOTLOADER_TEMPORARY_MEMORY_HOB_GUID \
{ 0xbbcff46c, 0xc8d3, 0x4113, { 0x89, 0x85, 0xb9, 0xd4, 0xf3, 0xb3, 0xf6, 0x4e } }


//
// 0x21 - 0xf..f are reserved.
//
#define BOOT_WITH_FULL_CONFIGURATION     0x00
#define BOOT_ON_S3_RESUME                0x11
```

Intel FSP Binary Format

Since Intel FSP is a binary file, it needs to be organized in a standard way that the data inside can be easily found and retrieved. What are things you need to find inside the Intel FSP? The two most important interface points are the application programming interface (API) and the configuration region.

Intel FSP chose to follow UEFI's Firmware Volume (FV) layout format. Don't be alarmed if you are not familiar with Platform Initialization (PI), UEFI, or FV. FV is just a layout format that dictates how the data inside is organized. If you want to learn more about FV, please find more information in the Appendix or look it up on the UEFI web site. The diagram in Figure 3-2 shows the FV layout format.

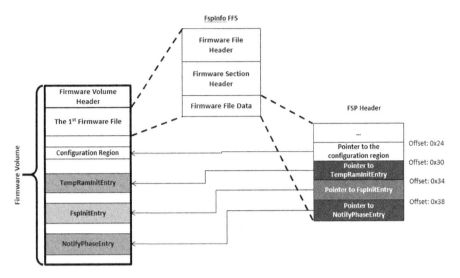

Figure 3-2. *Intel FSP binary Firmware Volume (FV) layout*

Figure 3-2 shows an FV where Intel FSP resides, but Intel FSP can be split into multiple FVs due to the needs of secure boot and other features. For example, there can be one FV that contains part of the code that needs to be certified and signed, and there can be another part of the code that is customizable for developers; therefore, the latter can exist in a different FV so that the second part can be certified or signed separately from the first one. The other case that warrants the separation of the FVs is where one part can be masked after production and the other part can be updated in the field. Intel FSP provides the flexibility to be used in different ways.

A few key ingredients are in the Intel FSP binary:

- FSP information header region for configuration data

- Offsets pointing to API entry points and the configuration data region

- The APIs themselves

The FSP information header provides a basic FSP image signature, a base, size information, and the offsets pointing to the API entry points and the configuration region.

The following shows the FSP information header:

```
typedef struct {

        UINT32  Signature;       // Off 0x94
        UINT32  HeaderLength;
        UINT8   Reserved1[3];
        UINT8   HeaderRevision;
        UINT32  ImageRevision;
```

```
CHAR8    ImageId[8];          // Off 0xA4
UINT32   ImageSize;
UINT32   ImageBase;

UINT32   ImageAttribute;   // Off 0xB4
UINT32   CfgRegionOffset;
UINT32   CfgRegionSize;
UINT32   ApiEntryNum;

UINT32   NemInitEntry;        // Off 0xC4
UINT32   FspInitEntry;
UINT32   NotifyPhaseEntry;
UINT32   Reserved2;
```

} FSP_INFO_HEADER;

As you can see, offset numbers are provided here in the sample header structure: 148 bytes (0x94 is the hexadecimal number) from the top of the file is the starting point of the FSP_INFO_HEADER; 164 bytes (0xA4 is the hexadecimal number) from the top is the identification string of the FSP binary; 180 bytes (0xB4 is the hexadecimal number) from the top is the location that contains the offset to the configuration region; and 196 bytes (0xC4 is the hexadecimal number) from the top is where the three pointers to the three APIs are located. Later on, we will talk about why the offset values are important to know. These numbers may change based on the platform. Please check the documentation that comes with each Intel FSP release—particularly the Intel FSP Integration Guide—to obtain the latest offset values.

The configuration data region stores platform-specific information; some parameters are customizable during runtime by the firmware stack, and some are fixed once configured—thus static once they are manipulated by the BCT. Details will be discussed later. The pointers to the APIs and the APIs themselves are part of the FV, and they will be discussed in later sections as well.

Sample Boot Flow

The boot process starts from the Reset Vector after power is applied. In modern computers, many things have already happened before the first fetch of the opcode located at the Reset Vector of the CPU, such as microcontroller firmware and management engine firmware. In a secure boot implementation, the management engine in the system can hold the reset signal to the CPU until it deems that the firmware running the CPU is trustworthy and safe to run.

As shown in Figure 3-3, once the firmware stack is allowed to execute, the CPU will fetch its first instruction from the Reset Vector, which is located at top of the 4-gigabyte physical memory space, minus 16 bytes (or FFFFFFF0, in hexadecimal value). This address is hardwired in the Intel microprocessors during reset, and the location should fall inside the Flash ROM if you have designed your board correctly. In the design of future microprocessors, this physical address of FFFFFFF0 may change to allow more flexibility.

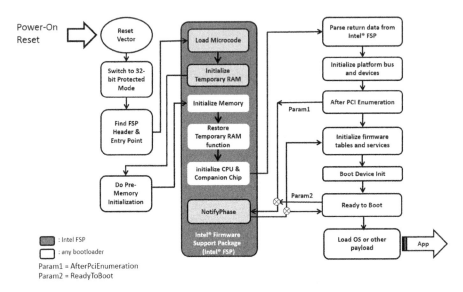

Figure 3-3. *A sample boot flow involving Intel FSP*

At this point, the firmware stack inside the Flash ROM will begin to execute; the first thing it needs to do is quickly exit the "reset mode" and enter a more permanent 32-bit Protected Flat Mode. This "32-bit Protected Flat Mode" is a loaded term, but it is basically a mode that allows you to access 4 gigabytes of "flat" physical address space with the existing segment register and selector settings. After entering this 32-bit Protected Flat mode, the firmware stack has a powerful execution environment to access code and memory mapped I/O anywhere within the 4-gigabyte range.

However, even with the power to access the 4-gigabyte address range, you still cannot do too much without memory and I/O devices; therefore, the firmware stack should be initializing the memory controller and the companion I/O controllers as soon as possible so that it can actually run its code inside the faster DRAM (instead of the slow Flash ROM) and access I/O devices in the system. This is where you will run into the first headache in dealing with a new silicon from a silicon vendor. In Intel's case, you may use Intel's Memory Reference Code (MRC) directly if you can get one, or you can download Intel FSP that contains the MRC.

Since MRC is very complicated, we recommend you not to touch MRC. If you understand DDR (Double Data Rate) memory technology, you know that MRC contains the memory training algorithm to try to find the sweet spot of the operating speed, signal strength, and other parameters for the DRAMs in the system; whatever algorithm Intel (or any other silicon vendor) has developed inside MRC, it is robust, optimized, and validated. You should not touch the code if you don't have a reason to do so. However, you might want to customize your design; for example, bypassing memory training when you have a soldered-down or fixed memory configuration. But this so-called "Fast Boot" path is also provided inside MRC; it is typically an option provided by the Intel FSP BCT configuration tool. You can achieve this "Fast Boot" by simply turning a bit on and off inside the tool. FSP will automatically apply the fast boot option when a valid NVS (Non-Volatile Storage) data region is provided by the firmware stack. The NVS data region contains the memory parameters that can be used repeatedly by Intel FSP.

▪ **Note** DDR technology is quite delicate; the training algorithm exists for a reason. The "sweet spot" of operation may change over time due to temperature, aging, and other factors in the environment; therefore, the parameters stored in the NVS may not work all the time unless careful error margins are built in, and a failover mechanism is provided when the parameters in NVS no longer work. The memory training may need to be executed again to acquire new parameters when old parameters do not function.

As shown in Figure 3-3, Intel FSP does more than just memory initialization; you should use it rather than dealing with MRC directly. Intel FSP also loads microcode patches and initializes companion I/O controllers for you. In addition, it sets up a small amount of temporary memory using cache or SRAM before DRAM is initialized, so that you can execute code more efficiently before the system memory is fully initialized.

Therefore, once the host firmware stack transitions to the 32-bit Protected Flat Mode, it can look for the first Intel FSP entry point and jump into it. The first thing that Intel FSP does inside the first FSP API is load microcode patches, and then initialize a small region of temporary memory. Once the temporary memory is set up, Intel FSP returns control back to the host firmware stack. Why? Because the next step Intel FSP is about to do is to initialize DDR memory, where a memory training algorithm will be conducted, and it can take 100 milliseconds to 300 milliseconds to finish, depending upon the board layout, the amount of memory, and which DDR technology is used. If you have something important and urgent or devices that can be turned on early to allow the electronics to be stabilized before the OS starts (e.g., the LED backlight, HDD spin-up, etc.), you can do it before memory is initialized. Some firmware stacks take this opportunity to verify the integrity of the next stage of boot code to ensure that the code running next is secure and trust worthy.

Once pre-memory initialization work is done by the host firmware, it can once again call into the second entry point of Intel FSP. This time, Intel FSP is going to finish the memory initialization and the companion chip initialization altogether. Once this is done, upon return, the host firmware will be able to see 4 gigabytes of memory available for them to use. There are many techniques in firmware to look beyond 4 gigabytes, such as memory hoisting (moving memory above 4 gigabyte to fill the memory holes created by Memory Mapped I/O); but the best way to access memory above 4 gigabyte is to transition to 64-bit long mode, although most embedded firmware stacks don't do that unless they are designed to boot a 64-bit OS. Some firmware stacks will remain in 32-bit mode until the last minute before booting a 64-bit OS; it is up to the firmware developer to decide when to switch to 64-bit mode if it is necessary.

At this point, Intel FSP has done its job and leaves the rest of the platform initialization work to the host firmware. The following chapters will be walking you through two firmware stacks as examples for carrying out the platform initialization work.

There is another entry point of Intel FSP that we have not talked about—NotifyPhase. NotifyPhase is an entry point for the host firmware to call back to Intel FSP after PCI bus enumeration and before booting an OS, because there are things to be adjusted, locked down, and cleaned up; as an example, the TSEG register will be locked so that no one can mess it up after booting an OS.

Once NotifyPhase returns the control to the host firmware, the firmware is ready to transition control to a payload or an interface to boot an OS.

Is this the only way to go through the boot process? Of course not; this is a typical boot process for a system based on PC architecture. For a system without PC bus or graphics, or closed without expansion, the boot process can be different or simpler, and Intel FSP can still be part of the boot process to initialize silicon features.

One thing should be very clear to you now: Intel FSP is not a firmware stack itself. It needs to be integrated into one. And, Intel FSP contains only the basic silicon initialization code; more sophisticated features need to be carried out by the host firmware stack; for example, power management, bus enumeration, ACPI, and so forth.

A rough estimation of the Intel FSP size is between 100 and 300 kilobytes, and it can finish all the tasks within 100 to 300 milliseconds. These size and performance estimations are all tied to the CPU type, and the size and performance of MRC dominate the overall estimation because it is the biggest and slowest code inside Intel FSP.

The boot flow shown in Figure 3-3 may change in the future, when new requirements for Intel FSP show up; for example, Intel FSP may provide more hooks to allow host firmware to carry out actions in between various Initialization tasks.

Locating the Entries of Intel FSP

Since Intel FSP is a binary image, the host firmware stack needs to find the image of Intel FSP soon after it starts running from the reset vector. Once Intel FSP is found, it needs to find the entry points pointing to the three APIs that we mentioned in the section about Boot Flow. There are two ways to find the pointers to these APIs.

The Hard Way to Find Intel FSP APIs: Use Data Structure

A developer can certainly follow the predefined and standard FV data structure to parse the data in an FV binary. All you have to do is trace through the data structure and look for header and data regions that contain relevant FSP data.

The first step is to find the base address of the FV where Intel FSP resides. This is where you physically put the FSP binary image. Many Intel FSP binary images are designed to exist at a physical address, such as 0xFFFF8000. A developer can customize the location by rebasing Intel FSP to a different location by running the BCT, which will be discussed later. As you read the data out of the FV and match it against the data structure of EFI_FIRMWARE_VOLUME_HEADER, defined in a standard UEFI header file for FV, you can basically follow the hierarchy of the data structure and look for the data you need.

```
typedef struct {
        UINT8 ZeroVector[16];
        EFI_GUID FileSystemGuid;
        UINT64 FvLength;
        UINT32 Signature;
        EFI_FVB_ATTRIBUTES_2 Attributes;
        UINT16 HeaderLength;
        UINT16 Checksum;
        UINT16 ExtHeaderOffset;
        UINT8 Reserved[1];
        UINT8 Revision;
        EFI_FV_BLOCK_MAP BlockMap[];
} EFI_FIRMWARE_VOLUME_HEADER;
```

FSP_INFORMATION_HEADER is a firmware file that is placed as the first firmware file within the FV. All firmware files have a GUID that can be used to identify the files, including the FSP header file. The FSP header firmware file GUID is defined as 912740BE-2284-4734-B971-84B027353F0C.

The host firmware stack can find the offset of the FSP header within the FSP binary by following these steps:

1. Use EFI_FIRMWARE_VOLUME_HEADER to parse the FSP FV header and skip the standard and extended FV header.

2. The EFI_FFS_FILE_HEADER with the FSP_FFS_ INFORMATION_FILE_GUID is located at the 8-byte aligned offset following the FV header.

3. The EFI_RAW_SECTION header follows the FFS File Header.

4. Immediately following the EFI_RAW_SECTION header is the raw data. The format of this data is defined in the FSP_INFORMATION_HEADER structure.

The following is a sample code snippet that does the previous steps in a stackless environment. Since the code will be executed in a stackless environment, assembly code is preferred. In this example, we use the C language for easier readability.

```
//
// Validate FV signature _FVH
//
        if (((EFI_FIRMWARE_VOLUME_HEADER *)ptr)-> Signature != 0x4856465F) {
              ptr = 0;
               goto NotFound;
        }
//
// Add the Ext Header size to the Ext Header base to go to the
// end of FV header
```

```
//
        ptr += ((EFI_FIRMWARE_VOLUME_HEADER *)ptr)->ExtHeaderOffset;
        ptr += ((EFI_FIRMWARE_VOLUME_EXT_HEADER *)ptr)->ExtHeaderSize;
//
// Align the end of FV header address to 8 bytes
//
        ptr = (UINT8 *)(((UINT32)ptr + 7) & 0xFFFFFFF8);
//
// Now ptr is pointing to thr FFS Header. Verify if the GUID
// matches the FSP_INFO_HEADER GUID
//
        if ( (((UINT32 *)&(((EFI_FFS_FILE_HEADER *)ptr)->Name))[0] !=
0x912740BE) ||
        (((UINT32 *)&(((EFI_FFS_FILE_HEADER *)ptr)->Name))[1] != 0x47342284) ||
        (((UINT32 *)&(((EFI_FFS_FILE_HEADER *)ptr)->Name))[2] != 0xB08471B9) ||
        (((UINT32 *)&(((EFI_FFS_FILE_HEADER *)ptr)->Name))[3] != 0x0C3F3527) ) {
                ptr = 0;
                goto NotFound;
        }
//
// Add the FFS Header size to the base to find the Raw section
// Header
//
        ptr += sizeof(EFI_FFS_FILE_HEADER);
        if (((EFI_RAW_SECTION *)ptr)->Type != EFI_SECTION_RAW) {
                ptr = 0;
                 goto NotFound;
        }
//
// Add the Raw Header size to the base to find the FSP INFO
// Header
//
        ptr += sizeof(EFI_RAW_SECTION);
NotFound:
        __asm__ __volatile__ ("ret");
```

All of these data structures are provided in FSP header files in the package; therefore, you can develop a generic solution to locate FSP APIs.

The Easy Way to Find FSP APIs: Use Hard-Coded Constants

If you are more concerned more about saving a few bytes here and there, or a few nanoseconds or microseconds here and there, and you are not worrying about changing code for every platform you build, you may consider using hard-coded constants to find the FSP APIs.

For example, the offset constant OFFSET_OF(FSP_INFO_HEADER) is defined as 0x94 for BayTrail platforms. It is the offset from the beginning of the FSP binary. The next important offset constant is OFFSET_OF(FSP_BASE), which is defined as 0x1C (28 bytes from the beginning of FSP_INFO_HEADER). The FSP_BASE must match the location where you put the FSP image in Flash. Then we have three pointers pointing to Intel FSP's three APIs located at offset constants from the beginning of FSP_INFO_HEADER: 0x30, 0x34, and 0x38, respectively. They are 4 bytes apart because these offsets are 32 bits long.

Using these offset constants, you may find the following:

- The first API (TempRAMInit) entry point at the physical location of (FSP_BASE + *(UINT32 *)(FSP_BASE + OFFSET_OF(FSP_INFO_HEADER) + 0x30))

- The second API (FspInit) entry point at the physical location of (FSP_BASE + *(UINT32 *)(FSP_BASE + OFFSET_OF(FSP_INFO_HEADER) + 0x34))

- The last API (NotifyPhase) entry point at the physical location of (FSP_BASE + *(UINT32 *)(FSP_BASE + OFFSET_OF(FSP_INFO_HEADER) + 0x38))

Programming Interface: The APIs of Intel FSP

Now you know how to find the three APIs inside of Intel FSP. It is time to understand what they are and how you should interface with them.

TempRamInit

As described in the "Sample Boot Flow" section, this FSP API will load the microcode patches, enable the code cache region specified by the host firmware, and set up a temporary stack to be used until the main memory is initialized. There are a couple of input parameters for passing in: the microcode patch base address and its size, and the host firmware code region base address and its size. The microcode patch mechanism built in FSP will try to load the correct microcode patches for the silicon by matching its CPUID and the ID of the patches; if no matching one is found, the API will return an error code. This is a typical error that the developer will face when he or she is not familiar with Intel microprocessors and the microcode patching mechanism.

The other input parameters are firmware code region base and size. They are used to enable the code cache to speed up the execution of the code in Flash. Here is the data structure of the input parameters:

```
typedef struct {
        UINT32 MicrocodeRegionBase,
        UINT32 MicrocodeRegionLength,
        UINT32 CodeRegionBase,
        UINT32 CodeRegionLength
} FSP_TEMP_RAM_INIT_PARAMS;
```

Since the host firmware is supposed to blindly jump into TempRamInit after finding its address, how does Intel FSP know where to return to after TempRamInit is done? A trick called "ROM-based stack" is used here. It is basically a trick to point the ESP (Stack Pointer) register to a location in ROM where a return address is stored. When the TempRamInit code is done, all it has to do is execute a "ret" instruction, which will pop the return address from the location pointed by the ESP register, and the Instruction Pointer will point to the next instruction that the host firmware specifies. Besides the return address, the input parameters will also be stored there so that TempRamInit can simply look at the "stack" and retrieve the input parameter as if it is running a subroutine written in the C language.

The following is an example of what the ROM-based stack looks like. ESP will be loaded with the address tempRamInitStack, where it contains the return address as temp_RamInit_done, and also the pointer to the input parameters—tempRamInitParams. The microcode patches-based address and length are passed in here.

```
tempRamInitParams:
        .long _ucode_base # Microcode base address
        .long _ucode_size # Microcode size
        .long 0xfff00000 # Code Region Base
        .long 0x00100000 # Code Region Length
tempRamInitStack:
        .long temp_RamInit_done # return address
        .long tempRamInitParams # pointer to parameters
```

This API should be called only once after the system comes out of the reset, and it must be called before any other FSP APIs. The system needs to go through a reset cycle before this API can be called again; otherwise, unexpected results may occur. The sample implementation of find_fsp_info_header and tempRamInit are listed next as an example:

```
# prepare to find FSP header
        lea findFspHeaderStack, %esp
        lea _fsp_rom_start, %eax
        jmp find_fsp_info_header
findFspHeaderDone:
        mov %eax, %ebp # save fsp header address in ebp
        mov 0x30(%ebp), %eax # TempRamInit offset in the header
        add 0x1c(%ebp), %eax # add FSP base to get the API address
        lea tempRamInitStack, %esp # initialize to a rom stack
#
# call FSP PEI to setup temporary Stack
#
        jmp *%eax
        temp_RamInit_done:
        addl $4, %esp
        cmp $0, %eax
        jz continue
```

```
#
# TempRamInit failed, dead loop
#
        jmp .
continue:
#
# Save FSP_INFO_HEADER in ebx
#
        mov %ebp, %ebx
#
# setup bootloader stack
# ecx: stack base
# edx: stack top
#
        lea -4(%edx), %esp
#
# call C based early_init to initialize meomry and chipset.
# pass the FSP INFO Header address as a paramater
#
        push %ebx
        call early_init
#
# should never return here
#
        jmp .
.align 4
findFspHeaderStack:
        .long findFspHeaderDone
tempRamInitParams:
        .long _ucode_base # Microcode base address
        .long _ucode_size # Microcode size
        .long 0xfff00000  # Code Region Base
        .long 0x00100000  # Code Region Length
tempRamInitStack:
        .long temp_RamInit_done # return address
        .long tempRamInitParams # pointer to parameters
```

If this function is successful, ECX and EDX registers will be returned to point to a temporary but writeable memory range available to the host firmware with FSP_SUCCESS stored in register EAX. Register ECX points to the start of this temporary memory range and EDX points to the end of the range. At this point, the host firmware is free to use the whole range described. Typically, the host firmware can reload the ESP register to point to the end of this returned range so that it can be used as a standard stack now, and the C-style function call can now be used; in other words, the programming language can be switch to the C language after this API is called. Since there is only limited space, the host firmware should not try to do crazy things using this memory range. Stack is probably the only function that the host firmware should consider using until the main memory is initialized by the next API.

Developers should also be aware that this returned range is just a subregion of the whole temporary memory initialized by the TempRamInit function; Intel FSP maintains and consumes the remaining temporary memory. It is important for the host firmware not to access the temporary memory beyond the returned boundary.

FspInitEntry

As shown in the sample boot flow diagram in the previous section, once Intel FSP hands over control back to the host firmware after TempRamInit is executed, the host firmware can choose to do a few things before calling the next API—FspInitEntry. Since this upcoming API initializes the memory, the CPU, and the companion chips, it may take a few hundred milliseconds before the host firmware gains control again; therefore, the host firmware can utilize this opportunity to carry out some pre-memory initialization work; for example, turn on the LED backlight, spin up the hard drive, or turn on other hardware components that need time to stabilize their electronic and mechanical states. The host firmware can also choose to verify components for secure boot purposes before continuing.

Since FspInitEntry deals with CPU, memory controller, and companion chips, it is highly dependent on the silicon it is associated with. Therefore, even though the input parameter is consistent among all Intel FSP as a pointer to a data structure, the contents of the data structure will be defined differently by each FSP release. They will be documented in the Integration Guide. The prototype of the input parameter is as follows:

```
typedef
FSP_STATUS
(FSPAPI *FSP_FSP_INIT) (
        INOUT FSP_INIT_PARAMS *FspInitParamPtr
);
```

And, the data structure is shown as the following:

```
typedef struct {
        VOID *NvsBufferPtr;
        VOID *RtBufferPtr;
        CONTINUATION_PROC ContinuationFunc;
} FSP_INIT_PARAMS;
```

Within the data structure, *NvsBufferPtr* points to the data buffer with data that needs to be stored into and retrieved from a non-volatile storage device. In the very beginning—the first time the host firmware calls the API—this parameter is NULL, and Intel FSP will return the data in the Hand-Off Block (HOB) after this API is executed. The data can then be stored in the non-volatile storage device for later usage by the host firmware. For subsequent boots, the data can be passed in by the host firmware to the FSP to handle special cases, such as S3 resume or fast boot.

RtBufferPtr points to the data buffer used for runtime configuration. For example, the "StackTop" pointer pointing to the top of the host firmware stack after memory is available; the pointer pointing to the configuration data region that contains customized configuration settings; and the boot mode, which is the flag to tell Intel FSP to optimize its initialization flow. This S3 resume path (i.e., resume from a sleep state using existing memory contents) is used to optimize the boot speed by using the memory parameters passed in (instead of going through the memory training code). It can also be used for soldered-down memory configuration, or after the first boot when there is no change in memory configuration and when memory training parameters remain valid. There is not a "Fast Boot" flag to reflect the need to skip memory training, but FSP will look at the input parameter, NvsBufferPtr, to determine if it should skip memory training or not. If it is NULL, it will not skip, and if there is a valid pointer stored in NvsBufferPtr, it will skip the memory training code. This can save potential boot time up to 100 milliseconds.

```
typedef struct {
        UINT32 *StackTop;
        UINT32 BootMode;
        VOID *UpdDataRegPtr;
        UINT32 Reserved[7];
} FSP_INIT_RT_COMMON_BUFFER;
```

ContinuationFunc is a pointer to the "continuation function" address, where Intel FSP will jump back to after the execution of this API is done. After the FspInitEntry API completes its execution, it does not return to the host firmware from where it was called, but instead returns control to the host firmware by jumping to the continuation function. The jump is accompanied by two parameters: the Status and the Pointer of a HOB list that contains the hand-off data from Intel FSP to the host firmware.

```
typedef VOID (* CONTINUATION_PROC)(
        IN FSP_STATUS Status,
        IN VOID *HobListPtr
);
```

Why are we using an input parameter, continuation function's address, as the return address? The reason why a simple return is not used after FspInitEntry is done in this case is because after memory is initialized, the old stack using temporary memory will be destroyed, and a new stack will be set up in its place. The transfer of contents in a stack can be done, but this is very risky due to compiler compatibility issues, and the old stack may no longer have valid contents after the transition; for example, a pointer to a local variable in the old stack will still point to the old stack. Even after migration, it is more reliable if we simply jump to an address passed in as a parameter.

Like the previous API, this API should be called only once.

NotifyPhase

This API is used by the host firmware to notify the FSP after finishing certain phases during the boot process, so that Intel FSP can take appropriate actions as needed for these phases. The actions and phases are platform dependent and will be documented with each FSP release. Examples of boot phases include "post pci enumeration" and "ready to boot."

The FSP will lock the configuration registers to ensure system security and reliability.

```
#define FSPAPI __attribute__((cdecl))
typedef UINT32 FSP_STATUS;
typedef FSP_STATUS (FSPAPI *FSP_NOTFY_PHASE)
(NOTIFY_PHASE_PARAMS *NotifyPhaseParamPtr);
typedef enum {
        EnumInitPhaseAfterPciEnumeration = 0x20,
        EnumInitPhaseReadyToBoot = 0x40
} FSP_INIT_PHASE;
typedef struct {
        FSP_INIT_PHASE Phase;
} NOTIFY_PHASE_PARAMS;

void FspNotifyPhase (UINT32 Phase)
{
        FSP_NOTFY_PHASE NotifyPhaseProc;
        NOTIFY_PHASE_PARAMS NotifyPhaseParams;
        FSP_STATUS Status;

        /* call FSP PEI to Notify PostPciEnumeration */
        NotifyPhaseProc = (FSP_NOTFY_PHASE)(fsp_info_header->ImageBase +
fsp_info_header->NotifyPhaseEntry);
        NotifyPhaseParams.Phase = Phase;
        Status = NotifyPhaseProc (&NotifyPhaseParams);
        if (Status != 0) {
                printf("FSP API NotifyPhase failed for phase %d!\n",Phase);
        }
}
```

Intel FSP Output

As initialization progresses, a lot of system information and configuration data are collected in the process. The data needs to be passed to the host firmware so that it does not need to rediscover this data on its own. While Intel FSP is discovering the data, it builds a series of data structures called Hand-Off Blocks, or HOBs, and fills them with useful information, such as total memory size and so forth. The data structures conform to the HOB format, as described in the PI specification Volume 3: Shared Architectural Elements, which can be downloaded from www.uefi.org/specifications/ under the latest specification listed on the page. HOBs are the only conduits between Intel FSP and the host firmware once Intel FSP is done with its work. Therefore, the user of the FSP binary is strongly encouraged to go through the specification mentioned earlier in order to understand the HOB design details and create a simple infrastructure to parse the HOBs, because the same infrastructure can be reused with different FSPs across different platforms.

The specification mentioned earlier describes about nine different HOBs; most of the information may not be relevant to a particular host firmware. It's up to the host firmware to decide how to consume the information passed through the HOBs produced by the FSP.

Regarding how you know which information is important and which information is not important, you need to examine the data structures and decide what is needed by the platform initialization code, and then retrieve the data from the data structures, as needed. The data structures can be different from platform to platform, and new data can be available as new features and new requirements are developed.

API Execution Status

The host firmware can check the status after each API call. The following are the statuses for TempRamInit:

- FSP_SUCCESS: Temp RAM was initialized successfully.

- FSP_INVALID_PARAMETER: Input parameters are invalid.

- FSP_NOT_FOUND: No valid microcode was found in the microcode region.

- FSP_UNSUPPORTED: The FSP calling conditions were not met.

- FSP_DEVICE_ERROR: Temp RAM initialization failed.

The following are the statuses for FspInit:

- FSP_SUCCESS: The FSP execution environment was initialized successfully.

- FSP_INVALID_PARAMETER: Input parameters are invalid.

- FSP_UNSUPPORTED: The FSP calling conditions were not met.

- FSP_DEVICE_ERROR: FSP initialization failed.

The following are the statuses for NotifyPhase:

- FSP_SUCCESS: The notification was handled successfully.

- FSP_UNSUPPORTED: The notification was not called in the proper order.

- FSP_INVALID_PARAMETER: The notification code is invalid.

Temporary Memory Data HOB

A few paragraphs ago, we talked about the temporary stack being destroyed after main memory initialization, but there could be data that interests you that is still in the stack. Intel FSP will save the subregion where the host firmware data is stored, and pass it back to the host firmware using a HOB data structure with a unique GUID, defined as follows:

```
#define FSP_BOOTLOADER_TEMPORARY_MEMORY_HOB_GUID \
{ 0xbbcff46c, 0xc8d3, 0x4113, { 0x89, 0x85, 0xb9, 0xd4, 0xf3,
0xb3, 0xf6, 0x4e } };
```

Non-Volatile Storage HOB

Another HOB worth mentioning is the Non-Volatile Storage HOB, which is used to pass data to the host firmware to save for S3 resume or fast boot. The host firmware needs to parse the HOB list to see if such a GUID HOB exists once the continuation function is regaining control from Intel FSP. If so, the host firmware should extract the data portion from the HOB and save it into a platform-specific NVS device, such as Flash, EEPROM, and so forth.

During the following boot process, the host firmware should load the data block back from the NVS device to temporary memory and populate the buffer pointer into the FSP_INIT_PARAMS.NvsBufferPtr field before calling into the FspInit() API. If the NVS device is memory mapped, the host firmware can initialize the buffer pointer directly to the buffer.

Sample Code for Parsing HOBs

This is sample code that parses HOBs to look for memory size below the 4 gigabyte boundary:

```
VOID
GetLowMemorySize (
UINT32 *LowMemoryLength
)
{
        EFI_PEI_HOB_POINTERS Hob;
        *LowMemoryLength = 0x100000;
        //
        // Get the HOB list for processing
        //
        Hob.Raw = GetHobList();
        //
        // Collect memory ranges
        //
        while (!END_OF_HOB_LIST (Hob)) {
                if (Hob.Header->HobType == EFI_HOB_TYPE_RESOURCE_DESCRIPTOR)
{
                        if (Hob.ResourceDescriptor->ResourceType ==
                        EFI_RESOURCE_SYSTEM_MEMORY) {
                         //
                         // Need memory above 1MB to be collected here
                         //
```

```
            if (Hob.ResourceDescriptor->PhysicalStart >=
            0x100000 &&
            Hob.ResourceDescriptor->PhysicalStart <
            (EFI_PHYSICAL_ADDRESS) 0x100000000) {
                    *LowMemoryLength += (UINT32)
                    (Hob.ResourceDescriptor-
                    >ResourceLength);
            }
        }
    }
    Hob.Raw = GET_NEXT_HOB (Hob);
  }
  return;
}
```

For memory above 4 gigabytes, the following code is used in place of the code looking a PhysicalStart element:

```
if (Hob.ResourceDescriptor->ResourceType == EFI_RESOURCE_SYSTEM_MEMORY) {
//
// Need memory above 4GB to be collected here
//
        if (Hob.ResourceDescriptor->PhysicalStart >=
        (EFI_PHYSICAL_ADDRESS) 0x100000000) {
                *HighMemoryLength += (UINT64) (Hob.ResourceDescriptor-
                >ResourceLength);
        }
}
```

Customization of Intel FSP

Even though Intel FSP can carry out CPU, memory, and companion chip initialization, it needs the cooperation from the host firmware to pass in crucial information about the platform. And developers can also customize Intel FSP by changing the hardware configuration settings when necessary.

The way Intel FSP organizes the configurable region is to separate it into two areas: a static area and a dynamic area. The static area is called VPD (Vital Product Data) and the dynamic area is called UPD (Updatable Product Data). Both areas can be customized using the BCT; however only the UPD area can be overridden by the host firmware during runtime.

The way to override the UPD data is to copy the UPD data structure to the temporary memory (remember that this is before FspInit is called), modify the data you want to alter, and then pass the pointer in as an input parameter. The FspInit API parameter includes a pointer that can be initialized to point to the UPD data structure. If this pointer is initialized to NULL when calling the FspInit API, the FSP will use the default UPD data that is available in the FSP configuration region. If it is not NULL, the FSP will use the data structure in temporary memory. Whatever data you have modified will be used to configure the hardware when FspInit executes.

The following shows an example of the VPD data structure:

```
typedef struct _UPD_DATA_REGION {
        UINT64 Signature; /* Offset 0x0000 */
        UINT32 RESERVED1; /* Offset 0x0008 */
        UINT8 Padding0[20]; /* Offset 0x000C */
        UINT16 PcdMrcInitTsegSize; /* Offset 0x0014 */
        UINT16 PcdMrcInitMmioSize; /* Offset 0x0016 */
        UINT8 PcdMrcInitSPDAddr1; /* Offset 0x0018 */
        UINT8 PcdMrcInitSPDAddr2; /* Offset 0x0019 */
        UINT8 PcdeMMCBootMode; /* Offset 0x001B */
        UINT8 PcdEnableSdio; /* Offset 0x001C */
        UINT8 PcdEnableSdcard; /* Offset 0x001D */
        UINT8 PcdEnableHsuart0; /* Offset 0x001E */
        UINT8 PcdEnableHsuart1; /* Offset 0x001F */
        UINT8 PcdEnableSpi; /* Offset 0x0020 */
        UINT8 PcdEnableLan; /* Offset 0x0021 */
        UINT8 PcdEnableSata; /* Offset 0x0023 */
        UINT8 PcdSataMode; /* Offset 0x002E */
        UINT8 PcdEnableAzalia; /* Offset 0x002F */
        UINT32 AzaliaConfigPtr; /* Offset 0x0030 */
        UINT8 PcdEnableXhci; /* Offset 0x0034 */
        UINT8 PcdEnableLpe; /* Offset 0x0029 */
        UINT8 PcdLpssSioEnablePciMode; /* Offset 0x002A */
        UINT8 PcdEnableDma0; /* Offset 0x002B */
        UINT8 PcdEnableDma1; /* Offset 0x002C */
        UINT8 PcdEnableI2C0; /* Offset 0x002D */
        UINT8 PcdEnableI2C1; /* Offset 0x002E */
        UINT8 PcdEnableI2C2; /* Offset 0x002F */
        UINT8 PcdEnableI2C3; /* Offset 0x0030 */
        UINT8 PcdEnableI2C4; /* Offset 0x0031 */
        UINT8 PcdEnableI2C5; /* Offset 0x0032 */
        UINT8 PcdEnableI2C6; /* Offset 0x0033 */
        UINT8 PcdEnablePwm0; /* Offset 0x0034 */
        UINT8 PcdEnablePwm1; /* Offset 0x0035 */
        UINT8 PcdEnableHsi; /* Offset 0x0036 */
        UINT8 PcdIgdDvmt50PreAlloc; /* Offset 0x0043 */
        UINT8 PcdApertureSize; /* Offset 0x0044 */
        UINT8 PcdGttSize; /* Offset 0x0045 */
        UINT16 PcdRegionTerminator; /* Offset 0x003A */
} UPD_DATA_REGION;
```

Whereas a sample VPD data structure is shown here:

```
typedef struct _VPD_DATA_REGION {
        UINT64 PcdVpdRegionSign; /* Offset 0x0000 */
        UINT32 PcdImageRevision; /* Offset 0x0008 */
        UINT32 PcdUpdRegionOffset; /* Offset 0x000C */
```

```
        UINT8 Padding0[16]; /* Offset 0x0010 */
        UINT32 RESERVED1; /* Offset 0x0020 */
        UINT8 PcdPlatformType; /* Offset 0x0024 */
        UINT8 PcdEnableSecureBoot; /* Offset 0x0025 */
        UINT8 PcdMemoryParameters[16]; /* Offset 0x0026 */
} VPD_DATA_REGION;
```

These two examples are from the Intel FSP for Intel Atom E3800 Product family. In this VPD data structure, each element has a matching member provided in a Binary Setting Flag file, which specifies the layout of the configuration region.

Downloading Intel FSP

Now you understand the basic plumbing and interface of Intel FSP. More practice exercises will be provided in later chapters using coreboot and EDK II codebase to show how they integrate Intel FSP, including the handling of input parameters and output parameters. During these exercises, you will need to download a copy of Intel FSP. Here are the steps:

1. Figure out which CPU and Chipset combo you are designing your firmware for. If you are working on a SoC, you need to figure out which SoC family you are using.

2. Go to www.intel.com/fsp/ and select the "Download an Intel FSP" link, as shown in Figure 3-4.

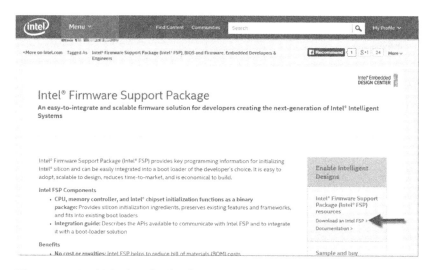

Figure 3-4. *Intel FSP download web site*

3. Once you click the "Download an Intel FSP" link, it takes you to the next screen, as shown in Figure 3-5. Select the kind of package you want: Windows or Linux.

Figure 3-5. *Intel FSP download selection*

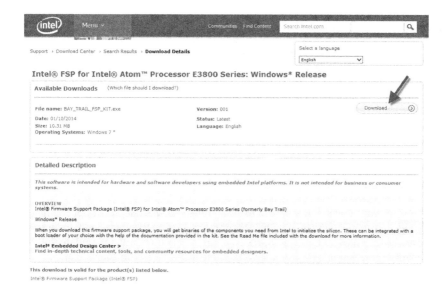

Figure 3-6. *Intel FSP download action*

4. After accepting the licensing agreement, the download will start. After downloading, unpack it.

Name	Date modified	Type	Size
BCT	5/11/2014 10:27 AM	File folder	
Documentation	5/11/2014 10:07 AM	File folder	
FSP	5/11/2014 10:28 AM	File folder	
Graphics	5/11/2014 10:07 AM	File folder	
Microcode	5/11/2014 10:07 AM	File folder	
Uninstall	5/11/2014 10:07 AM	File folder	
BAY_TRAIL_FSP_KIT.exe	5/11/2014 10:06 AM	Application	10,562 KB
bct-3.1.2-i686.win32.exe	5/11/2014 10:26 AM	Application	12,382 KB
bct-3.1.2-x86_64.fc14.tar.gz	5/11/2014 11:06 AM	GZ File	22,268 KB
FSP Kit Production RULAC click-through License.pdf	2/21/2014 5:57 PM	Adobe Acrobat D...	173 KB
FSP Kit Production RULAC click-through.txt	2/24/2014 12:09 PM	Text Document	27 KB
ReadMe.pdf	3/25/2014 10:27 AM	Adobe Acrobat D...	128 KB

Figure 3-7. *Intel FSP package layout and contents*

5. Depending upon which source code codebase you are using, you can start copying them to the appropriate folders under the host firmware directory trees.

Now, you are ready to create code, change the code, and build the code.

Microcode Patches

Microcode is a unique machine code that runs inside a CPU and many other silicon chips to initialize its internal states and features. Since the year 2000, all modern CPUs have been using microcode updates to fix issues that are frequently documented in erratum by silicon vendors.

The microcode update format is not documented and it cannot be easily read or understood by engineers who are not specialized in microprogramming. For example, one microinstruction could carry out a "Connect this register to that side of the ALU" task, and the other one might "Set ALU's carry input to zero". Each microinstruction may be doing something completely tied to the silicon at the logic level, and will only make sense to the silicon designers who actually designed the chip.

As shown in Figure 3-8, one of the Intel FSP folders is called Microcode, and it has the microcode updates that are available at the time Intel FSP was released. Intel FSP has the microcode update mechanism already incorporated. During the microcode update step, it will check the CPUID of the microprocessor on the circuit board and update the appropriate microcode update file into the CPU. There is the possibility that you are using a newer board with a newer stepping of the CPU, and thus the microcode updates inside Intel FSP do not match the stepping of your CPU; therefore, it will not be able to find the appropriate microcode update to update your CPU, and the system will hang as a result. If this is the case, you will need to go to Intel's support web site and look for the latest microcode updates for the CPU you have on board, convert it from a raw text file to an `.h` or an `.inc` text file, and copy it to the corresponding microcode folder in the host firmware directory tree.

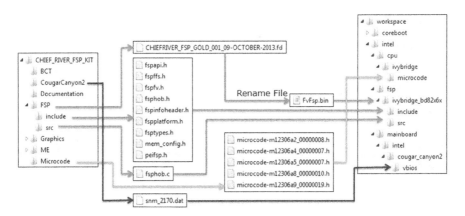

Figure 3-8. Intel FSP file movement to the host firmware folders

If you are familiar with Linux commands, here are two commands to convert from a .txt file to .h or .inc files:

```
cat name.txt | awk ' { print $1 ; print $2 ; print $3; print $4 } ' > name.h
cat name.txt | sed 's/,//'| awk ' { print " .long " $1 } '
```

There is also a utility in the coreboot tree to convert the microcode file for you; there may be other tools available to do the same thing.

The microcode updates–based address and the length are passed into the TempRamInit API as an input parameter, which is stored in ROM and is part of the ROM-based stack that we described earlier. In a multiprocessor environment, FSP supports BSP (Boot Strap Processor) and AP (Application Processor) microcode loading. The microcode range can contain multiple back-to-back microcode binaries, and the FSP will check them one by one and load all applicable patches. The microcode code patches for BSP will be loaded inside the TempRamInit API, and the patches for AP will be loaded in the FspInit API.

Relocating Intel FSP

After you download and start building your host firmware, you are told to put the Intel FSP binary at the physical location described in the FSP integration guide. However, if you decide to move Intel FSP, you will need to run BCT and change the base address of FSP to the location you prefer to use. This step is needed because many internal references to the base address need to be corrected by a tool, since they do not dynamically resolve address assignment at runtime.

Integration and Build

At this point, you should have all the elements from Intel in place to do an integration with your host firmware stack. Once you have done the integration, the build process and testing will begin. Hopefully, you will spend most of time developing your value-added features, rather than debugging Intel silicon code. Intel FSP should have taken care of your basic silicon initialization needs at this point.

The Future of Intel FSP

Intel FSP is only the first step in the direction that Intel wants to take to help embedded and IoT developers to adopt Intel Architecture easily and quickly, so that they aren't spending precious time studying, implementing, and debugging silicon-related configurations and issues. Going forward, Intel FSP will continue its evolution toward a more flexible, scalable, and customizable silicon initialization module, and will cover more silicon on the Intel roadmap. We do realize that there are different needs in the developer community. Unfortunately, these needs are distributed on a scale with two opposite extremes on the spectrum. On one end are the developers who want completely open source code available to them so that they can play with the source code with total freedom and total control. On the other end are the developers who just want a turnkey solution so that they don't have to know anything about firmware; "knobs" for tuning parameters and for turning on and off features are all that they need.

The best way to satisfy everyone is to keep opening up source code for collaboration and customization and to provide different levels of turnkey solutions where it makes sense.

What Is Coming in the Following Chapters

By now, if you have been reading this chapter carefully, you should know what Intel FSP is, why it was created, what it can do, and how it carries out the work, as well as how to customize Intel FSP and how to integrate it into the host firmware stack of your choice.

Even though there are only three APIs (this number may change in a future Intel FSP) that you need to interface with in your firmware stack, you still need to prepare input parameters and deal with output parameters carefully, and learn how to build the firmware with the right tools. It is best if you continue by reading the following hands-on chapters to get familiar with the practical knowledge about building successful firmware stacks.

■ ■ ■

## CHAPTER 4

Building coreboot with Intel FSP

Empowerment of individuals is a key part of what makes open source work, since in the end, innovations tend to come from small groups, not from large, structured efforts.

—Tim O'Reilly

The Introduction of coreboot

Since 1999, developers from around the world, some as individual contributors and others working on behalf of businesses and corporations, have formed a community around coreboot, an open source firmware project. *coreboot* is boot firmware primarily focused on x86 processors and chipsets, but other processors, like Alpha, PPC, and ARM-based systems are supported. The coreboot logo is a European Brown Hare, Figure 4-1.

Figure 4-1. *coreboot logo*

coreboot firmware deals directly with system hardware configuration. As silicon has become more complicated, with more features and integrated peripherals, firmware developers have had to rely more and more on the silicon vendors for reference code and binaries for the latest silicon releases. Many silicon vendors have tried different solutions to help the developers in the community; for example, AMD's AGESA (AMD Generic Encapsulated Software Architecture), and now, Intel FSP (Firmware Support Package). With the support of silicon vendors, coreboot developers are able to develop and release current silicon devices and to concentrate on peripheral and platform customization.

We are excited to introduce you to the coreboot project. In this chapter, we will cover many of the different aspects of coreboot. The first few sections of this chapter lay the groundwork for working with the coreboot community. We cover the history of coreboot, coreboot's open source software development practices—including details on using Git, and how to build a sample coreboot image. Later in the chapter, we examine the technical details of coreboot, including the binary image structure, the execution flow, and the source code organization. The final sections include information about payloads, debugging, and optimizations for coreboot. Feel free to skip ahead and come back to these sections if you want.

The Philosophy of coreboot

coreboot is built on the belief that users and vendors deserve an open, fast, customizable, and purpose-built firmware for silicon and mainboard initialization. coreboot is designed to do critical hardware initialization before passing control to a payload.

The coreboot philosophy aligns with the Intel FSP philosophy. The coreboot hardware initialization framework handles the FSP silicon initialization API, configures system peripherals, and loads the payload.

Since coreboot is focused on hardware initialization, it does not contain any BIOS or other runtime services. Services, runtime code, and the operating system boot are provided by a payload. coreboot supports a number of different payloads, for disk boot, network boot, and legacy BIOS services. coreboot is often used to boot Linux, but depending on the payload, it can also boot most versions of BSD, Windows, or any other OS. While not part of coreboot, payloads are integral to a complete coreboot firmware image.

coreboot source code is licensed under the GNU General Public License, version 2 (GPLv2). This is the same license that the Linux kernel is released under. The GPL is a share-alike license, which means that each developer benefits from the efforts and the knowledge of the entire community, adding to the success and growth of the project. There are several restrictions about what you can and cannot do with GPL source code, which are clearly documented on the GNU web site at http://www.gnu.org/licenses/licenses.html#GPL. You need to be aware of this and should consult legal experts before integrating GPL code into your own proprietary code.

■ **Note**   Payloads are separate projects and have their own license requirements.

A Brief History

coreboot has a long history, stretching back more than 15 years to when it was known as LinuxBIOS. While the project has gone through lots of changes over the years, many of the earliest developers still contribute today.

v1: 1999–2000

The coreboot project originally started as LinuxBIOS in 1999 at Los Alamos National Labs (LANL) by Ron Minnich. Ron needed to boot a cluster made up of many x86 mainboards without the hassles that are part of the PC BIOS. The goal was to do minimal hardware initialization in order to boot Linux as fast as possible. Linux already had the drivers and support to initialize the majority of devices. Ron and a number of other key contributors from LANL, Linux NetworX, and other open source firmware projects successfully booted Linux from flash. From there, they were able to discover other nodes in the cluster, load a full kernel and user space, and start the clustering software.

v2: 2000–2005

After the initial success of v1, the design was expanded to support more CPU architectures (x86, Alpha, PPC) and to support developers with increasingly diverse needs. One of the early design goals was to have as little assembly code as possible. With new and more complex CPUs and DDR initialization requirements, the developers realized that there would be too much assembly code in the firmware. The problem with assembly code is that it is difficult to write and maintain. It also lacks the flexibility and maintainability of a higher language like C. The reason standard C cannot be used in the initial firmware code is because the C compiler requires memory to store variables on a stack.

The first supported CPU memory initialization could be done in just a few instructions of assembly code, but the newer DDR memory controllers required significantly more configuration and a lot more assembly code. To address this problem, Eric Biederman wrote a special "precompiler" called ROMCC that turns C code into stackless assembly code. ROMCC works around the stack issue by turning the C code into assembly code and using the internal CPU registers to hold all variables. ROMCC is extremely limited in the number of variable and function calls it can support, due to the small number of registers that a CPU has available. The ROMCC-generated assembly is included as an .inc file, and then compiled as part of LinuxBIOS. ROMCC could be used until the memory was initialized, and then LinuxBIOS used standard C for the majority of the firmware device configuration code.

As part of the v2 implementation, the LinuxBIOS device tree was introduced. The device tree is based on the PCI bus hierarchy and outlines the system devices. The concept is similar to the Linux kernel's PCI device driver hierarchy and uses some of the same concepts as the Linux tree and driver initialization.

Many target systems had flash devices that were too small to hold both the hardware initialization code and the Linux kernel. Image size was not the only issue. The needs of the users were changing, and additional boot device support was required. Payloads were created for flexible boot device support. A network boot solution was the obvious choice for clusters, so the "etherboot" project was modified to run directly from LinuxBIOS as a payload. Later, a disk-based boot option called FILO was added.

During this period, there were substantial silicon development contributions from Intel, VIA, SIS, Linux NetworX, SUSE, and AMD.

v2+: 2005–2008

The next advancement was the introduction of Cache as RAM (CAR) in 2005. With CAR, the CPU cache was used as temporary memory prior to memory controller initialization. It was a delicate process, but allowed the use of C code after a few hundred lines of assembly.

■ **Note** For more information, see the white paper *CAR: Using Cache as RAM in LinuxBIOS* at http://rere.qmqm.pl/~mirq/cache_as_ram_lb_09142006.pdf.

In 2005, Stefan Reinauer, a developer on the project, formed a company named coresystems GmbH to support LinuxBIOS. Stefan was one of the primary developers and co-leaders of LinuxBIOS with Ron Minnich. Stefan's significant contributions included the first AMD64 port, the original ACPI implementation, the original SMM implementation, the flashrom utility, and the FILO payload development and maintainer.

In 2005 the Free Software Foundation (FSF) started the Free BIOS campaign to support LinuxBIOS development. Ward Vandewege, of the FSF, ported LinuxBIOS to the FSF servers and other mainboards.

During this time, the AMD processors become the silicon of choice due the availability of good documents and vendor support. This support included the AMD K-8, Geode, and AMD Family 10 CPUs.

v3: 2006–2008

By 2006, LinuxBIOS had already supported hundreds of mainboards. With so many boards, there were problems with porting additional silicon and systems. Based on lessons learned from v2, LinuxBIOS v3 was a fresh start and a place to experiment and fix major problems. Developers fixed and clarified many driver and bus support issues in the device tree. New features included the new build configuration with Kconfig and a firmware image archive called LAR (LinuxBIOS ARchiver). LAR was improved upon and led to the more refined and flexible concept of CBFS.

v3 had a lot of great technical advancements, but it didn't support many mainboards and it was too unstable for commercial developers. For these reasons, it wasn't the main development branch; it was essentially an R&D branch, where the best ideas were backported to v2.

2008 LinuxBIOS Renamed "coreboot"

LinuxBIOS gained popularity and recognition within the open source community. The name became a bit of a misnomer, since Linux was no longer booted directly from flash, and other payloads and bootloaders had been substituted in its place. Since the original idea was about hardware initialization (core init) and booting quickly, it made sense to rename the project as "coreboot". At this time, co-leader Stefan Reinauer took over as the primary leader of the project, as Ron Minnich focused on other projects.

v4: 2009–2012

coreboot turned 10 years old in 2009. Open source projects should be measured in dog years, and 10 years was a major milestone. In early 2010, coreboot moved from SVN to Git for source control, and during that transition, the community took the opportunity to recognize the advancements of the past 10 years and updated to version 4.0.

coreboot continued to add developers and expanded its user base. Many mainboards were added; one of the largest contributions came from AMD, with the open source release of AMD Generic Encapsulated Software Architecture (AGESA), which started in 2004. AGESA reference code needed to be integrated with coreboot, but at the same time stand alone, as it was code directly from the silicon vendor and the same code used by the BIOS vendors. The initial support was for the AMD Family 14 silicon, but soon grew to include Family 15, Family 16, and the accompanying chipsets.

v4+: 2012–2014

In recent years, several other big vendors have become directly involved as contributors to and supporters of coreboot. The involvement of these vendors has pushed coreboot to be a viable firmware competitor on x86 processor systems at product launch.

In 2012, Google introduced the first x86-based Chromebook with coreboot as the firmware and Chrome OS as the operating system. Since then, Google, in cooperation with multiple computer manufacturers, has released several generations of Chromebooks—all using coreboot. Google is also porting and upstreaming an ARM port of coreboot to promote a consistent and common codebase.

In early 2013, Intel released coreboot FSP support with cooperation and support from Sage Electronic Engineering. Sage has been a coreboot contributor and commercial vendor since 2011, and has developed several coreboot ports with its partners AMD, Google, and Intel.

The coreboot community is also experiencing many new contributors joining it and providing new patches and support. There is a new distribution based on coreboot called *libreboot*. It is a nonproprietary software distribution for the Thinkpad T60. It is a major contribution to the coreboot source code and has the support and endorsement of Free Software developers around the world.

The following are statistics on coreboot (source: `http://www.ohloh.net/p/coreboot`, May 23, 2014):

- It has had 10,207 commits made by 285 contributors

- It represents 1,597,818 lines of code

- It is mostly written in C

- It has a very well-commented source code

- It has a well-established, mature codebase

- It is maintained by a very large development team

- It is with stable Y-O-Y commits

- It took an estimated 461 years of combined effort (COCOMO model) to create

- It has a codebase of 1,597,818 lines

- It has an estimated cost of $25,353,695

Further Reading

For more information on the history of coreboot, visit the following:

- `$ git log`: All coreboot history is easily accessible

- `http://review.coreboot.org`

- `http://www.linuxjournal.com/article/4888`

- `http://www.linuxjournal.com/article/7170`

- `http://www.linuxjournal.com/magazine/coreboot-your-service`

- `http://www.socallinuxexpo.org/scale8x/blog/interview-ron-minnich-coreboot.html`

- `https://archive.fosdem.org/2007/interview/ronald+g+minnich`

- http://2012.latinoware.org/2012/10/ron-minnich-and-details-of-coreboot/

- http://www.h-online.com/open/features/The-beginnings-746825.html

Prerequisites for Working with coreboot

coreboot uses a typical open source development process. The source code is developed by a community made up of individual contributors. It is submitted to the community for public review prior to being committed to the tree. The code is reviewed for bugs, style, and other improvements. Anyone (even you) can comment and make suggestions during the code review. Developers iterate the code and resubmit it for further review until it is accepted. Once accepted by a senior member, the source is submitted to the coreboot repository.

The coreboot web site (http://coreboot.org) contains a lot of valuable information about the project and it is the first place a new developer should go for information.

The coreboot community does the majority of its communication on the mailing list (http://www.coreboot.org/mailman/listinfo/coreboot) and in IRC (#coreboot on freenode.net).

All code reviews are done in Gerrit (more about Gerrit in a little bit) at http://review.coreboot.org.

If you are using Windows, you might also consider running a Linux virtual machine for coreboot development.

Community Organization

The coreboot community is a flat organization. There is a small leadership group that is informally organized, with Stefan Reinauer as the current chairman, but anyone can review or contribute code to the project. The community is led by developers with commit rights; commit rights are awarded to developers who act in the best interests of the community. These developers participate in the community regularly by developing high-quality code, reviewing other developers' code, and acting as mentors and liaisons for coreboot.

Git and Gerrit

The coreboot source code is maintained at coreboot.org in a Git repository. Git is a distributed SCM (Source Control Management) system that is commonly used in the open source community. We will cover some basic Git commands as part of the development process, but you will want to explore the power and flexibility of Git for your own development (see http://git-scm.com and http://git-scm.com/book).

The coreboot source review process uses the Gerrit tool. Gerrit provides a web-based review of source code with side-by-side differences and user-comment functionality (it also integrates very well with Git). Each Git commit is identified by a SHA-1 hash unique to that change and commit message. The hash is a 40-character hexadecimal sequence, recalculated with every update to the code or commit message so that Gerrit can't use the hash to track a revision of code already under review. Instead of the commit hash, Gerrit uses a Change-ID hash in the commit message to track a patch through the source code review iteration process. The Change-ID in the commit message doesn't change; and when source is updated and pushed, Gerrit replaces the old version with the new version to be reviewed. The coreboot Git setup automatically adds a Change-ID to the commit message if one doesn't already exist (see https://code.google.com/p/gerrit/).

Git Commit Messages

Each git commit has an accompanying commit message. This is extremely helpful to the community; it allows you to see what changed without parsing all the code. Here are a few guidelines for git commit messages:

- The first line of the commit message has a short summary of the change. It should have helpful information about the subsection and what changed. It should be no more than 75 characters long.

- Skip the second line.

- The third line is the start of a detailed description. There should be enough information provided that other developers can understand what was going wrong, what changed, and any other relevant details. The description should be informative and clear enough that developers don't need to guess what happened when they read it five years later. Again, lines should never be longer than 75 characters.

- The next line is empty (no whitespace at all).

- The Change-Id line to let Gerrit track this logical change (this is generated by the commit hook).

- The Signed-off-by line according to the development guidelines. (Use git commit -s to have Git add your Signed-off-by line automatically. Also see the following "coreboot Sign-off Procedure" section and coreboot's development procedures at http://www.coreboot.org/Development_Guidelines#Sign-off_Procedure).

The following is an example of a well-formatted commit message from coreboot (note the additional lines inserted by Gerrit):

```
commit 48a749a89844ba76ff1564d5009e81d4d8e06db8
Author: Marc Jones <marc.jones@se-eng.com>
Date:   Tue Oct 29 22:13:38 2013 -0600

    intel/cougar_canyon2: Intel CRB FSP based mainboard

    Cougar Canyon 2 is a Ivybridge/PantherPoint reference board.
```

This implementation uses the Intel FSP (Visit the Intel FSP website for details on FSP architecture and support).

> The FSP does not support s3 at this time. S3 may be added
> when it is available in the FSP. All other features and IO
> ports are functional. Booted on Ubuntu 12.04 and 13.04,
> Fedora 18 with SeaBIOS payload. Memtest86, FWTS, and
> other tests pass.
>
> Board support page will be updated on acceptance.
>
> Change-Id: I26c0b82d7ac295498376ad4c3517a9d6660d1c01
> Signed-off-by: Marc Jones <marc.jones@se-eng.com>
> Reviewed-on: http://review.coreboot.org/4018
> Tested-by: build bot (Jenkins)
> Reviewed-by: Stefan Reinauer <stefan.reinauer@coreboot.org>

coreboot Sign-off Procedure

Before the code can be pushed to coreboot Gerrit for review, the author must follow a sign-off procedure. This procedure is very similar to the Linux sign-off procedure, and the sign-off is enforced by Git and Gerrit tools. You must use your real (legal) name in the Signed-off-by line and in any copyright notices that you add.

By adding your sign-off, you agree to the Developer's Certificate of Origin 1.1.

Developer's Certificate of Origin 1.1

By making a contribution to this project, I certify that:

    a.   The contribution was created in whole or in part by me and I have the right to submit it under the open source license indicated in the file; or

    b.   The contribution is based upon previous work that, to the best of my knowledge, is covered under an appropriate open source license and I have the right under that license to submit that work with modifications, whether created in whole or in part by me, under the same open source license (unless I am permitted to submit under a different license), as indicated in the file; or

    c.   The contribution was provided directly to me by some other person who certified (a), (b) or (c) and I have not modified it; and

    d.   In the case of each of (a), (b), or (c), I understand and agree that this project and the contribution are public and that a record of the contribution (including all personal information I submit with it, including my sign-off) is maintained indefinitely and may be redistributed consistent with this project or the open source license indicated in the file.

■ **Note**　The Developer's Certificate of Origin 1.1[1] is licensed under the terms of the Creative Commons Attribution-ShareAlike 2.5 License[2].

For more information, see the following web sites:

- `http://web.archive.org/web/20070306195036/http://osdlab.`
  `org/newsroom/press_releases/2004/2004_05_24_dco.html`
- `HTTP://CREATIVECOMMONS.ORG/LICENSES/BY-SA/2.5/`

Adding Your Sign-off

`git commit -s` will add your sign-off (as set in your git config) to the commit message; for example:

`Signed-off-by: Random J Developer <random@developer.example.org>`

■ **Note**　See `http://www.coreboot.org/Development_Guidelines#Sign-off_` `Procedure` for additional sign-off procedure information.

Working with the coreboot Community

An active and productive community is a major component of a successful open source project. As part of any community, it is most constructive if people are civil and considerate of others. This is particularly important in online communities, where people are coming together from different cultures, backgrounds, and levels of technical expertise. Be mindful of one's own place as one among many within the community—in order to be a productive and worthy-of-respect contributor.

coreboot Do's

The following should be done in the coreboot community:

- DO engage the coreboot community e-mail list and IRC channel.
- DO review patches and engage in development discussion.
- DO publish source code for review by the community.
- DO publish small, logical, and understandable patches.

coreboot Don'ts

The following should *not* be done in the coreboot community:

- DON'T violate the GPL or other open source licenses.

- DON'T demand support from the coreboot community.

- DON'T expect every (your) device to have complete support.

- DON'T submit code and ignore the reviews (dump and run).

Nonsource Binaries in coreboot

Even though nonsource binaries have been part of the x86 ecosystem for many years, it remains a touchy subject to incorporate binaries into coreboot. coreboot attempts to use as few proprietary binaries as possible while still providing the base level of support for coreboot users. Binaries are located on the flash with coreboot, without being linked to coreboot. Binaries may include PCI Option ROMs, Video BIOS, payloads, or silicon-specific binaries (like the Intel FSP). Binaries are optional at build time and are not part of the coreboot repository, although some are stored in a SubModule repository called *3rdparty/*. Users may forgo binaries if the feature or capability isn't required. For users looking for a completely free source, the libreboot.org distribution has removed all proprietary binaries.

   Intel FSP pairs with coreboot easily. The FSP binary is located at a fixed address within the coreboot image and is accessed with a coreboot driver interface based on the FSP requirements described in Chapter 3. The specific details of where the FSP is located and how the FSP are accessed are covered later in this chapter.

A Hands-on Example: Building coreboot for the MinnowBoard MAX Mainboard

This chapter is meant to provide hands-on training, so we will dive right in, get the code, and use it as reference as we guide you through building and modifying coreboot. There are a few things you will need prior to diving in.

Environment

It is expected that you are building coreboot in a Linux environment and that you are familiar with the standard application and kernel tools. coreboot can be built under most common shells (bash, csh, zsh). coreboot can also be built on BSD and on Windows with Cygwin or MinGW, but that is outside the scope of this book. If you are using Windows, you might also consider running a Linux virtual machine for coreboot development.

- Fedora: `$ sudo yum groupinstall "Development Tools" "Development Libraries"`

- Debian/Ubuntu: `$ sudo apt-get install build-essentials`

The following tools are required to get started:

- GCC/G++

- make

- Git

- ncurses-dev

- flex and bison

Please read the information at `http://www.coreboot.org/Build_HOWTO`.

Note: Ubuntu dash, the default Ubuntu shell, may have strange failures with the coreboot sh scripts. While coreboot has addressed these issues in the scripts, you might want to update to full bash.

```
$ sudo dpkg-reconfigure dash
```

Hardware: MinnowBoard MAX

The MinnowBoard MAX (MinnowMax) is a low-cost, open hardware development board. It uses the Intel E38xx 'Bay Trail-I' SoC. The compact, low-power, and affordable mainboard is idea for coreboot with FSP development (see `http://www.minnowboard.org/meet-minnowboard-max/` for more information).

MinnowBoard MAX Platform Details

Please note the following information on the MinnowBoard MAX:

- SoC: 64-bit Intel E38xx 'Bay Trail-I'

- Video: HDMI Intel Integrated Graphics

- Memory: 1GB or 2GB DDR3

- IO: MicroSD, SATA2, USB3.0, USB2.0, 10/100/1000 Ethernet

- Low-speed expansion ports: SPI, I2C, I2S Audio, 2xUART, 8xGPIO

- High-speed expansion ports: 1xPCIe, 1xSATA, 1xUSB2.0, I2C, GPIO, JTAG

■ **Note** A Bus Pirate or similar device is required to get serial debug information via the low-speed expansion port.

Development Directory

For our example, we do development in ~/fsp_coreboot/:

```
~/$ mkdir fsp_coreboot
~/$ cd fsp_coreboot
```

You may use any directory that you prefer.

Downloading Intel FSP

The E3800 (Bay Trail) FSP is distributed directly from Intel. You need to download it, uncompress it, and agree to the license before you can use it with coreboot. There is more extensive FSP download information in Chapter 3. The FSP download is at http://intel.com/fsp.

```
Download an Intel Firmware Support Package
 Intel® Atom™ processor E3800 product family (formerly Bay Trail)
   Linux* release version 003 >
```

Installing Intel FSP

Uncompress the .tgz file to the development folder. Then, install the FSP.

```
~/fsp_coreboot$ tar -xzvf ~/Downloads/BAY_TRAIL_FSP_KIT_GOLD3.tgz
~/fsp_coreboot$ ./BAY_TRAIL_FSP_KIT.se
                         INTEL CORPORATION
                  RESTRICTED USE LICENSE AGREEMENT
           INTEL(R) PRODUCTION FIRMWARE SUPPORT PACKAGE
                        (Intel Confidential)

IMPORTANT - READ BEFORE COPYING, INSTALLING OR USING.

...<SNIP>...
```

```
Do you accept the license terms (y/n)? y
Extracting into ~/fsp_coreboot/BAY_TRAIL_FSP_KIT
Finished
```

■ **Note**   Be aware that you will need to modify your paths later in the process if you install the FSP somewhere else.

The FSP package contains a number of important components besides the FSP binary. It also contains additional supporting software and binaries, including the Video BIOS and CPU microcode. Again, the FSP package is described in detail in Chapter 3.

Downloading the coreboot Source

The coreboot source download may take a few minutes.

```
~/fsp_coreboot$ git clone http://review.coreboot.org/coreboot
Cloning into 'coreboot'...
remote: Counting objects: 35863, done
remote: Finding sources: 100% (24537/24537)
remote: Total 167717 (delta 11917), reused 163083 (delta 11917)
Receiving objects: 100% (167717/167717), 47.14 MiB | 2.60 MiB/s, done.
Resolving deltas: 100% (121812/121812), done.
Checking connectivity... done
```

This will create a directory called coreboot/ in the directory that the command was run.

```
~/fsp_coreboot$ cd coreboot/
~/fsp_coreboot/coreboot$ ls
3rdparty  documentation  Makefile.inc  README  toolchain.inc
COPYING   Makefile       payloads      src     util
```

coreboot Toolchain

To help alleviate build problems with many different distribution toolchains, coreboot builds its own small toolchain. The toolchain contains all the tools required to build coreboot and most payloads. We can use a make target to run the coreboot/utils/buildgcc/buildgcc script. It builds gcc, libraries, binutils, iasl, and checks for the required tool dependencies.

```
~/fsp_coreboot/coreboot$ make crossgcc-i386
Welcome to the coreboot cross toolchain builder v1.25 (November 19th, 2014)
```

```
Target arch is now i386-elf
Will skip GDB ... ok
Downloading tar balls ...
...<SNIP>...
Unpacked and patched ... ok
Building GMP 5.1.2 ... ok
Building MPFR 3.1.2 ... ok
Building MPC 1.0.1 ... ok
Building libelf 0.8.13 ... ok
Building binutils 2.23.2 ... ok
Building GCC 4.8.3 ... ok
Skipping Expat (Python scripting not enabled)
Skipping Python (Python scripting not enabled)
Skipping GDB (GDB support not enabled)
Building IASL 20140114 ... ok
Cleaning up... ok
```

You can now run your i386-elf cross toolchain from the following directory:
~/fsp_coreboot/coreboot/util/crossgcc/xgcc.

You can make crossgcc-arm to build the ARM toolchain, but it isn't required for FSP-based mainboards. There is a make crosstools target, which builds additional tools that are not required to compile coreboot.

coreboot Commit Hooks

Back in the "Git and Gerrit" section of this chapter, we discussed the need for a Change-ID to be added to each git commit. This is added by the commit-msg hook. coreboot also has a pre-commit hook that runs lint on the patch. The commit hooks are set up by the following coreboot make target:

```
~/fsp_coreboot/coreboot$ make gitconfig
```

Creating a coreboot Development Branch

Create a branch in git to do the development on. For the purposes of this book, we will use a specific coreboot commit so that the code is consistent with the instructions and information within. Should you choose, you may use the HEAD code, but HEAD is being actively developed and it may have some differences. The following command creates the branch and sets it to the specific commit that works for the instructions in this book:
commit cf52f9761fef3a8e46ff28d6593e0d573ff1d4ac

```
~/fsp_coreboot/coreboot$ git checkout -b fsp_dev cf52f9
```

Building the Mainboard

The next step is to build the correct mainboard and to direct the build to the FSP and other binaries for inclusion. These settings are shown in Figures 4-2 through 4-5.

`~/fsp_coreboot/coreboot$ make menuconfig`

On the Menuconfig Menu

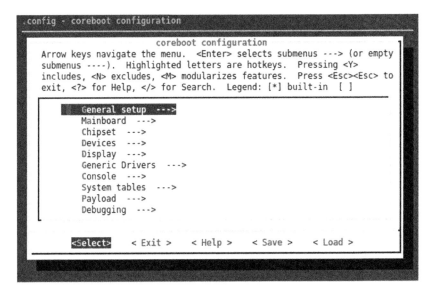

Figure 4-2. *Screenshot of coreboot menuconfig utility*

On the Mainboard Menu

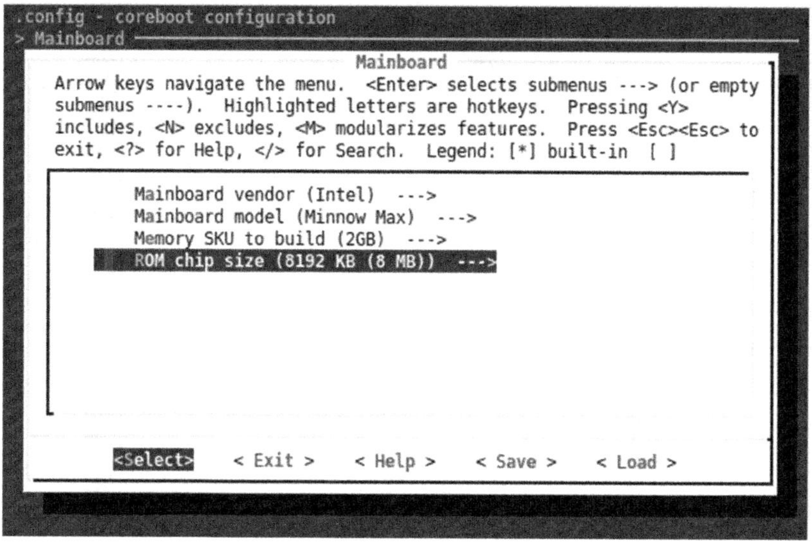

```
.config - coreboot configuration
> Mainboard
                              Mainboard
    Arrow keys navigate the menu.  <Enter> selects submenus ---> (or empty
    submenus ----).  Highlighted letters are hotkeys.  Pressing <Y>
    includes, <N> excludes, <M> modularizes features.  Press <Esc><Esc> to
    exit, <?> for Help, </> for Search.  Legend: [*] built-in  [ ]

            Mainboard vendor (Intel)  --->
            Mainboard model (Minnow Max)  --->
            Memory SKU to build (2GB)  --->
            ROM chip size (8192 KB (8 MB))  --->




        <Select>    < Exit >    < Help >    < Save >    < Load >
```

Figure 4-3. *Screenshot of coreboot menuconfig to select Mainboard*

```
Set Mainboard vendor (Intel)
Set Mainboard model (MinnowMax)
Set the Memory Size
Exit the submenu to return to the top level menu
```

On the Chipset Menu

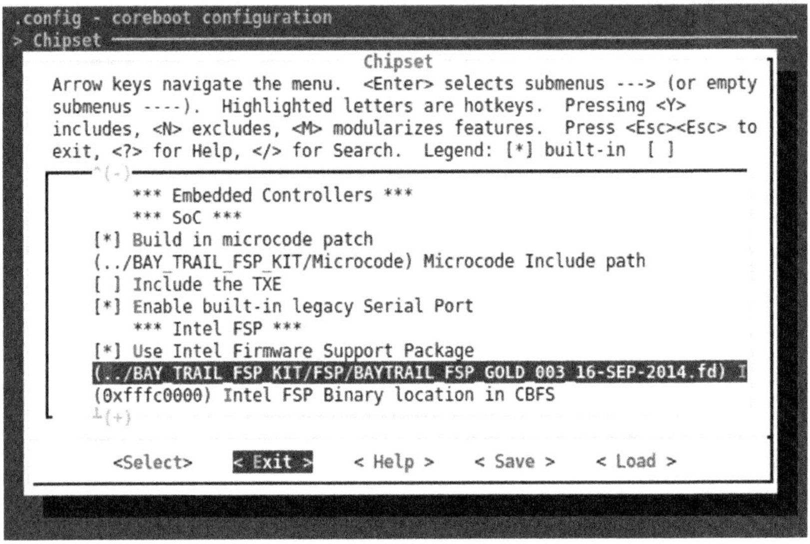

Figure 4-4. *Screenshot of coreboot menuconfig in selecting microcode and FSP path*

```
Set Microcode Path:  ../BAY_TRAIL_FSP_KIT/Microcode
Enable: Enable built-in legacy Serial Port
5Set the FSP file: ../BAY_TRAIL_FSP_KIT/FSP/BAYTRAIL_FSP_GOLD_003_16-
SEP-2014.fd
```

On the Devices Menu

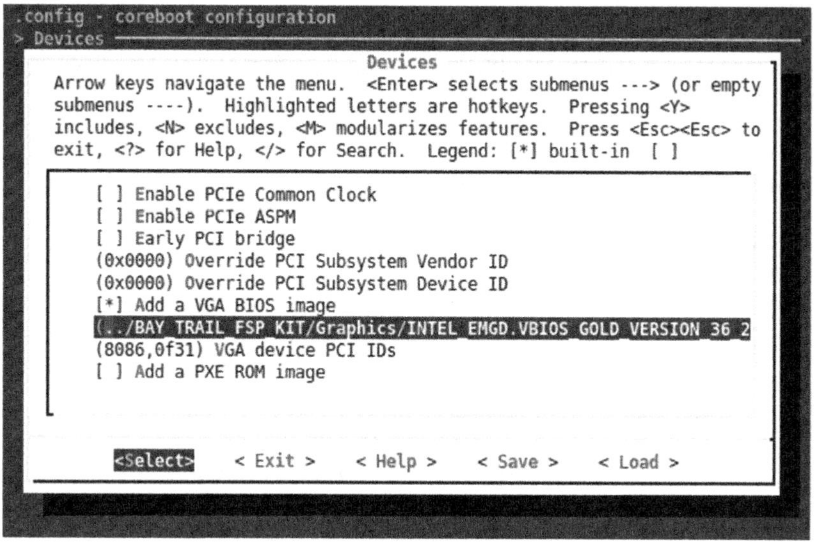

```
.config - coreboot configuration
> Devices
─────────────────────────────────────────────────────────────────
                              Devices
   Arrow keys navigate the menu.  <Enter> selects submenus ---> (or empty
   submenus ----).  Highlighted letters are hotkeys.  Pressing <Y>
   includes, <N> excludes, <M> modularizes features.  Press <Esc><Esc> to
   exit, <?> for Help, </> for Search.  Legend: [*] built-in  [ ]

      [ ] Enable PCIe Common Clock
      [ ] Enable PCIe ASPM
      [ ] Early PCI bridge
      (0x0000) Override PCI Subsystem Vendor ID
      (0x0000) Override PCI Subsystem Device ID
      [*] Add a VGA BIOS image
      (../BAY_TRAIL_FSP_KIT/Graphics/INTEL_EMGD.VBIOS_GOLD_VERSION_36_2
      (8086,0f31) VGA device PCI IDs
      [ ] Add a PXE ROM image


          <Select>    < Exit >    < Help >    < Save >    < Load >
```

Figure 4-5. *Screenshot of coreboot menuconfig to select VGA BIOS file*

Set the VGA BIOS file, as follows:

```
../BAY_TRAIL_FSP_KIT/Graphics/INTEL_EMGD.VBIOS_GOLD_VERSION_36_2_3_3698/
Vga.dat
```

Once the preceding steps to configure the components of the project are done, select Exit and Save to preserve the configuration for this project.

Build

The menuconfig target creates a .config file, which coreboot uses to build the correct options for a given mainboard.

Let's build the project now:

```
~/fsp_coreboot/coreboot$ make
#
# configuration written to .config
#
    HOSTCC      nvramtool/cli/nvramtool.o
    HOSTCC      nvramtool/cli/opts.o
    HOSTCC      nvramtool/cmos_lowlevel.

...<SNIP>...
```

```
CBFS       coreboot.rom
PAYLOAD    build/seabios/out/bios.bin.elf (compression: LZMA)
CONFIG     .config
CBFSPRINT  coreboot.rom
```

```
coreboot.rom: 2048 kB, bootblocksize 1024, romsize 2097152, offset 0x0
alignment: 64 bytes
```

Name	Offset	Type	Size
cmos_layout.bin	0x500000	cmos_layout	1352
pci8086,0f31.rom	0x500580	optionrom	65536
fallback/romstage	0x5105c0	stage	30444
fallback/ramstage	0x517d00	stage	65969
fallback/payload	0x527f00	payload	55583
config	0x535880	raw	4321
revision	0x5369c0	raw	693
(empty)	0x536cc0	null	1938200
cpu_microcode_blob.bin	0x710000	microcode	156736
(empty)	0x736480	null	105240
mrc.cache	0x74ffc0	(unknown)	65536
(empty)	0x760000	null	393112
fsp.bin	0x7bffc0	(unknown)	229376
(empty)	0x7f8000	null	31640

The build has completed successfully and the ROM image is here:

```
~/fsp_coreboot/coreboot/build/coreboot.rom
```

Summary of Commands

Here are the commands we have used so far to get a platform project configured and built:

```
$ mkdir fsp_coreboot
$ cd fsp_coreboot/
$ tar -xzvf ~/Downloads/BAY_TRAIL_FSP_KIT_GOLD3.tgz
$ git clone http://review.coreboot.org/coreboot
$ cd coreboot
$ ls
$ make crossgcc-i386
$ make gitconfig
$ git checkout -b fsp_dev cf52f9
$ make menuconfig
$ make
```

Flashing the ROM

flashrom is a utility for programming flash chips. It is one of the projects that has spun-off from the coreboot community. It is designed to program any type of firmware binary image (not only coreboot) onto a mainboard or other controller cards. It supports programming many flash devices in the system, including parallel, LPC, FWH, and SPI devices. It also supports many external programmers, including the commonly used Dediprog SF100 and BusPirate. It has common interface support for FT2232 and serprog-based devices. It is built for support on most operating systems.

Please check `http://flashrom.org` for more information.

■ **Note** It is strongly recommended that you have an external programmer for firmware development. At some point, you will "brick" your system and need to reflash the device.

For this example, we'll use the Dediprog SF100 to program the mainboard. Please see the mainboard user guide for additional programming requirements. The system may need to be powered on, powered off, or have a jumper set before you can program.

Preparing the Flash Programmer

The following are the steps to program System BIOS by using the Dediprog SPI flash programmer:

1. Power-off the board.

2. Port for BIOS flash update is J1 (MinnowBoard MAX).

3. No jumper settings.

4. Config the Dediprog voltage to 1.8V.

5. Program the device (W25Q64DW).

Save the entire existing flash image, just in case.

```
~/fsp_coreboot/coreboot$ flashrom -p dediprog -r backup.rom
flashrom v0.9.7-r1764 on Linux 3.11.0-20-generic (x86_64)
flashrom is free software, get the source code at http://www.flashrom.org

Calibrating delay loop... OK.
```

Flashing the ROM Image

The total coreboot ROM image is the same size as the SPI flash device—8MB. coreboot is not the only code in the SPI flash device and it may only use the BIOS section. For MinnowMax, the BIOS section is 3MB; the flash descriptor and the TXE binary are the other 5MB. We will discuss the descriptor and other binaries later in this chapter.

To update the flash with flashrom, we need to do the following:

1. Create an XML file with flashrom instructions.

2. Flash the device with the correct parameters (the MinnowMax flash device requires 1.8 volts from the Dediprog).

3. Create the XML instructions for flashrom:

   ```
   ~/fsp_coreboot/coreboot$ echo 00500000:007fffff cb > 8mb.xml
   ```

4. Write the image you have built to the BIOS region:

   ```
   ~/fsp_coreboot/coreboot$ sudo flashrom -p dediprog -l 8mb.xml -i
   cb -w build/coreboot.rom
   flashrom v0.9.7-r1764 on Linux 3.11.0-20-generic (x86_64)
   flashrom is free software, get the source code at http://www.
   flashrom.org

   Calibrating delay loop... OK.
   ```

■ **Warning**   You cannot program the entire flash with the coreboot image. There are other binaries located on the flash that are required to boot the system. Overwriting these files is bad. (You backed up the entire flash image as described earlier, right?)

Remove the Dediprog, replace the programming jumpers, and power up the system. The system should boot. If not, check out the "Troubleshooting and Debugging" section.

coreboot Internals

Now that you have a booting FSP coreboot MinnowMax, we can dig into the internals of coreboot. This section discusses what happens in the coreboot image during boot. We also cover how it is organized, the source tree, and the boot process.

Boot Stages

coreboot is made up of four boot stages. Each stage is a binary within the ROM image. From power-on, coreboot transitions from one binary stage to the next in the order shown in Table 4-1.

Table 4-1. *coreboot Boot Stages*

Stage	Description
bootblock	The reset vector and pre cache-as-RAM setup
romstage	Cache-as-RAM setup, early silicon initialization, memory setup
ramstage	Normal device setup and mainboard configuration
payload	The OS or application bootloader

Additional Files

The stage binaries require supporting files. These additional files are part of the coreboot image and critical for system functionality (see Table 4-2).

Table 4-2. *coreboot Supporting Files*

File Name	Description
fsp.bin	The FSP binary file.
pci8086,0166.rom	The video BIOS file; the name associates the binary to the PCI ID of the graphics device.
cmos_layout.bin	A map of the CMOS values used by coreboot. This file may be used by payloads or other utilities to safely manipulate CMOS.
config	The build options in the .config file are saved in the ROM image. This makes it possible to reproduce the image with the same options in the future.
mrc.cache	For saved memory configuration data. (More on this later.)

■ **Note** These are the file names in CBFS. They may be different than the menuconfig input path and file name.

CBFS

The coreboot stages and binaries require some organization in order to be found and loaded. This is accomplished in coreboot within CBFS, which is a scheme for managing independent binaries within a single firmware ROM image. Though not a true file system, the style and concepts are similar. CBFS binary headers contain information to help identify the binary by type, such as stage, optionROM, and payload, and indicate if the binary is compressed. It is important to understand that each file in the CBFS is compiled separately. These binaries are not linked and each file is located, loaded, uncompressed, and executed as required.

■ **Note** Please visit http://www.coreboot.org/CBFS.

An Example of CBFS

At the end of the preceding coreboot build, the contents of the coreboot.rom file are printed out. We can check it again using the cbfstool:

```
~/fsp_coreboot/coreboot$ ./build/cbfstool ./build/coreboot.rom print
coreboot.rom: 2048 kB, bootblocksize 1024, romsize 2097152, offset 0x0
alignment: 64 bytes
Name                         Offset      Type        Size
cmos_layout.bin              0x0         cmos_layout 1132
pci8086,0f31.rom             0x4c0       optionrom   65536
fallback/romstage            0x10500     stage       27029
fallback/ramstage            0x16f00     stage       58969
fallback/payload             0x255c0     payload     59940
config                       0x34040     raw         4221
(empty)                      0x35100     null        896728
cpu_microcode_blob.bin       0x110000    microcode   52224
(empty)                      0x11cc40    null        209752
mrc.cache                    0x14ffc0    (unknown)   65536
(empty)                      0x160000    null        393112
fsp.bin                      0x1bffc0    (unknown)   229376
(empty)                      0x1f8000    null        31640
```

There are a couple things to note about the CBFS output.

You can find that all the stages are listed except for the bootblock. The bootblock stage is a mandatory piece and handled as a special case. It is located in the last 20K of the ROM space with the reset vector. It contains the location of the master header and the entry point for the loader firmware. It doesn't have a CBFS header due to its location at the end and how it is accessed, via a direct jump from the reset vector.

■ **Note** This may change in the future as ARM and other support are added, and which have different reset requirements for the reset vector and bootblock.

CBFS can have a directory-like structure; for example, `fallback/romstage` and `fallback/ramstage`. This is useful for grouping files that should be used together or for a specific boot purpose. In the preceding example, `fallback/` is the default boot path in coreboot. An additional set of binaries could be added for an alternate boot path that would be selected by the bootblock. The SeaBIOS payload also uses the directory structure for coreboot options.

■ **Note**   For more information about SeaBIOS, please visit `http://www.coreboot.org/ SeaBIOS#SeaBIOS_and_CBFS`.

CBFS Size

The size of the coreboot.rom file is not required to be the size of the flash device. It only needs to be large enough to fit the required files within CBFS. This leaves room on the flash device for files that are not part of coreboot. On a FSP-based system, the `coreboot. rom` file should be the same size as the BIOS descriptor region indicated by the flash descriptor. The `coreboot.rom` must be located at the end of the flash device to execute the reset vector.

Special Binaries

In addition to Intel FSP and microcode, there are some important binaries located on the flash device that are not part of coreboot. This was briefly described in the flash and boot section of this chapter. These files are required for proper system operation, so it is important that they are not overwritten with coreboot (see Table 4-3).

Table 4-3. *Special Binaries for coreboot*

Binary	Description
descriptor.bin	The Intel Firmware Descriptor describes the content of the flash device. This includes the locations of the binaries, which areas are write protected, and bootstrap options.
TXE/ME	Trusted Execution Engine(TXE) or Management Engine (ME) binaries. These binaries are run by the security and management processor prior to starting the CPU.
GigEthernet	Intel integrated Ethernet binary. This is not a PXE option ROM, but device firmware.

▓ **Note**   The descriptor and other binaries can be queried by the coreboot `utils/ifdtool`.

Boot Flow Using Intel FSP

As mentioned earlier, each stage is called consecutively after the other. In this section, we will follow the flow from the reset vector to loading a payload.

Reset Vector and Bootblock

On x86 systems, there is a lot of legacy cruft, which makes for some tedious details that must be dealt with by early boot firmware. To start with, the very first instruction executed by an x86 CPU is in 16-bit reset mode (sort of like real mode, but with 4GB selectors loaded as default); the first instruction is fetched and executed by the CPU at memory location FFFFFFF0, in hexadecimal value, 16 bytes below 4GB of the 32-bit architecture's addressing limit. There's a lot of history behind this design; therefore, we won't go into more detail in this book.

coreboot's reset vector contains a single jump instruction to the 16-bit entry code of the bootblock. coreboot then transitions immediately to 32-bit flat protected mode. This switch makes it much easier to use the 32-bit registers and to access the entire 4GB memory space.

The reset vector and bootblock code is run directly from ROM, doing what is called "execute in place" (XIP). The first few instructions are written in assembly code. As discussed in the preceding history section, assembly code is difficult to read and debug, so coreboot starts using C code within a few hundred instructions. This is accomplished by using a special compiler/assembler called ROMCC. ROMCC translates C code to a stackless assembly `.inc` file that is then compiled and linked by the assembler/linker. It must be stackless because there is no memory for stack at this point in the boot process, and normal C compilers assume memory and use the stack to pass variables.

The early C code in bootblock has a few basic functions. If required by the system, it can do very early silicon setup. For example, routing the Port 80h debug output, enabling the chipset flash features, or checking a signal to indicate which stage should be loaded next. The bootblock parses CBFS, locates the romstage, and jumps to its starting point.

romstage

The early part of romstage is very similar to the bootblock. It is execute in place (XIP) code written in assembly. The only difference is that coreboot is already in 32 bit protected flat mode. There is no system memory available, so the first step in romstage is to set up "Cache as RAM" (CAR). This allows coreboot to use the CPU cache as system RAM for a stack location. The FSP handles the CAR setup and has some very specific requirements to run. This is fully explained in the Intel FSP chapter, but we will do a quick review.

To call the first Intel FSP entry, coreboot contains a stack area that contains a pointer to the Intel FSP parameter structure and the return address to get back to coreboot when Intel FSP is finished. The parameter structure contains the microcode address and length, and start address and length of the ROM area that should be cached. With the stack pointer prepared, coreboot locates the FSP, verifies that the FSP headers are as expected for the platform and jumps to the FSP TempRamInit API entry point. The FSP executes, works its magic, sets up CAR, and returns to coreboot. coreboot sets the stack pointer and makes the first C-style call to do romstage system setup and memory setup.

Most x86 systems require a significant amount of setup to configure the hardware. This is even more the case in integrated silicon and System on a Chip (SoC) systems. Most integrated subsystem devices require additional configuration prior to being accessed in the normal methods (PCI Configuration Space, Memory Mapped I/O, System I/O, etc.). Romstage is where the few devices required for memory initialization are configured. It is also the first change to get additional debug information from the system. With most Intel FSP based systems, including MinnowMax, the serial port is configured and debug information can be streamed to the developer.

With a little bit of mainboard specific hardware initialized, coreboot is almost ready to make the second call into Intel FSP for memory initialization and the initial setup of the various peripherals. In order to do this, coreboot locates the UPD/VPD structures as discussed in Chapter 3. After getting the UPD/VPD data, coreboot modifies these based on mainboard specific configuration data from devicetree.cb. This allows coreboot to inform Intel FSP which devices should be enabled or disabled and what mode the devices should be configured in. The FspInit entry sets up the memory and disables CAR before it returns to the coreboot's return function. Intel FSP also passes back a Hand-Off Block (HOB), which contains data Intel FSP and coreboot may use later. coreboot saves the HOB data location and prepares for ramstage. The romstage code locates the ramstage in CBFS, copies it to memory and jumps to the entry point.

ramstage

Ramstage is a bare-metal application. The CPU and memory are functional and ramstage is running from memory with a normal stack and can use heap, global variables, and so forth. The purpose of ramstage is to configure the I/O devices, additional application processors, SMM, and to set up tables that may be passed to payloads or operating systems.

The heart of ramstage is a state machine running in the hardwaremain function and the device tree. The state machine states are defined by the standard stages of PCI device configuration and enumeration. There are additional states for chip and mainboard configuration to allow customization of device prior to the normal initialization process. The state machine also has pre and post hooks at each state, so chipset and mainboards can be customized as needed. The states and state machine are explained in detail later in this chapter.

The device tree is the hierarchical structure of the PCI and legacy devices in the system. The device tree is prepopulated at build time through the entries in the mainboard's devicetree.cb file and amended runtime as devices are discovered in the PCI enumeration process. The device tree structure has function pointers for every device for each state in the state machine. This allows chipset and onboard devices to have customer driver functions run during the enumeration process. We will discuss the specific of the state machine and device tree later in this chapter.

There are two calls to the FspNotifyPhase entry point in ramstage, AfterPCIEnumeration and ReadyToBoot. After all the devices are enumerated, the coreboot calls FspNotifyPhase(AfterPCIEnumeration). coreboot then sets up SMM, does legacy table setup, and finally ACPI table setup. The final call to Intel FSP is made, FspNotifyPhase(ReadyToBoot), where the lock registers are set to protect SMM and other sensitive registers. Then, ramstage locates the primary payload in CBFS, decompresses it to memory, and executes it.

Payload

The last part of coreboot is to execute a payload. The payload functions and features are not defined by coreboot. A payload could be a bare-metal application or it could boot an operating system. There may be more than one payload in a coreboot image. Some common payload options are discussed later in the chapter.

coreboot Source

coreboot contains initialization code for several different architectures, many different silicon devices, and hundreds of mainboards. This can be overwhelming for new coreboot developers, so we will highlight the areas of focus for coreboot FSP-based mainboards. Again, we focus on the MinnowMax mainboard.

coreboot Device Tree

Each device supported by coreboot has a corresponding driver. In order to associate the hardware to the driver, coreboot describes the onboard devices in the coreboot device tree. The mapping of devices to their custom functions is done in the mainboard devicetree.cb file. The devicetree.cb is evaluated during the build process by the sconfig tool (`coreboot/util/sconfig`), which creates a linked list of devices in the `build/mainboard/VENDOR/BOARD/static.c` file. During the boot process, the coreboot scans the devices, adds any found devices to the device tree, and links the drivers to the devices found. The device tree is an integral part of the coreboot build and boot process. The device tree code is located in the coreboot device tree source directory at `coreboot/src/device`.

The device tree has two root busses, the CPU bus and the PCI bus. The start of the device tree is called the *root complex*, which links the top level CPU bus and PCI bus 0. The CPU bus contains systems local APICs (Advanced Programmable Interrupt Controllers). PCI bus 0 contains all other system devices, including legacy and IO devices.

■ **Note**   The coreboot device tree is not a Flattened Device Tree used by Linux ARM kernels.

Chips and Devices

The coreboot device tree has chip and device functions. A chip may be made up of one or more devices. Some chips require configuration prior to the device configuration. This is very common on southbridge devices. To accommodate the predevice setup, the chip functions are called prior to device functions. We will cover this in more detail in the section covering coreboot hardware state machines.

Device Tree Variables

Each device tree section starts with the variable name (see Table 4-4) and is closed with the 'end' keyword.

Table 4-4. coreboot Device Tree Variables

Variable Name	Description
chip	Path to the chip source. The chip variable comes prior to all devices in the device tree. The path also corresponds with a chip_operations structure.
device	Defines a device type at the indicated address.
register	Is used to pass mainboard customization to generic chip code as defined in its chip.h. This is different than a Kconfig build option.

Each device type has its own set of function pointers, as listed in Table 4-5.

Table 4-5. coreboot Device Types

Device Type	Description
domain	Sets the PCI bus number. All PCI devices must be within a domain keyword. Only bus 0 must be set up in a system, leaving all other busses to be configured using the default configuration.
cpu_cluster	Specifies the top-level APIC and the CPU root cluster.
pci	Devices with PCI configuration space.
i2c	Sets the 7-bit I2C address of a device on an I2C bus. This keyword must be within a PCI I2C/SMBUS controller device.
pnp	Devices in the legacy (ISA) memory and I/O range (e.g., SuperIOs).
ioapic	The ID of a chipset's IO APIC. A default configuration is used if this is not set in the device tree.
lapic	The ID of a CPU's Local APIC. One lapic is required in the device tree.

There are additional keywords used in the device tree, which are listed in Table 4-6.

Table 4-6. *coreboot Additional Keywords Used in the Device Tree*

Keyword	Description
subsystemid	Sets the PCI config register subsystem device and vendor IDs. This may be set at the top level and inherited, or within a specific device. See inherit.
inherit	Sets a value for all the devices after it. Used for subsystem ID.
io	Sets an IO register value for a pnp device.
irq	Sets an IRQ line for a pnp device.
drq	Sets a DRQ line for a pnp device.
ioapic_irq	Is used to generate mptable from the devicetree.cb.
on	Sets a device state to enabled.
off	Sets a device state to disabled (may hide device on some chipsets).
end	Closes a block.

A Device Tree Example

The following example is at coreboot/src/mainboard/intel/minoxmax/devicetree.cb.

```
chip soc/intel/fsp_baytrail
#### ACPI Register Settings ####
register "fadt_pm_profile"           = "PM_UNSPECIFIED"
register "fadt_boot_arch"            = "ACPI_FADT_LEGACY_FREE"

#### FSP register settings ####
register "PcdSataMode"               = "SATA_MODE_AHCI"
register "PcdMrcInitSPDAddr1"        = "SPD_ADDR_DEFAULT"
register "PcdMrcInitSPDAddr2"        = "SPD_ADDR_DEFAULT"
register "PcdMrcInitMmioSize"        = "MMIO_SIZE_DEFAULT"
register "PcdeMMCBootMode"           = "EMMC_FOLLOWS_DEVICETREE"
register "PcdIgdDvmt50PreAlloc"      = "IGD_MEMSIZE_DEFAULT"
register "PcdApertureSize"           = "APERTURE_SIZE_DEFAULT"
register "PcdGttSize"                = "GTT_SIZE_DEFAULT"
register "PcdLpssSioEnablePciMode"   = "LPSS_PCI_MODE_DEFAULT"
register "AzaliaAutoEnable"          = "AZALIA_FOLLOWS_DEVICETREE"
register "LpeAcpiModeEnable"         = "LPE_ACPI_MODE_DISABLED"
register "IgdRenderStandby"          = "IGD_RENDER_STANDBY_ENABLE"
register "EnableMemoryDown"          = "MEMORY_DOWN_ENABLE"
register "DRAMSpeed"                 = "DRAM_SPEED_1066MHZ"
```

```
register "DRAMType"                = "DRAM_TYPE_DDR3L"
register "DIMM0Enable"             = "DIMM0_ENABLE"
register "DIMM1Enable"             = "DIMM1_DISABLE"
register "DIMMDWidth"              = "DIMM_DWIDTH_X16"
register "DIMMDensity"             = "DIMM_DENSITY_2G_BIT" # Setting for 1GB
board - modified runtime for 2GB board in romstage.c to DIMM_DENSITY_4G_BIT
register "DIMMBusWidth"            = "DIMM_BUS_WIDTH_64BIT"
register "DIMMSides"               = "DIMM_SIDES_1RANK"
register "DIMMtCL"                 = "11"
register "DIMMtRPtRCD"             = "11"
register "DIMMtWR"                 = "12"
register "DIMMtWTR"                = "6"
register "DIMMtRRD"                = "6"
register "DIMMtRTP"                = "6"
register "DIMMtFAW"                = "20"


device cpu_cluster 0 on
device lapic 0 on end
end


device domain 0 on
device pci 00.0 on end # 8086 0F00 - SoC router -
device pci 02.0 on end # 8086 0F31 - GFX micro HDMI
device pci 03.0 off end # 8086 0F38 - MIPI -

device pci 10.0 off end # 8086 0F14 - EMMC Port -
device pci 11.0 off end # 8086 0F15 - SDIO Port -
device pci 12.0 on end # 8086 0F16 - SD Port MicroSD on SD3
device pci 13.0 on end # 8086 0F23 - SATA AHCI Onboard & HSEC
device pci 14.0 on end # 8086 0F35 - USB XHCI - Onboard & HSEC  - Enabling
both EHCI and XHCI will default to EHCI if not changed at runtime
device pci 15.0 on end # 8086 0F28 - LP Engine Audio LSEC
device pci 17.0 off end # 8086 0F50 - MMC Port -
device pci 18.0 on end # 8086 0F40 - SIO - DMA -
device pci 18.1 off end # 8086 0F41 -   I2C Port 1 (0) -
device pci 18.2 on end # 8086 0F42 -   I2C Port 2 (1) - (testpoints)
device pci 18.3 off end # 8086 0F43 -   I2C Port 3 (2) -
device pci 18.4 off end # 8086 0F44 -   I2C Port 4 (3) -
device pci 18.5 off end # 8086 0F45 -   I2C Port 5 (4) -
device pci 18.6 on end # 8086 0F46 -   I2C Port 6 (5) LSEC
device pci 18.7 on end # 8086 0F47 -   I2C Port 7 (6) HSEC
device pci 1a.0 on end # 8086 0F18 - TXE -
device pci 1b.0 off end # 8086 0F04 - HD Audio -
device pci 1c.0 on end # 8086 0F48 - PCIe Port 1 (0) -
device pci 1c.1 off end # 8086 0F4A - PCIe Port 2 (1) -
device pci 1c.2 on end # 8086 0F4C - PCIe Port 3 (2) Onboard GBE
device pci 1c.3 on end # 8086 0F4E - PCIe Port 4 (3) HSEC
```

```
device pci 1d.0 on end # 8086 0F34 - USB EHCI - Enabling both EHCI and XHCI
will default to EHCI if not changed at runtime
device pci 1e.0 on end # 8086 0F06 - SIO - DMA -
device pci 1e.1 on end # 8086 0F08 -   PWM 1 LSEC
device pci 1e.2 on end # 8086 0F09 -   PWM 2 LSEC
device pci 1e.3 on end # 8086 0F0A -   HSUART 1 LSEC
device pci 1e.4 on end # 8086 0F0C -   HSUART 2 LSEC
device pci 1e.5 on end # 8086 0F0E -   SPI LSEC
device pci 1f.0 on end # 8086 0F1C - LPC bridge No connector
device pci 1f.3 on end # 8086 0F12 - SMBus 0 SPC
end
end
```

■ **Note**   These are not the only PCI devices in the system, but they are the only ones that require drivers. Devices may be added to slots and use the standard device initialization functions.

Chip Operations

The chip operations structure contains pointers to a function to initialize the chip and to enable a device, as well as a finalize function and a chip name string. The device enable function is called prior to the device operations (see Table 4-7). This is particularly important for devices that need to enable PCI devices before the initial scan and initialization. For example, some chipsets require additional setup for each device to be visible on the PCI bus.

Table 4-7. coreboot Chip Functions

Chip Function	Description
init	Chip initialization function.
enable_dev	The function called for each chip in the device tree.
final	The final function for each chip in the device tree. The last function before payload loading.

Device Operations

During the coreboot initialization process, each device operations function is run on the device in the order that it is scanned. Any device operation function pointer can be set to point to a custom device function. The device operations structure contains the function pointers listed in Table 4-8.

Table 4- 8. coreboot Device Operations

Device Operation	Description
read_resources	Read and save the device resources to be arranged and assigned.
set_resources	Assigned memory and IO space.
enable_resources	Enable memory and IO in the PCI command register.
init	Load the PCI device option ROMs.
finalize	Perform any final cleanup.
scan_bus	Bus or bridge devices scan and enable function.
enable	Activate the device (very late function call; not normally used).
disable	Deactivate the device, turning it off (very late function call; not normally used).
ops_pci	Sets the devices default operation functions.

Set the function pointer to NULL to skip the function for the device; otherwise, the default device function is used.

coreboot Hardwaremain State Machine

At the heart of the coreboot ramstage is a state machine for enumerating mainboard devices. coreboot starts device enumeration with the top-level device in the device tree and begins a bus scan. PCI devices that do not require special setup are added to the device tree as they are found during the scan, and are set up by the default PCI configuration functions. PCI devices that require special setup are linked with their custom drivers in the initial scan. Then, the state machine enumerates each PCI device's functions in five stages: read_resource, set_resource, enable_resource, init, and enable (see the "Device Operations" section). At each state, custom device functions can be called. The coreboot hardwaremain state machine source is coreboot/src/lib/hardwaremain.c.

State Machine States

Table 4-9 lists the state machine states used in coreboot.

Table 4-9. *coreboot State Machine States*

State	Descrtiption
BS_PRE_DEVICE	Before any device tree actions take place
BS_DEV_INIT_CHIPS	Init all chips in device tree
BS_DEV_ENUMERATE	Device tree probing
BS_DEV_RESOURCES	Device tree resource allocation and assignment
BS_DEV_ENABLE	Device tree enabling/disabling of devices
BS_DEV_INIT	Device tree device initialization
BS_POST_DEVICE	All device tree actions performed
BS_OS_RESUME_CHECK	Check for OS resume vector
BS_OS_RESUME	Resume to OS
BS_WRITE_TABLES	Write coreboot tables
BS_PAYLOAD_LOAD	Load payload into memory
BS_PAYLOAD_BOOT	Boot to payload

State Machine Callbacks

Each state has an Entry Callback and an Exit Callback, which may be used by any coreboot code to hook any state; for example, the Bay Trail FSP mrc.cache is saved during the table write state, after all devices have been setup.

```
Enter State  -> Entry Callback  -> Execute State  -> Exit Callback  ->
Next State
```

■ **Note**   Do not use multiple hooks to the same state callback. The order in which multiple hooks to the same state's callback are executed is undetermined.

Mainboard

The coreboot mainboard directory is the primary location that new mainboard developers will begin working in. It is located in the mainboard vendor directory and contains the files that make one mainboard unique from another (see Table 4-10). coreboot is architected to share as much common code as possible. The mainboard files access the CPU's, the chipset's, and the device driver's common code to do the majority of the work. Let's review the contents of the MinnowMax directory and break down the purposes of these key files.

Table 4-10. *coreboot Mainboard Files*

File Name	Description
acpi_tables.c	Functions that patch the DSDT and other ACPI table runtime.
cmos.layout	CMOS entries used by the mainboard.
devicetree.cb	Prepopulate mainboard chips and devices used to configure and enable and disable certain device options.
dsdt.asl	The mainboard ACPI ASL file.
fadt.c	Generates and checksums the ACPI FADT file.
gpio.c	Sets the default configuration for the mainboards GPIOs. GPIO configuration is fairly complex on Bay Trail and there are a lot of options to set up.
irqroute.c	Required to compile the IRQ macros defined in IRQ.h.
irqroute.h	Macros for each device IRQ routing in APIC and PIC modes.
Kconfig	Selects the default build options for CPU-, chipset-, and mainboard-specific options.
mainboard.c	The mainboard-specific file called in ramstage.
mainboard_smi.c	The mainboard-specific SMI calls.
Makefile.inc	Required to build the mainboard directory.
onboard.h	Mainboard-specific SMBIOS table settings.
romstage.c	The mainboard-specific function for romstage.
thermal.h	Critical temperature definitions for ACPI.
acpi/ ec.asl mainboard.asl superio.asl video.asl	Contains mainboard-specific ACPI ASL files that are included by the chipset ASL files.

The directory is `coreboot/src/mainboard/intel/<mainboard>/`.

It is easiest to begin working on a new mainboard using the reference design. It will already have the basic calls to the chipset and other devices.

The Chipset Driver

When the coreboot device enumeration finds a new device, it checks for a custom driver to set up the device. For Bay Trail, the basic setup is handled by the romstage and ramstage files located in the SoC directory. When Intel FSP access is required, the chipset code and the Intel FSP driver cooperate to send the correct information for the chipset-specific Intel FSP.

The Bay Trail FSP source files are at `coreboot/src/soc/intel/fsp_baytrail`. Key files are listed in Table 4-11.

Table 4-11. *Key Chipset Files Under coreboot*

File Name	Description
northcluster.c	Memory and PCIe resource allocation
southcluster.c	I/O device resource allocation
ramstage.c	
romstage/romstage.c	FSP early_init() call and return point
chip.h	Bay Trail FSP variables, includes UPD options
fsp/chipset_fsp_util.c	

■ **Note** Bay Trail is an SoC, so it has northcluster and southcluster files within the `src/soc/` directory. A typical chipset pair would have their files in `src/northbridge/` and `src/southbridge/` directories.

Chipset FSP UPD Options

The chipset UPD options in Intel FSP are defined in chip.h and set in the mainboard-specific devicetree.cb. See the section discussing UPD in Chapter 3 for more details on the options that are passed.

The FSP Driver

The coreboot FSP driver handles standard access functions to Intel FSP. While the access functions are standardized per the API, each chipset and mainboard may have custom FSP requirements, capabilities, and options. Chipset-specific options such as configuring the UPD data are handled by calls from the driver back to the chipset's FSP files. The mainboard-specific configuration is set in the devicetree.cb file, and then can be customized further during the romstage callback, as previously mentioned. The FSP driver is based on the reference code provided in Intel FSP documentation, but resides in coreboot. The driver runs in both romstage and ramstage. The first FSP API call to TempRAMInit is part of the normal driver code, but is included in early romstage, cache_ as_ram.inc.

The FSP driver source directory is located at `coreboot/src/drivers/fsp`.

Table 4-12 lists the coreboot fsp_util functions.

Table 4-12. *coreboot Functions that Interface with Intel FSP*

Function Name	Description
find_fsp	Function to find the FSP in memory.
fsp_early_init	FSP memory and early device setup function. Called in romstage by the chipset driver.
romstage_fsp_rt_buffer_ callback	Callback from fsp_early_init for mainboard-specific RT buffer customizations (soldered down memory timings, etc.).
FspNotify	There are two notify calls in ramstage.
	AfterPCIEnumeration during device finalize and
	ReadyToBoot during chip finalize.
save_mrc_data	Called in romstage after fsp_early_init to save the memory configuration to CBMEMh.
update_mrc_cache	Moves the mrc data from CBMEM to NVRAM in late ramstage.

Kconfig

coreboot uses the Linux build configuration tool, Kconfig, to select build options. Kconfig files are in nearly all coreboot source directories. The Kconfig options are used by the makefiles to include the correct source files. In the preceding coreboot mainboard build section, you used the Kconfig Text User Interface—menuconfig—to select options for your example coreboot build. Typically, there are options for the mainboard, chipsets, debugging, and which payload to include in the coreboot.rom image file. The Kconfig options are saved as .config file and converted to a config.h for definitions to be used by the coreboot source code. The file is also saved in the `coreboot.rom` image, where it can be extracted and used to build with the same coreboot options.

The Kconfig tool is built by the coreboot make process and is located here: `coreboot/util/kconfig`

xcompile

The coreboot make process needs to locate a compatible toolchain. This is done by the xcompile script. On each build, the coreboot makefile checks for the `.xcompile` file, which is generated by the `utils/xcompile/xcompile` script, and if it is not found, the makefile calls the script to generate it. The xcompile script locates the coreboot toolchain and copies the path into the `.xcompile` file. The generated `.xcompile` file is included in the make to set variables `CC, CFLAGS, CPP, AS, LD, NM, OBJCOPY, OBJDUMP, READELF, STRIP, AR`.

■ **Warning** The `.xcompile` file isn't built on every make. If the file already exists, the script will not be re-run. This is a problem if you didn't have the toolchain built previously and the `.xcompile` is empty. Without a "make clean," the old path to the distribution toolchain is used.

Payloads

A payload may be any ELF binary. It must be able to execute on bare metal and without any support services. Payloads are typically separate projects from coreboot and have their own development community (although there is some obvious overlap with coreboot developers). As a separate project and binary, payloads may have a different license than coreboot. The cbfstool supports converting the ELF format to the SELF format, which can be loaded by coreboot. SeaBIOS is the default payload, but any ELF may be added in the Payload section of the menuconfig.

See `http://www.coreboot.org/Payloads` and `http://www.coreboot.org/SELF` for more information.

There are several Payloads available for you to choose from.

SeaBIOS

SeaBIOS provides the legacy BIOS services for booting most operating systems. The coreboot build process makes it easy to use SeaBIOS by downloading and building it if it is selected. SeaBIOS supports booting from SATA and USB. It also supports loading Option ROMs and additional payloads. SeaBIOS runtime options, like boot order, are added to configuration files in CBFS.

SeaBIOS has been tested with Linux, NetBSD, OpenBSD, FreeDOS, and Windows XP/Vista/7. Classic GRUB, GRUB2, lilo, and isolinux work well with SeaBIOS. Other x86 bootloaders and operating systems will likely also work.

The SeaBIOS development license uses GPLv2+.

See `http://www.coreboot.org/SeaBIOS` and `http://www.seabios.org/SeaBIOS` for more information.

GRUB 2

You can use GRUB2 as a coreboot payload to boot an operating system from a hard drive, for instance. You can also boot via an existing GRUB2 MBR on your hard drive by using SeaBIOS as your coreboot payload.

The GRUB2 development license uses GPLv3. See http://www.coreboot.org/GRUB2 and https://www.gnu.org/software/grub/grub.html for more information.

FILO

FILO is a simple bootloader with filesystem support. It can boot from hard drives and USB mass storage. It does not require any legacy BIOS callbacks.

The FILO development license uses GPLv2. See http://www.coreboot.org/FILO for more information.

iPXE

iPXE is a network bootloader and is a fork of GPXE/Etherboot. It provides a direct replacement for proprietary PXE ROMs. It can be run as a payload or as an OptionROM by SeaBIOS.

The iPXE development license uses GPL v2+.

See http://www.coreboot.org/IPXE and http://ipxe.org/ for more information.

TianoCore

There is limited porting and support work in the community for TianoCore, a bootloader providing the UEFI interface.

The TianoCore development license uses BSD.

See http://www.coreboot.org/TianoCore for more information.

Depthcharge

Depthcharge is a payload for the Google Chromebooks.

The Depthcharge development license uses GPLv2 (or later).

See https://chromium.googlesource.com/chromiumos/platform/depthcharge for more information.

U-Boot

The U-Boot bootloader can be configured as a coreboot payload for Google Chromebooks.

The U-Boot development license uses GPLv2.

See http://www.denx.de/wiki/U-Boot for more information.

Memtest86+

Aimed at memory failures detection, this memory test is available as a coreboot payload as well.

See `http://www.coreboot.org/Memtest86` and `http://memtest.org/` for more information.

libpayload

Libpayload is a library to assist with developing and building custom payloads. It contains entry point, build options, and basic libc functions. libpayload is built separately from the developers' payload code and it is statically linked. libpayload may be built with a number of different options configured with a libpayload-specific Kconfig. See the FILO or TINT payloads for an example.

The libpayload development license uses BSD.

See `http://www.coreboot.org/Libpayload` for more information.

coreboot Troubleshooting and Debugging

There are lots of complicated parts to modern systems, and silicon initialization and development and testing don't always go smoothly. There are a number of troubleshooting and debugging options when debugging with coreboot.

Postcodes

The earliest debug information available from coreboot is postcodes on port 80h. Many CRBs have integrated postcode hardware to display this early debug information. coreboot's first instruction after the reset vector is an out 01h (POST_RESET_VECTOR_CORRECT) to port 80h. There are two common failures early in coreboot with FSP:

- postcode 00h: The system is on, but no there are no postcodes. This is usually a problem with the flash device. Check that the flash jumpers are correctly populated.

The other problem is that the flash image descriptor.bin and TXE/ME have been overwritten. Reflash the backup image and only update the last 2MB of the MinnowMax flash device with coreboot.

- postcode BBh: The system is alternating between BBh and one of the following postcodes:

```
00h - FSP_SUCCESS: Temp RAM was initialized successfully.
02h - FSP_INVALID_PARAMETER: Input parameters are invalid.
03h - FSP_UNSUPPORTED: The FSP calling conditions were not met.
07h - FSP_DEVICE_ERROR: Temp RAM initialization failed
0Eh - FSP_NOT_FOUND: No valid microcode was found in the
      microcode region.
14h - FSP_ALREADY_STARTED: Temp RAM initialization has been invoked
```

The most common failure is 0Eh, no valid microcode was found. Check that you are using the latest Intel microcode for your silicon version. The Intel FSP package may not have the latest version and you need to update it.

Serial Debug

Serial debug is the most common method of debug in coreboot. The serial port and console configuration is one of the earliest functions after CAR (TempRAMInit) is set up. coreboot can be configured to output different levels of information on the serial port. A typical development coreboot build defaults to DEBUG level, which outputs a lot of information for the developer. The level can be turned up to SPEW, which is way too much information, and it can also be turned down to ERROR or other lower settings to speed up the boot process by printing less information to the serial port. Intel FSP also supports serial output for sending debug information.

EHCI USB Debug

If a serial port is not available for normal debug, coreboot may set up the EHCI controller USB port 0 for debug mode. The EHCI debug port provides a special mode of operation that requires neither RAM nor a full USB stack. It requires additional hardware, like the Ajays NET20DC USB Debug Device, and drivers for the device for the target to send the logging information to. The debug mode is not yet supported by Intel FSP for debug information.

Summary

The coreboot firmware philosophy is about building up with small, fast, target-specific needs. The developers have created a framework to build on and do not make assumptions about the users' needs. Intel FSP and coreboot together allow system designers to customize their solutions down to the smallest details. We look forward to what the next generation of coreboot developers will bring.

## CHAPTER 5

Chrome book Firmware Internals

"The world as we have created it is a process of our thinking. It cannot be changed without changing our thinking."

—Albert Einstein

About Chrome book and Chrome OS

When the first version of Chrome OS became available, many people were asking the same questions: Why? What can it be used for? How is it different from Android? Out of curiosity, many people downloaded it and played with an earlier version. People quickly discovered that it is a neat idea to build an application environment for connected devices that is bounded by a browser-like framework.

Chrome OS takes advantage of the numerous Google cloud-based applications. Why would an OS be designed to depend on the idea that everything would be stored and manipulated in the cloud? Yes, that is the idea. Today's Chrome book and Chrome OS have the offline capabilities to allow users to write e-mails, view appointments, take notes, manipulate documents, edit photos, read offline web pages, and even play games offline without connection, but it is a machine and operating system built to work with Google's cloud. Whatever you work on offline is synchronized with whatever is online, once you are connected. While there is a wide range of Chrome OS devices, the look and feel and experience is uniform across the whole product spectrum.

The reason why we include Chrome book and Chrome OS in this book is because of Google's choice of coreboot as the vehicle to boot its OS. Chrome book may not be designed to be like a typical laptop that can boot multiple operating systems, and it does not have the capability to add and remove internal devices like a PC can, but it is designed to do one thing (if interfacing with cloud is considered as "one thing") and do it well, and that is all that matters. This idea is what IoT devices are about, with a few dedicated functions, and to maximize its benefits and usability for those functions. Chrome book looks like a PC and smells like a PC, but it is deviating itself from the typical PC paradigm. And its choice of coreboot to simplify and secure the firmware stack not only makes sense, but also matches with Google's open source philosophy from top to bottom.

As you read this chapter, you will also learn that Chrome devices are designed to be experimented with. Google has held classes to do just that—showing people how to change the internal firmware and software of a Chrome book. After reading this chapter (and the previous chapter about coreboot), as long as you always preserve a way to restore the original firmware and OS image, you should feel free to experiment with the firmware and OS stack.

Chrome OS Firmware Overview

Chrome OS uses coreboot for all its supported CPU architectures (currently, several different flavors of x86 and ARM devices). This allows for a consistent codebase and designed behaviors across all architectures. Google is committed to open source solutions, and coreboot contains the requisite features and capabilities for booting Chrome OS. coreboot, the firmware layer, provides maximum customization for the optimization of power, performance, and security, with a flexible and consistent firmware OS interface, via ACPI.

The internal operations of coreboot was discussed in the previous chapter, so in this chapter, we will highlight any differences and extensions that have been made to coreboot for Chrome OS devices. You should revisit the previous chapter for specific information about the internals of coreboot.

The Chrome OS firmware image is made up of several pieces: the coreboot hardware initialization code, the Google Depth charge payload, and support binaries and libraries required to boot Chrome OS. The image as a whole is called *Chrome OS firmware* and it should not to be confused with the embedded controller (EC) firmware or other firmware images within the flash device.

Chrome OS Security Philosophy

Google has designed Chrome OS from the ground up with users' data security in mind. Chrome OS devices use the Google verified boot security library for the chain of trust, which starts in write-protected coreboot romstage.

Chrome OS Security Guiding Principles

The following are Chrome OS security guiding principles:

- *The perfect is the enemy of the good.* By realizing that there will never be a perfect solution, the developers of Chrome systems can always ship something good enough to protect the users.

- *Deploy defenses in depth.* There are a variety of defenses to prevent attacks at different levels, so that even if the attacker can penetrate one level, he can be stopped at other levels, making it difficult for the attacker to persist.

- *Make devices secure by default.* Security should not be optional, and it should not be a trade-off item competing with performance and ease-of-use. Since firmware, Chrome OS, and software are well-integrated by the developers, there can be a seamless security implementation from top to bottom by default, not as an afterthought.

- *Don't scapegoat the user.* The design helps the user make decisions only about things they can comprehend, and ensures a fail-safe to make the choice go away when the user does not understand.

Further details are documented at `http://www.chromium.org/chromium-os/chromiumos-design-docs/security-overview`.

Power wash

To further protect user data, a system may be *power washed*, which securely wipes the user's data on the device and returns the system to the default state. This may be performed at any time via the settings screen.

Chrome OS Boot Modes

Chrome OS supports three separate boot modes. The normal Verified Mode boots a Google-signed Chrome OS image. In case of image corruption or other device failure, Chrome OS has Recovery Mode to reinstall the signed image. The third boot mode is Developer Mode, which allows for advanced features and user-customized sources to be loaded.

Verified (Normal) Mode

Verified boot is the cornerstone for the Chrome OS security, which is implemented in concert with coreboot and the Depth charge payload. Google signs all the binary images that make up a Chrome OS device. This includes the coreboot firmware stages, the embedded controller firmware, and the kernel image. As the system boots, each binary image is cryptographically verified prior to running the image. To protect users, the firmware image enters Recovery Mode if any binary verification fails.

Recovery Mode

If something goes wrong in Chrome OS, the system will boot into Recovery Mode. Recovery Mode runs a protected version of coreboot and gives the user an opportunity to recover the system and return to Normal boot mode. Recovery Mode will only boot a Google-signed USB recovery image. Recovery Mode may be automatically initiated when a software or hardware issue occurs. It may also be initiated directly by the user, typically by pressing the Esc+Refresh+Power buttons.

To protect the system during Recovery Mode, the firmware runs the read-only protected version to defend against a problem with a system firmware update or in cases where the system may have been subject to some sort of attack. The read-only version of the firmware can't be overwritten without physical access to the machine, and then only by removing the write-protect screw (which voids the device warranty).

Developer Mode

Developer Mode allows the user to run the Chrome OS system in an unverified mode. This allows more significant software modifications and system controls at the expense of some security. The user may use the root shell, install unsigned and unverified software, run customized images, or even boot a different operating system.

Developer Mode is, essentially, a built-in jailbreak mode that keeps Chrome OS hardware open and enables fair use for all who want to get a Chrome OS device, but are not quite sure whether they want to commit to Chrome OS over the lifetime of the device.

▓ **Note**   Entering Developer Modeclears the private user data saved while the system is in Normal Mode. A warning screen is shown to the user on each boot, so they know that the device is not secure. Developer Mode may be entered by first entering Recovery Mode and then pressing Ctrl+D.

Once in Developer Mode, the user may wish to boot something other than Chrome OS. This may be done by enabling the Legacy Mode flags. This loads the SeaBIOS payload instead of the Depth charge payload. SeaBIOS supports USB and normal hard drive INT19 (legacy) –style booting.

To enable legacy boot, the following flag must be set via the root shell.

```
crossystem dev_boot_legacy=1
```

▓ **Note**   For more information, please check out the information at the following URL:

http://www.chromium.org/chromium-os/chromiumos-design-docs/developer-mode.

Chrome OS Coreboot

Chrome OS is developed on several CPU architectures. Currently, x86, ARM (including ARM64), and MIPS are supported; each architecture requires custom firmware.

x86

For the x86 architecture, the Chrome OS coreboot does not use the Intel FSP as described in the coreboot chapter. It has a smaller Intel firmware binary image, similar to the FSP, and the firmware binary image is specifically tailored to meet the performance and boot time requirements for Chrome OS. The Intel firmware binary image contains subsections of the Memory Reference Code (MRC) and System Agent code.

■ **Note**   As this book is written, Google has come down the path of using MRC binary in the firmware stack, and Intel FSP was made available later. There is an ongoing evaluation effort between Intel and Google to decide on the best solution for future projects. In other words, MRC and Intel FSP may converge in the near future.

ARM

x86 is well represented in the coreboot codebase. coreboot was originally designed around PCI standards first introduced in x86. Google has combined x86 and ARM support into a common codebase. ARM wasn't discussed in the previous coreboot chapter, so we will give a brief overview here.

The number of ARM SOCs supported in coreboot at this time is still significantly behind the number of x86 processors and chipsets, but the number is steadily increasing. The first ARM SOC that started off ARM architecture support in coreboot was the Samsung Exynos 5250, which was added as an experimental proof of concept. Since then, several SOCs have been supported, including newer Exynos, Nvidia Tegra, and Qualcomm devices. Similar to x86, some of the systems require certain binary-only components—like a signed first-stage bootloader or a microcode—to fully function.

■ **Note**   Please check out coreboot differences at `http://git.chromium.org/gitweb/?p=chromiumos/third_party/coreboot.git;a=summary`.

Depth charge Payload

The Google Depth charge payload has a single, focused goal: to securely boot Chrome OS. It is designed to be simple, small, and easy to learn. Being simple and small, it has a quick load time, fast execution, a small attack surface, and is generally very efficient. Depth charge uses two libraries: vboot and libpayload.

Depth charge is loaded by coreboot just as any other coreboot payload. It resides in CBFS and is loaded immediately after coreboot has initialized the hardware. The code flow is fairly simple, as shown in Figure 5-1.

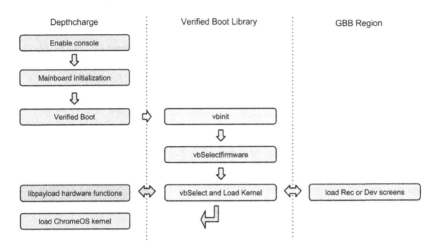

Figure 5-1. *Verified boot flow with Depthcharge payload*

Depth charge will only load Chrome OS and can't boot any other operating system. Depth charge can chain load other payloads in Developer Mode, which may be used to load an additional payload, like SeaBIOS, which may load other operating systems.

libpayload

Depth charge is built upon lib payload. As mentioned in the "Payloads" section of Chapter 4, lib payload is a library of common payload functions and hardware drivers provided by coreboot. It is used by Depth charge and has the following lib payload features:

- A subset of libc and other utility functions

- malloc/free, printf, "string" functions, rand, *delay, etc.

- Tiny ncurses implementation for console and Developer Mode display

- Functions to read and parse the coreboot tables

- LZMA compression

- CBFS utility functions (see Chapter 4 for more information on CBFS)

- Device drivers

  - PCI/PCIe: USB ver. 1, 2, 3—HID, mass storage, hubs; SD and eMMC; SATA (hard drive)

  - CBMEM: Serial console and frame buffer console; CMOS; PC keyboard

Verified Boot

Verified boot is used within coreboot and Depth charge to ensure that only signed code is executed. It is based on security standards starting with a Root of Trust. The Root of Trust on Chrome OS devices is in read-only (RO) firmware protected by physical hardware write protection. The device reset vector (the first instructions executed) is in the RO area of flash (see Figure 5-2). Then, the RO firmware verifies a signed read-write (RW) firmware (VB_Firmware). (The RW firmware may be updated to fix issues in the field). The RW firmware verifies the Chrome OS kernel signature (VB_Kernel) prior to loading it.

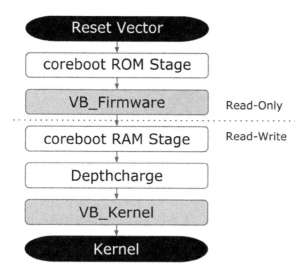

Figure 5-2. *coreboot boot flow from reset to kernel*

Verified Boot and Kernel Security

After the firmware has verified and loaded the kernel, the Root hash is passed to the kernel-on-kernel command line by Depthcharge. The kernel continues the Root of Trust-based security model and mounts the root filesystem as read-only (see Figure 5-3). The kernel security hashes each block in the image. The block hashes are bundled and structured in a tree, and subsequent read blocks are hashed and checked against the tree. The hash tree is stored in the page cache.

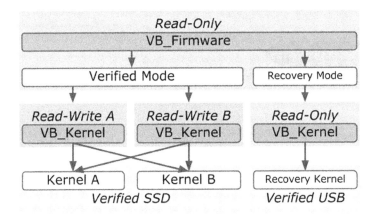

Figure 5-3. *Verified boot and kernel security*

■ **Note**   Reference implementation is available in the Chrome OS source code:
http://git.chromium.org/gitweb/?p=chromiumos/platform/depthcharge.git;a=summary.

Chrome OS Firmware Boot Log

Traditionally, coreboot sends its boot console log messages to a serial port. The coreboot and Depth charge firmware boot log is saved to CBMEM on Chrome OS systems. This log is extremely helpful in debug and it contains useful information to the curious user.

In Chrome OS, the boot log is available in the system information at chrome://system and by then clicking on the Expand button under bios_log.

In Developer Mode, the boot log is easy to access in /sys/firmware/log:

```
# cat /sys/firmware/log
```

Boot Times Log

In addition, the firmware boot times are available under bios_times:

There are 23 entries total:

```
1:start of rom stage              50,048
2:before ram initialization       52,139 (2,091)
3:after ram initialization        73,927 (21,787)
4:end of romstage                 74,426 (499)
5:start of verified boot          74,706 (280)
6:end of verified boot            329,652 (254,946)
8:start of copying ram stage      330,040 (387)
9:end of copying ram stage        346,012 (15,972)
10:start of ramstage              346,040 (28)
30:device enumeration             346,115 (74)
40:device configuration           400,461 (54,346)
50:device enable                  404,182 (3,721)
60:device initialization          405,091 (908)
70:device setup done              459,755 (54,663)
75:cbmem post                     459,770 (14)
80:write tables                   467,590 (7,820)
90:load payload                   468,743 (1,152)
99:selfboot jump                  494,047 (25,304)
1000:depthcharge start            496,598 (2,551)
1002:RO vboot init                496,605 (7)
1020:vboot select&load kernel     498,680 (2,074)
1100:crossystem data              1,031,758 (533,077)
1101:start kernel                 1,032,895 (1,136)
```

In Developer Mode, the boot log is easy to access in var/log/bios_times.txt:

```
# cat /var/log/bios_times.txt
```

Chrome OS Firmware Event Log

The coreboot boot log in CBMEM contains a lot of detailed information about the current boot, but it is lost when the system reboots and cannot be accessed when the system is in a nonbootable state. In order to debug issues across several reboots, all coreboot-based Chrome OS systems have a persistent log of system events.

The event log is based on SMBIOS Type 15 Event Log format, but uses a number of OEM events to provide additional information. The mosys application that is part of Chrome OS can be used to read and decode the log by running the mosys event log list as the root user in Chrome OS if the device is in Developer Mode, or by opening chrome://system and looking for the event log entry in Normal/Verified mode.

```
# mosys eventlog list
12 | 2013-01-15 10:47:43 | ACPI Wake    | S5
13 | 2013-01-15 10:47:43 | EC Event     | Lid Open
14 | 2013-01-15 10:47:43 | System boot  | 142
15 | 2013-01-15 11:51:42 | ACPI Enter   | S3
16 | 2013-01-15 21:05:37 | ACPI Wake    | S3
17 | 2013-01-15 21:05:37 | Wake Source  | GPIO | 11
18 | 2013-01-15 21:05:38 | Kernel Event | Oops
19 | 2013-01-15 21:05:38 | Kernel Event | Panic
20 | 2013-01-15 21:05:39 | System boot  | 143

10:47 - Power on because lid was opened
11:51 - System is suspended
21:05 - Wake from suspend due to GPIO 11 (Touchpad)
21:05 - Kernel oops+panic on resume
```

Google SMI Linux Kernel Driver

The Google SMI kernel driver implements a kernel interface to talk to the firmware's System Management Interrupt (SMI) handler. It allows kernel events to be stored in the firmware event log. The driver hooks into kernel notifier chains and records the following conditions to the log:

- panic
- thermal
- reboot
- die

Chrome OS Extensions to the Firmware Image

As discussed in previous sections, Google has added a number of features and capabilities that are beyond a standard coreboot firmware image. These extensions cohabitate within the firmware image along with coreboot, payloads, and vendor binaries. The extensions in the following subsections were added to help facilitate the many features in the flash image.

FMAP

FMAP is a simple specification for the layout of flash devices. It doesn't make assumptions about the underlying technology. For example, it may be used by coreboot, Legacy BIOS, UEFI, and EC images. FMAP only defines regions in flash. Unlike the coreboot file system CBFS, FMAP defines fixed-size regions.

```
fmap structure:
struct fmap_header {
  char      fmap_signature[8];   /* "__FMAP__" */
  uint8_t   fmap_ver_major;      /* Major version number of this structure */
  uint8_t   fmap_ver_minor;      /* Minor version number of this structure */
  uint64_t  fmap_base;           /* Physical address of the flash chip */
  uint32_t  fmap_size;           /* Size of the flash chip in bytes */
  char      fmap_name[32];       /* Descriptive name of this flash device */
  uint16_t  fmap_nareas;         /* Number of areas described by fmap_areas[] */

  struct fmap_area_header {
  uint32_t    area_offset;       /* Offset of this area in flash device */
  uint32_t    area_size;         /* Size of this area in bytes */
  char        area_name[32];     /* Descriptive name of this area */
  uint16_t    area_flags;        /* Flags for this area */
  } fmap_areas[0];
} __packed;

#define FMAP_AREA_STATIC        0x0001  /* Area contents will not change */
#define FMAP_AREA_COMPRESSED    0x0002  /* Area holds potentially
compressed data */
#define FMAP_AREA_RO            0x0004  /* Area is considered read-only */
```

A Chrome OS firmware FMAP example is shown in Table 5-1.

Table 5-1. *FMAP Example*

Base	Size	Section	Description
0x000000	0x200000	SI_ALL	Descriptor + ME
0x200000	0x0f0000	RW_SECTION_A	Read-Write Firmware A
0x2f0000	0x0f0000	RW_SECTION_B	Read-Write Firmware B
0x3e0000	0x010000	RW_MRC_CACHE	Memory Training Cache
0x3f0000	0x004000	RW_ELOG	Event Log
0x3f4000	0x004000	RW_SHARED	Shared Data
0x3f8000	0x002000	RW_VPD	Read-Write VPD
0x400000	0x200000	RW_LEGACY	Legacy Firmware
0x600000	0x004000	RO_VPD	Read-Only VPD
0x610000	0x000800	FMAP	Flash Map
0x610800	0x000040	RO_FRID	RO Firmware ID
0x611000	0xef0000	GBB	Google Binary Block
0x700000	0x100000	BOOT_STUB	Read-Only Firmware

BOOT_STUB FMAP Section

The BOOT_STUB section contains the reset vector location at the end of the rom (for x86), as well as all the read-only firmware. This includes the coreboot rom stage and verified boot image used by the normal verified boot path. It also contains the complete RO firmware for Recovery Mode, which includes read-only versions of coreboot ram stage and Depth charge.

Chrome OS Firmware RW FMAP Sections

Chrome OS firmware contains two read-write sections. These are updated separately in case there is a problem with the update process. When a firmware update happens, only one of the sections is updated with a new image. Once the system has booted successfully with the new firmware, the old firmware in the other section is overwritten with the new firmware. If the firmware update fails, the system will automatically fall back to the old, known good firmware. A Chrome OS firmware FMAP RW Section example is shown in Table 5-2.

Table 5-2. *FMAP Read-Write Section Example*

RW_SECTION_A	Size	Type	Description
0x200000	0x010000	VBLOCK_A	Key Block
0x210000	0x0c0000	FW_MAIN_A	BIOS Image A
0x2d0000	0x01ffc0	EC_MAIN_A	EC Image A
0x2effc0	0x000040	RW_FWID_A	RW Firmware ID
RW_SECTION_B			
0x2f0000	0x010000	VBLOCK_B	Key Block
0x300000	0x0c0000	FW_MAIN_B	BIOS Image B
0x3c0000	0x01ffc0	EC_MAIN_B	EC Image B
0x3dffc0	0x000040	RW_FWID_B	RW Firmware ID

The FMAPorganization is defined by the `fmap.dts` file located in the Depthcharge payload (see the following example).

An fmap.dts (RW_SECTION_A) Example

```
rw-a {
      label = "rw-section-a";
      reg = <0x00200000 0x000f0000>;
};
rw-a-vblock {
      label = "vblock-a";
      reg = <0x00200000 0x00010000>;
      type = "keyblock boot,ecrwhash,ramstage,refcode";
      keyblock = "firmware.keyblock";
      signprivate = "firmware_data_key.vbprivk";
      version = <1>;
      kernelkey = "kernel_subkey.vbpubk";
      preamble-flags = <0>;
};
rw-a-boot {
      label = "fw-main-a";
      reg = <0x00210000 0x000c0000>;
      type = "blob boot,ecrwhash,ramstage,refcode";
};
rw-a-ec-boot {
      label = "ec-main-a";
      reg = <0x002d0000 0x0001ffc0>;
      type = "blob ecbin";
};
rw-a-firmware-id {
      label = "rw-fwid-a";
      reg = <0x002effc0 0x00000040>;
      read-only;
      type = "blobstring fwid";
};
```

The FMAP reference implementation is available at http://flashmap.googlecode.com.

Google Binary Block (GBB)

The Google Binary Block (GBB) is a simple binary storage interface for Chrome OS devices. It is stored in a region in read-only firmware and located via the FMAP. It contains the following information:

- Hardware Identification (HWID)

- Firmware Root Key

- Recovery Key

- Bitmaps for firmware screens and translations of firmware messages

- A Flags setting to enable/disable Chrome OS–related features and boot configuration

GBB: HWID v3

The Hardware identifier is unique for each Chrome OS device model. It is generated by an algorithm that catalogs all HW and FW components, as well as the platform name, build phase, and the RO firmware version. It is generated for each board during the factory process. HWID is used to uniquely identify each platform hardware variant to ensure compatibility during recovery and updates.

GBB: Firmware Bitmaps

The firmware image screens for Recovery Mode help and Developer Mode warnings are included in the GBB area. These images have localized text overlays for the transition to and from Recovery and Developer modes. The user can switch between locales with arrow keys. The images are LZMA-compressed bitmaps to minimize space and they must be available for the RO firmware.

GBB: Firmware Keys

Public keys in GBB are used for verification of the binaries, which are signed by the Google private keys during the build process. The binary data is not encrypted; it is only hashed. The GBB contains the Root and Recovery Public Keys, which are RSA-8192 + SHA-512. Subsequent keys are smaller. Each signing key is versioned and the Verified boot will reject lower versions.

GBB: Boot Flags

The boot flags are flags that alter the Chrome OS boot path. They override the nonvolatile flags set with the crossystem tool. The flags are used to enable alternate booting for the factory process, but they can also be used by the end user to customize a boot after entering Developer Mode and disabling write protect. A list of the boot flags is located in Table 5-3.

Table 5-3. *GBB Boot Flag Types*

Flag Name	Flag Value	Description
GBB_FLAG_DEV_SCREEN_SHORT_DELAY	0x00000001	Reduce Developer screen delay to 2s
GBB_FLAG_LOAD_OPTION_ROMS	0x00000002	Load option ROMs from arbitrary PCI devices (obsolete)
GBB_FLAG_ENABLE_ALTERNATE_OS	0x00000004	Allow booting of non-Chrome OS kernel (obsolete)
GBB_FLAG_FORCE_DEV_SWITCH_ON	0x00000008	Force enable Developer Mode
GBB_FLAG_FORCE_DEV_BOOT_USB	0x00000010	Allow booting from USB in dev mode even if dev_boot_usb is 0
GBB_FLAG_DISABLE_FW_ROLLBACK_CHECK	0x00000020	Disable firmware rollback protection
GBB_FLAG_ENTER_TRIGGERS_TONORM	0x00000040	Allow Enter key to trigger mode transition to Normal Mode on Developer Mode warning screen
GBB_FLAG_FORCE_DEV_BOOT_LEGACY	0x00000080	Allow Legacy Mode boot even if dev_boot_legacy is 0
GBB_FLAG_FAFT_KEY_OVERRIDE	0x00000100	Allow use of alternate keys for firmware testing
GBB_FLAG_DISABLE_EC_SOFTWARE_SYNC	0x00000200	Disable EC read-write firmware update
GBB_FLAG_DEFAULT_DEV_BOOT_LEGACY	0x00000400	Boot legacy OS in Developer Mode by default
GBB_FLAG_DISABLE_PD_SOFTWARE_SYNC	0x00000800	Disable PD MCU read-write firmware update

111

Vital Product Data (VPD)

There are two types of the Vital Product Data in the flash image. There is a region in read-only and read-write areas of flash and the two VPDs hold separate information, as follows.

- RO_VPD
    - Serial Number
    - Initial Locale
    - Initial Time Zone
    - Keyboard Layout
    - Ethernet MAC address
- RW_VPD
    - Activation Date
    - Registration Codes

Firmware TPM Usage

TPM stands for Trusted Platform Module. It is a specialized chip on an endpoint device that stores RSA encryption keys specific to the host system for hardware authentication. Chrome OS's verified boot library uses the TPM for the following tasks:

- Preventing software and firmware version rollback
- Maintaining information to detect transitions between Normal and Developer Modes
- Protecting user data encryption keys
- Protecting certain user RSA keys ("hardware-backed" certificates)
- Providing tamper evidence for installation attributes
- Protecting state ful partition encryption keys
- Attesting TPM-protected keys
- Attesting device mode

The TPM is not directly available outside of Chrome OS for any purpose; that is, no remote software or system may have access to the TPM.
Chrome OS does not use the TPM for the following:

- *Trusted boot*: The TPM is not used as part of the Chrome OS verified boot solution.
- *Hardware*: Strength platform configuration reporting.
- *Whole-disk encryption or similar*: In particular, the TPM is not used to unwrap an encryption key during the boot process.

Chrome OS Firmware Update

The Chrome OS read-write area of the flash may be updated by the auto-update process. When required, Chrome OS downloads the firmware update as a self-contained firmware update package. All the binaries and scripts embedded into the shell archive, as well as the firmware images for the system flash and the EC flash. The flashrom utility is part of the package and is used to flash both the Chrome OS firmware image and the EC image.

As shown in the "FMAP" section of this chapter, the Chrome OS firmware has two read-write images. The update process begins with flashing one region, rebooting, verifying that the new image works, and then flashing the second region. This process should prevent the system from becoming unusable if there is an update issue. Figure 5-4 shows the process of the RW image update process.

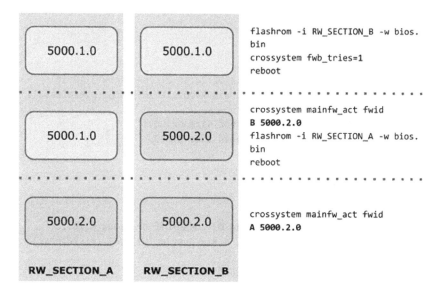

Figure 5-4. *RW image update process*

Chrome OS Utilities

Chrome OS uses several customized utilities behind the scenes. Users are able to access these utilities to make system modifications in Developer Mode:

- flashrom
- gbb_utility
- mosys
- crossystem

flashrom

flashrom is an open source flash chip programmer utility (flashrom.org). It supports many chipsets, flash devices, and programmers. The Chrome OS version has been customized for Chrome OS needs, which includes updates to FMAP regions.

```
FTDI (-p ft2232_spi:servo-v2)
Dediprog (-p dediprog)
Embedded Controllers (-p ec)
FMAP integration (-i region)

Usage: flashrom [-h|-R|-L|-p <programmername>[:<parameters>] [-c <chipname>]
[-E|(-r|-w|-v) <file>] [-l <layoutfile> [-i <imagename>]...] [-n] [-f]]
[-V[V[V]]] [-o <logfile>]
```

Read Chrome OS firmware image:

```
# flashrom -p host -r fw_backup.bin
flashrom v0.9.4  : 141a262 : Jan 08 2014 02:24:30 UTC on Linux 3.10.18
(x86_64), built with libpci 3.1.10, GCC 4.8.x-google 20130905 (prerelease),
little endian
Mapping BYT IBASE at 0xfed08000, unaligned size 0x200.
Mapping BYT SBASE at 0xfed01000, unaligned size 0x200.
Reading flash... SUCCESS
```

Write Chrome OS firmware image:

```
# flashrom -p host -w image.bin
flashrom v0.9.4  : 141a262 : Jan 08 2014 02:24:30 UTC on Linux 3.10.18
(x86_64), built with libpci 3.1.10, GCC 4.8.x-google 20130905 (prerelease),
little endian
Mapping BYT IBASE at 0xfed08000, unaligned size 0x200.
Mapping BYT SBASE at 0xfed01000, unaligned size 0x200.
Erasing and writing flash chip... Verifying flash... VERIFIED.
SUCCESS
```

gbb_utility

gbb_utility is the utility to manage the Google Binary Block (GBB) region of the firmware image.

■ **Note**   The internal write protect screw on the mainboard must be removed to write the GBB region.

```
Usage: gbb_utility [-g|-s|-c] [OPTIONS] bios_file [output_file]
```

Read current BIOS from flash into bios.bin:

```
# flashrom -r bios.bin
```

Extract and display HWID from bios.bin:

```
# gbb_utility --get --hwid bios.bin
hardware_id: RAMBI TEST A-A 0120
```

Extract and display GBB flags from bios.bin:

```
# gbb_utility --get --flags bios.bin
flags: 0x00000000
```

Set GBB flags in bios.bin to 0x39 (factory default):

```
# gbb_utility --set --flags=0x39 bios.bin
- flags changed from 0x00000000 to 0x00000039: success
successfully saved new image to: bios.bin
```

Write updated bios.bin back to flash:

```
# flashrom -i GBB -w bios.bin
```

GBB Flags Utility Script: set_gbb_flags.sh

set_gbb_flags.sh is a script to automate the gbb_utility to change the flags. It can be used in place of the preceding GBB flags example.

```
Usage: set_gbb_flags.sh [option_flags] GBB_FLAGS_VALUE
```

crossystem

The crossystem tool is used to gather information about the Chrome OS device's system flags, boot modes, VPD, GBB, NVRAM information, and binary versions.
Get vital system data:

```
# crossystem
arch                     = x86       # Platform architecture
clear_tpm_owner_request  = 0         # Clear TPM owner on next boot
clear_tpm_owner_done     = 0         # Clear TPM owner done
cros_debug               = 1         # OS should allow debug features
dbg_reset                = 0         # Debug reset mode request (writable)
ddr_type                 = unknown   # Type of DDR RAM
debug_build              = 1         # OS image built for debug features
```

115

```
dev_boot_usb           = 0                        # Enable developer mode
                                                     boot from USB/SD
                                                     (writable)
dev_boot_legacy        = 0                        # Enable developer mode
                                                     boot Legacy OSes
                                                     (writable)
dev_boot_signed_only   = 0                        # Enable developer mode
                                                     boot only from official
                                                     kernels (writable)
devsw_boot             = 1                        # Developer switch
                                                     position at boot
devsw_cur              = 1                        # Developer switch current
                                                     position
disable_dev_request    = 0                        # Disable virtual dev-mode
                                                     on next boot
ecfw_act               = RW                       # Active EC firmware
fmap_base              = 0xffe10000               # Main firmware flashmap
                                                     physical address
fwb_tries              = 0                        # Try firmware B count
                                                     (writable)
fwid                   = Google_Rambi.5216.239.0  # Active firmware ID
fwupdate_tries         = 0                        # Times to try OS firmware
                                                     update (writable, inside
                                                     kern_nv)
hwid                   = RAMBI TEST A-A 0128      # Hardware ID
kern_nv                = 0x00000000               # Non-volatile field for
                                                     kernel use
kernkey_vfy            = sig                      # Type of verification
                                                     done on kernel key block
loc_idx                = 0                        # Localization index
                                                     for firmware screens
                                                     (writable)
mainfw_act             = A                        # Active main firmware
mainfw_type            = developer                # Active main firmware type
nvram_cleared          = 1                        # Have NV settings been
                                                     lost?  Write 0 to clear
oprom_needed           = 0                        # Should we load the VGA
                                                     Option ROM at boot?
platform_family        = BayTrail                 # Platform family type
recovery_reason        = 0                        # Recovery mode reason
                                                     for current boot
recovery_request       = 0                        # Recovery mode request
                                                     (writable)
recovery_subcode       = 0                        # Recovery reason subcode
                                                     (writable)
recoverysw_boot        = 0                        # Recovery switch position
                                                     at boot
```

```
recoverysw_cur        = (error)                # Recovery switch current
                                                 position
recoverysw_ec_boot    = 0                      # Recovery switch position
                                                 at EC boot
ro_fwid               = Google_Rambi.5216.239.0 # Read-only firmware ID
savedmem_base         = 0x00f00000             # RAM debug data area
                                                 physical address
savedmem_size         = 1048576                # RAM debug data area size
                                                 in bytes
sw_wpsw_boot          = 0                      # Firmware write protect
                                                 software setting enabled
                                                 at boot
tpm_fwver             = 0x00010001             # Firmware version stored
                                                 in TPM
tpm_kernver           = 0x00010001             # Kernel version stored
                                                 in TPM
tried_fwb             = 0                      # Tried firmware B before
                                                 A this boot
vdat_flags            = 0x00000c56             # Flags from VbSharedData
vdat_timers           = LFS=185474800,273111920
                        LF=274161584,415809776
                        LK=1,2856282           # Timer values from
                                                 VbSharedData
wpsw_boot             = 1                      # Firmware write protect
                                                 hardware switch position
                                                 at boot
wpsw_cur              = 1                      # Firmware write protect
                                                 hardware switch current
                                                 position
```

mosys

mosys is the firmware and hardware inspection utility. It is customized for each chipset, so the capabilities and information vary from system to system. Generally, the following commands are available with mosys:

```
ec          EC information
eeprom      EEPROM Information
gpio        GPIO Information
memory      Memory Information
nvram       NVRAM information
platform    Platform Information
smbios      SMBIOS Information
eventlog    Event Log

usage: mosys [options] [commands]
```

Get the SMBIOS BIOS information table:

```
# mosys smbios info bios
coreboot | Google_Rambi.5216.239.0 | 07/11/2014 | 8192 KB
```

Google Embedded Controller

Besides the Application processor firmware, coreboot, Google has developed open source embedded controller (EC) firmware.

The primary responsibilities of the EC are as follows:

- Application processor power sequencing

- Battery charging

- Thermal management

- Keyboard controller

- Buttons and switches

- Backlights, indicator LEDs

- Additional board-specific peripherals

■ **Note**   For more information about the Google EC, visit http://git.chromium.org/
gitweb/?p=chromiumos/platform/ec.git;a=summary.

Like other areas of Chrome OS, the Chrome EC is designed for security. It has read-only and read-write regions. The read-write binary update is called Software Sync. The sync is handled by Depth charge and verified boot. The Chrome EC firmware has support for several different ARM SOCs, including Texas Instruments Stellar is Cortex-M4 and the ST Micro STM32 Cortex-M3.

Power Sequencing

Each application processor family has its own power sequencing requirements. The EC must manage and respond to all those requirements across the different system states, like boot, sleep, and idle. It also ensures that some peripherals are brought up and down as directed by system drivers; for example, USB and Wi-Fi devices.

Battery Charging

Most Chrome books use Smart Battery technology. This is a fairly simple system, where the battery asks for specific voltage and current, and the charger circuitry responds accordingly. The EC handles a few special cases:

- Trickle charge a fully discharged battery

- Custom charge requirements for high- or low-power conditions

- Keeping temperatures within safe operating ranges

■ **Note**   Reference materials are located at http://sbs-forum.org/specs/sbdat110.pdf.

Thermal Management

The Chrome EC firmware supports several different thermal modes. It can act on independent thresholds and deliver host events via ACPI and the system PROCHOT signal. It also has configuration for fan speeds and can force the system power off, based on any sensor readings.

Keyboard Controller

For x86-based systems, the EC provides a "standard" 8042 AT-style interface. ARM-based systems use a binary format that merely sends the scan matrix up to the kernel. In either case, the keyboard scan matrix is defined in the board-specific firmware configuration.

Other Peripheral Controls

The Chrome EC also controls the following devices:

- LED behavior (battery charging, full, power on, etc.)

- Backlight

- Wi-Fi/USB power

- Light bar, accelerometer, dedicated hardware buttons

Chrome EC Software Sync

It is important that the AP firmware (coreboot) and the EC firmware remain compatible through upgrades. During every Normal Mode boot, the EC firmware is verified by the AP firmware and updated, if required. In Recovery Mode, the EC and AP firmware stay in read-only mode.

Software Sync Steps

The following are the software sync steps:

1. The EC boots its RO firmware and powers on the AP.

2. The AP boots its RO firmware.

3. The AP verifies its RW firmware and jumps to it.

4. The EC computes a hash of its RW firmware.

5. The AP RW firmware contains a copy of the EC's RW firmware.
   The AP compares its hash with the EC's hash.

If they differ, the AP gives the EC the correct RW firmware, which the EC writes to its flash. The EC jumps to its RW firmware.
In Developer Mode, set the flag in the GBB to disable Software Sync:

```
# set_gbb_flags.sh 0x239
0x00000001 GBB_FLAG_DEV_SCREEN_SHORT_DELAY
0x00000008 GBB_FLAG_FORCE_DEV_SWITCH_ON
0x00000010 GBB_FLAG_FORCE_DEV_BOOT_USB
0x00000020 GBB_FLAG_DISABLE_FW_ROLLBACK_CHECK
0x00000200 GBB_FLAG_DISABLE_EC_SOFTWARE_SYNC
```

Summary

We are hoping that after reading this chapter, you have realized that the Chrome book and other Chrome devices are not only interesting and convenient to use, but are also devices that you can play with to experiment your new firmware and software ideas. This chapter has provided you enough information to start your journey, but do check out Google web sites to learn up-to-date and more detailed technical information.

By the way, this chapter's text and graphics were written on a Chrome OS device in Google Docs.

■ **Note** This chapter contains some modified materials from the Chromium OS wiki (http://www.chromium.org/chromium-os). This falls under the Creative Commons Attribution 2.5 license (http://creativecommons.org/licenses/by/2.5/).

CHAPTER 6

■ ■ ■

Intel FSP and UEFI Integration

"In theory, there is no difference between theory and practice. But, in practice, there is."

—Yogi Berra

This chapter will provide a bridge from the earlier chapters on FSP and coreboot to Unified Extensible Interface (UEFI)-based technologies. These UEFI technologies include the UEFI Platform Initialization (PI)-based modules in the EFI Developer Kit II (EDK II) found on tianocore.org. EDK II elements can "consume" an Intel FSP binary to build a complete platform. In addition, EDK II can be used as a payload for coreboot-style systems. Finally, there are examples of EDK II–based open hardware platforms, such as Minnow and MinnowMax, which demonstrate the Intel FSP and EDK II platform elements.

Introduction to EFI

EFI (Extensible Firmware Interface) and coreboot began around the same time in the late 1990s. They started with two different purposes. One of the objectives of EFI was moving legacy BIOS to a modern interface with a modular driver model that allowed components to be added and removed with ease.coreboot, on the other hand, was mostly created from scratch to keep a minimum set of hardware initialization to boot Linux, and it was designed to be an open source project from the beginning. EFI was later adopted by many industry leaders, and turned into UEFI (Unified Extensible Firmware Interface). Along with the UEFI evolution, the EDK (EFI Development Kit) was created to help firmware development projects based on UEFI. Today's EDK II is the second generation of the original EDK, as the name suggests. You may also find UDK (UEFI Development Kit) as the name representing the same codebase, which designates specific validated instances of the EDK II tree.

We have talked about coreboot and Intel FSP in the last few chapters, and we will focus on EDK II and Intel FSP integration in this chapter. Figure 6-1 shows an overview of the development flow of different firmware ingredients in route to make the final target ROM. As stated before, the goal of this book is to teach you how to put these ingredients together so that you have the freedom to explore and develop your value-added features.

The life cycle of firmware creation is shown in Figure 6-1. The flow starts from the left, with the silicon reference code formatted as PEI Modules (PEIMs). These PEIMs are, in turn, built into a firmware volume with the appropriate FSP interfaces via the FSP SDK. This SDK includes elements of the MDE Module Package (`https://svn.code.Sf.net/p/edk2/code/trunk/edk2/MdeModulePkg`) and the Intel FSP Package (`https://svn.code.Sf.net/p/edk2/code/trunk/edk2/IntelFspPkg/`). The latter package encapsulates the interfaces that a FSP binary needs to publish, as defined in the FSP External Architecture Specification at `http://www.intel.com/fsp`.

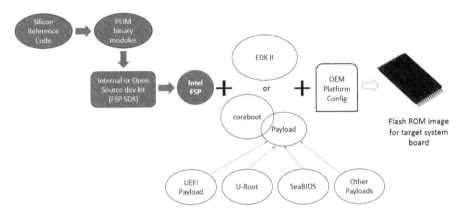

Figure 6-1. *Work flow of FSP and EDK II*

Even though UEFI/PI-based EDK II and core boot are distinctly different code bases, conceptually, they share similar boot phases. Table 6-1 compares core boot and UEFI/PI-based EDK II from a boot phase and terminology perspective. The left most column describes the common capability, the middle column lists the core boot mapping, and finally, the right most column contains the UEFI PI-based firmware mapping.

Table 6-1. *Comparison of coreboot and UEFI PI*

Capability	coreboot	UEFI PI
The reset vector and pre cache-as-RAM setup.	boot block	Security Phase (SEC)
Cache-as-RAM setup, early silicon initialization, memory setup. Covered largely by Intel FSP.	rom stage	Pre-EFI Initialization (PEI) Create HOBs
Normal device setup and main board configuration. Publishes SMBIOS/ACPI tables.	ram stage	Early Driver Execution Environment (DXE)
Memory map hand-off.	CBMEM	UEFI Memory Map
The OS or application boot loader.	pay load	DXE BDS and UEFI Drivers

The reality is that EDK II is necessarily rich and expansive because it supports the specifications at www.uefi.org and a large set of capability sets to meet the various business demands. To that end, EDK2 and UEFI have been successful in the broad market.

Even UEFI/EDK II stalwarts have expressed complexity, including anecdotal commentary at http://uefi.blogspot.com/2014/04/the-tale-of-three-conferences.html.

Many discussions around UEFI have to do with complexity. And there is something to these discussions, since the very power and flexibility of UEFI has led to implementations (like that on TianoCore) that are broken into hundreds of pieces, where assembling the right one requires the appropriate recipes. Most embedded vendors don't need their firmware distribution to be as complicated as their Linux distribution (see yoctoproject.org).

Alternate firmware communities like core boot (www.coreboot.org) have Source Control Management (SCM), a simpler workflow and number of files, and many public main boards with full source. This poses an opportunity to embrace some of those properties in our extant EDK II community. Specifically, the challenge for this effort is to balance the richness of the present EDK II source, standards, and http://tianocore.org, but provide simplified views or "recipes."

The Firmware Support Package (FSP) is a recipe for aggregating a series of PEI Modules (www.uefi.org) into a firmware volume. More information on the interface to the FSP, including the hand-off state and additional APIs, can be found at http://www.intel.com/content/www/us/en/intelligent-systems/intel-firmware-support-package/fsp-architecture-spec.html in the FSP EAS. We refer to this internally as "FSP 1.0" since the evolution of FSP to include the migration of code to the reset vector and other state management will be provided on the path toward the vision of "FSP2.0."

FSP allows for the reuse of the validated EDK II code from the Intel product groups providing silicon-initialization reference code. So the FSP + coreboot, or the FSP + EDK II boot loader allow for amortizing the validation listed earlier.

There are presently efforts underway to assess open sourcing the closed-source silicon reference code (SiRC) in Figure 6-1. If that happens, does that mean that the FSP is no longer of value? No. Instead, FSP provides a simple means by which to segregate the CPU and chipset-specific initialization code from the platform initialization (board-specific elements) and the boot loader (OS-interface specific). This provides a clean separation of duty from the ecosystem.

Introduction to FSP

The Intel® Firmware Support Package (Intel® FSP) provides key programming information for initializing Intel® silicon. It can be easily integrated into a firmware boot environment of the developer's choice.

Different Intel hardware devices may have different Intel FSP binary instances, so a platform user needs to choose the right Intel FSP binary release. The FSP binary should be independent of the platform design, but specific to the Intel CPU and chipset complex. We refer to the entities that create the FSP binary as the *FSP producer* and the developer who integrates the FSP into some platform firmware as the *FSP consumer*.

Despite the variability of the FSP binaries, the FSP API caller (a.k. A. FSP consumer) could be a generic module to invoke the three APIs defined in FSP EAS. This allows for rich differentiation in the platform silicon, but it provides for a single set of interface code in the consuming firmware base, whether it be coreboot or EDK II based. In other words, the interface to the FSP binary can be like a class-driver or generic code, written for any FSP binary. This allows for the ease of maintaining generic open source firmware code that can absorb FSPs from different lines of business within a given manufacturer or other manufacturers.

Figure 6-2 describes the FSP architecture, with the FSP binary from the FSP producer in the center of the figure, and the platform code that integrates the binary, or the FSP consumer, in blue. The fixed APIs published by the center FSP producer code, which is the center of the figure, allow for a consistent set of invoking "consumer" code in the adjacent boxes on the left and right.

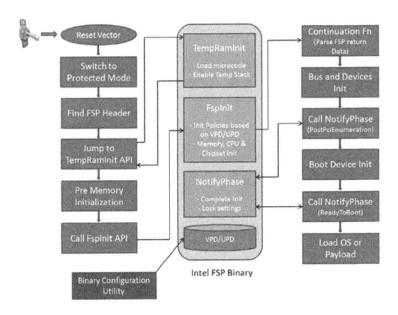

Figure 6-2. *Platform flow with FSP*

The FSP EAS describes the API interface to the FSP binary that the consumer code will invoke, but it also describes the hand-off state from the execution of the FSP binary. The latter information is conveyed in Hand-Off Blocks, or HOBs. The Hand-Off Block generic definition can be found in the UEFI Platform Initialization (PI) specification at www.uefi.org, and the generic FSP EAS contains additional definitions of the HOB, as do silicon-specific integration guides. Both the HOB definition and the binary layout of the FSP.bin, namely as a Firmware Volume (FV), are the same as that defined in the UEFI PI specification. Both the reuse of the PI specification artifacts and the EDK II open source are used in the FSP production.

The FSP consumption, which is the topic of this chapter, can be a plurality of firmware environments, of which an EDK II-style consumer will be described in more detail. This EDK II consume will be a mixture of generic code from Tiano Core and platform-specific PEI and DXE modules.

Introduction to EDK II

EDK II is the open source implementation for UEFI firmware, which can boot multiple UEFI OS. This document will introduce how to use EDK II as a FSP consumer module to build a platform BIOS.

Summary

This section provided an overview of Intel FSP and EDK II. Specifically, the use of open source http://www.Tianocore.org/ elements that provide UEFI and UEFI PI interfaces—along with consumer code of the FSP APIs—will be treated. TianoCore/ is a package-based firmware architecture that provides an open source implementation of industry-standard APIs in order to provide a "BIOS Core" that can be used in the construction of platforms. The more generic, open source packages of TianoCore/, such as the Module Development Environment (MDE) and the associated modules of the MDE Module Package, should be reusable across a broad class of architectures, from ARM Ltd to AMD to Intel. Chapter 2 of the UEFI 2.4 specification describes the various bindings for which UEFI can be built.

For the Intel FSP, the https://svn.code.Sf.net/p/edk2/code/trunk/edk2/IntelFspWrapperPkg/ is the package that provides an abstraction into an FSP.bin file. The FSP.bin is included in a firmware build by importing the binary into the directory and including a reference to the DSC file, along with the other necessary packages from TianoCore/.

FSP Components

In EDK II, there are two different FSP-related packages. One is the producer, IntelFspPkg, which is used to produce FSP.bin together with other EDK II packages and silicon packages. The other is consumer, IntelFspWrapperPkg, which consumes the API exposed by FSP.bin.

This chapter only focuses on IntelFspWrapperPkg and how it consumes FSP.bin. This chapter will not describe IntelFspPkg or how it produces FSP.bin because the upcoming chapter on Tiny Quark describes the construction of a full initialization binary very much like a FSP binary. The core boot consumption of FSP was described in Chapter 4. Figure 6-3 shows the EDK II work flow for the production of an FSP (on the left) and the resultant paths to consume the FSP (on the right).

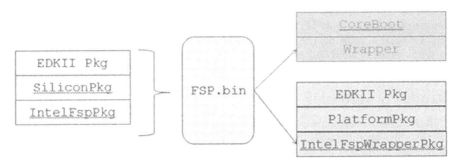

Figure 6-3. *FSP components*

FSP Wrapper Boot Flow

According to the FSP EAS, an FSP.bin exposes three APIs: TempRamInitApi, FspInitApi, and FspNotifyApi (PciEnumerationDone and ReadyToBoot).

When should they be invoked in EDK II BIOS? There are three options for integrating the FSP into an EDK II-style firmware. Details on the three options are described next, with a grading that can be found in Table 6-2.

There are many architectural choices. The choices of FSP integration include having a SEC core that directly invokes the FSP binary, and a second implementation that includes a full PEI firmware volume with a PEI core. The former would be for a simple system without other features in the PEI firmware volume (FV), such as Capsule Update or Recovery.

With the SEC integration of FSP, which is shown in Figure 6-4, the SecCore can call TempRamInitApi and FspInitApi immediately, and then skip the entire PEI phase and jump to DxeLoad. DxeLoad can consume the FspHob, produce HOBs for DXE, and then enter DxeCore directly. Afterward, FspNotifyDxe will register for a notification on the PciEnumerationDone and ReadyToBoot callback function.

Finally, the FspNotifyApi is called in the callback function.

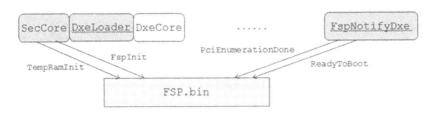

Figure 6-4. *FSP wrapper boot flow option 1*

For the option described in Figure 6-5, SecCore calls TempRamInitApi and FspInitApi immediately, and then enters PeiCore as normal. One PEIM will consume FspHob and produce the HOBneeded by DXE. At the end of PEI, DxeIpl is launched and enters DxeCore. The FspNotifiyDxe is the same as the example shown in Figure 6-4.

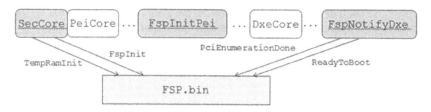

Figure 6-5. *FSP wrapper boot flow option 2*

In the final integration option shown in Figure 6-6, SecCore calls TempRamInitApi only, and then enters the PeiCore. The FspInitPei module calls FspInitApi. However, once FspInitApi is back, all PEI context saved in CAR is destroyed. So FspInitPei has to enter PeiCore again to continue the PEI phase boot. Then, the rest of the initialization activities will be same as a normal UEFI PI firmware boot flow. In addition, FspNotifyDxe is the same as option 1 listed above in Figure 6-4.

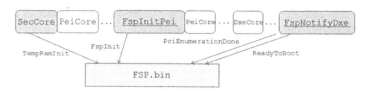

Figure 6-6. *FSP wrapper boot flow option 3*

Table 6-2 compares the pros and the cons for each solution.

Table 6-2. *Comparison of the FSP Integration Options*

FSP Wrapper Flow	Pros	Cons
Option 1	Small firmware size.	No generic Dxe Loader. Hard to support a different PI boot mode.
Option 2	All generic code.	Hard to support a different PI boot mode.
Option 3	All generic code. Supports all PI boot modes.	Complex. Needs to enter PEI Core twice.

In EDK II, the default option is the last one. That means the IntelFspWrapperPkg can support multiple PI boot modes, like Normal boot, S3 resume, Capsule Update, and Recovery. Boot modes are describes in the UEFI PI Specification.

However, an EDK II developer can use option 2 if the platform is so simple that there is no need to support multiple boot modes. Or, a developer can use option 1 if the platform is simple enough to skip the PEI phase. And in this case, "simple" means PEI-phase features like platform Recovery, S3 Resume, Capsule Detection, and other platform-based PEI phase actions can be omitted or deferred to a later phase, such as the Driver Execution Environment (DXE).

Generic FSP Wrapper Boot Flow

Next is a deeper dive into the FSP wrapper boot flow. The detailed boot flow in each of the UEFI PI boot modes will be described, too.

Normal Boot

A Normal Boot is typically a restart of the system that passes control from the reset vector to the ensuing OS loader or payload. It is typically an ACPI S5 restart from a hardware perspective, as opposed to a wake event like ACPI S3 or a restart event that is intended to support a firmware update, such as the UEFI Capsule Update.

Boot Flow

In Normal boot mode, SecCore will firstcall theFSP API—TempRamInitApi, and then transfer control to the PeiCore. One platform PEIM will be responsible to detect the current boot mode and find some variable to finalize the boot mode selection. The Normal boot flow is shown in Figure 6-7.

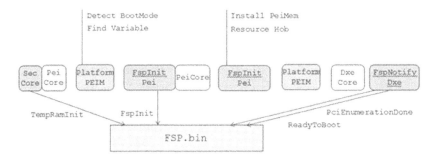

Figure 6-7. *FSP Normal boot flow*

FspInitPei has a dependency on MasterBootModePpi, so after the boot mode is determined, FspInitPei is invoked for the first time, and it will call the second FSP API—FspInitApi. In FSP.bin, the cache is torn down, so all previous PeiCore context is lost. In the FspInit continuation function, it will emulate SecCore to launch the PeiCore again, with a special PEIM-to-PEIM Interface (PPI)—FspInitDonePpi—as a parameter for the PeiCore. Then FspInitPei will be invoked for a second time. At that moment, since FspInitDonePpi is installed, FspInitPei will run into another path to parse the FspHob and install PEI memory.

PeiCore will continue dispatching the final PEIMs and jump into the DXE core. Then, DXE core will launch FspNotifyDxe, which registers a callback function for the last FSP API—FspNotifyApi, for both PciEnumerationDone and ReadyToBoot.

Memory Layout for a Normal Boot Flow

The memory layout for FSP Normal boot is shown in Figure 6-8. The left-hand side demonstrates the component on flash and the temporary memory, such as cache as RAM. On the right-hand side is the DRAM layout. The green part is for FSP.BIN. The blue part is for EDK II BIOS.

When SecCore calls TempRamInitApi, FSP binary sets up the temporary memory using the processor cache-as-RAM (CAR), uses part of them, and leaves the rest of these activities to the EDK II BIOS. This CAR information is reported as a return parameter of TempRamInitApi (see bottom left of Figure 6-8).

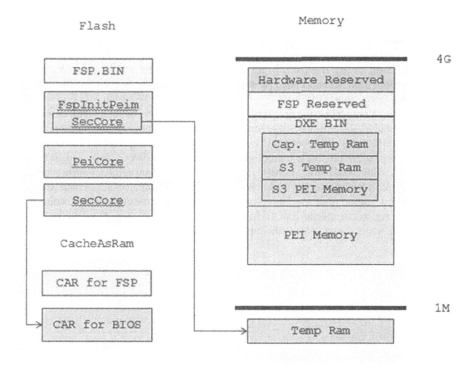

Figure 6-8. *FSP Normal boot flow memory layout*

Then FspInitPei calls FspInitApi, wherein the FSP binary will initialize silicon including DRAM and reserved portions of DRAM. The full memory layout, including full DRAM size, reserved DRAM location, and SMRAM location will be reported by the FspHob. After FspInitApi, it will return back to the Continue Function provided by FspInitPei, with the stack pointed to DRAM (because CAR is destroyed; see the bottom right of Figure 6-8).

In FspInitPei, the Continue Function will launch the second SecCore, with the temp ram pointed to DRAM. The second SecCore will launch the same PeiCore and continue dispatching the PEI firmware volume (see the top left of Figure 6-8 for more information). The purpose of the second PEI core is so that the FSP binary has its own small PI initialization flow. Regions in the figure are broken out by "who allocates the memory—FSP reserved at the top from FSP.bin, DXE code and data with DXE allocations in the middle, and PEI allocated at the bottom."

Finally, the system enters the DXE phase, and a platform module may allocate temporary ram for the S3 boot path and a capsule boot path to save the information in a tamper-proof, safe location.

FSP Normal Boot Data Structure

According to Figure 6-8, there are two SecCores involved. The first one is the normal SecCore and the second one is a small SecCore inside FspInitPei. Given the two SecCores, there needs to be a scheme where in the first SecCore passes information to the second one, like the Built-In Self-Test (BIST) data and the initial reading of the performance counter, or 'boot time ticker' needed for subsequent construction of the Firmware Performance Data Table (FPDT).

In IntelFspWrapperPkg, the first SecCore saves the BIST and ticker in CAR. Before FspInitApi is called, the platform may choose to save them in some special registers not touched by FSP.bin. One example could be IA CPU multimedia registers like MMX, or a PCI scratch register. In the implementations listed later, the MMX option is used, as shown in Figure 6-9, using MMX0 and MMX5/6 for BIST and performance ticker information, respectively. After FspInitApi, the FspInitPei launches the second SecCore, which will restore the information from special registers to a new stack in temp ram. The second SecCore also registers a special TopOfTemporaryRam PPI (a.k. A., TopOfCarPPI, as shown in Figure 6-9), which has pointer to the top of temp ram.

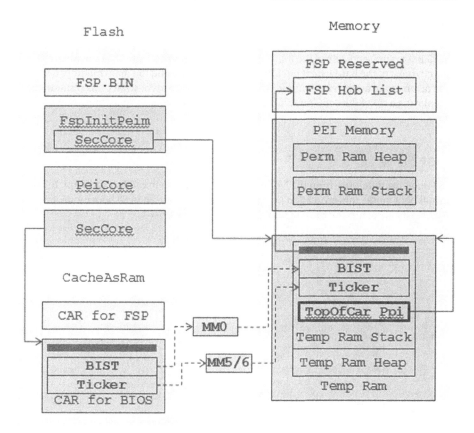

Figure 6-9. *FspInitPei data structure*

The reason to introduce TopOfTemporaryRam PPI is because the FspInitPei needs a way to ascertain the beginning of the FSP's HOB list, while the FspHobList pointer itself is saved to the top of temp ram. Also, the BIST and boot time ticker information are saved at the top of temp ram. It becomes easy to know the information by having a PPI to tell the temp ram location.

This section described the FSP wrapper boot flow in Normal boot mode. As part of enabling the Normal boot, several options were reviewed, with details on the present open source implementation (option 3), that supports all the UEFI PI PEI phase related features. The next section goes into the specific implementation of those features, such as S3, Recovery, and Capsule Update.

S3 Boot

TheS3 Boot represents one of the more involved restart mechanism. S3 is a wake event wherein most of the hardware it put into a low-power state and the main memory needs to be taken out of a self-refresh mode. The system firmware orchestrates this restoration by replaying a set of the configuration settings applied during a Normal Boot as one embodiment.

Boot Flow

In S3 boot, the difference from the Normal boot entails when to call FspNotifyApi. In Normal boot mode, this invocation occurs in the DXE phase, but in S3 boot mode, there is no DXE. Details of the FSP S3 boot flow are shown in Figure 6-10.

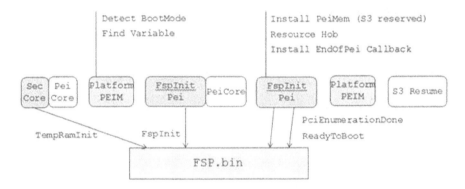

Figure 6-10. *FSP S3 boot flow*

In the IntelFspWrapperPkg, the FspInitPei routine will register EndOfPei callback in S3 boot mode. So when the boot script finishes execution, FspNotifyApi is invoked, and then the system invokes the OS waking vector.

S3 Memory Layout

In an S3 boot, the difference in the memory layout entails the temp ram location. In Normal boot mode, the temporary ram is at some low DRAM address, configured by Platform Configuration Database (PCD) settings, which is used by no one in PEI phase. In theS3 boot, usable DRAM is owned by OS, expected the one reported as ACPI reserved or ACPI NVS. The details of this memory layout are shown in Figure 6-11.

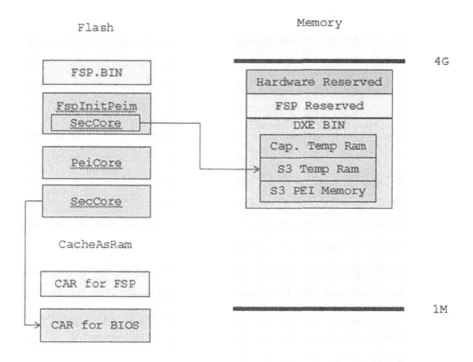

Figure 6-11. *FSP S3 memory layout*

In a Normal boot DXE phase, a platform driver should allocate S3 temp ram, marking it as reserved to OS. Then in the S3 phase, the FspInitPei can use it as temp ram for purposes of invoking the continuation function.

S3 NV Data Passing

In some platforms, S3 phase initialization needs the configuration saved in a Normal boot. Figure 6-12 is an example of how memory configuration data is passed from the MRC module in Normal boot to the MRC module in S3.

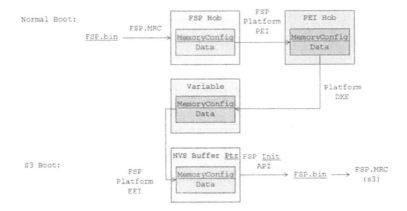

Figure 6-12. FSP S3 NVS data passing

In a Normal boot, the FSP Memory Reference Code (MRC) PEI module produces a MemoryConfigData HOB and saves it in the FSP HOB list. The resultant FSPlist is published after FspInitApi. Then an FSP platform PEI parses the FSP HOB, gets the MemoryConfigData, and saves it into the normal PEI HOB list. In the DXE phase, a platform module parses the PEI HOB list and saves MemoryConfigData into an NV variable.

In S3 boot, the FSP PEI module finds the MemoryConfigData from an NV variable region, constructs NvsBufferPtr as an FspInitApi parameter, and calls the FSP binary. Then, the FSP binary has the NvsBufferPtr, and the MRC module can get the MemoryConfigData from NvsBufferPtr and do the memory initialization in S3 phase.

This section describes the FSP wrapper boot flow in S3 boot mode. This section treated concerns about having memory reservation for purposes of invoking the OS wake vector and securely storing the configuration information necessary to restore the platform state prior to the hand-off to the OS.

Capsule Flash Update

The Normal Boot and S3 boot typically refer to hardware restarts, namely S5 and S3, respectively. The Capsule Flash Update is a logical boot flow that leverages an S5 or S3 hardware restart but applies some underlying logic to orchestrate receiving and applying a firmware update.

Boot Flow

In the Capsule Update boot, there is only a small difference with the Normal boot flow. In the Capsule Update flow, the FspInitPei needs to call CapsuleCoalesce before installing PEI memory, and it needs to install PEI memory for Capsule Update mode. Other differences from the Normal boot flow include the size and location of the PEI memory. The reason that the Capsule Update flow may need to sequester more memory is that the Capsule FV in memory is loaded by the PEI phase and thus consumes additional resources from the PEI usages of DRAM. Details of the FSP Capsule Update boot flow can be found in Figure 6-13.

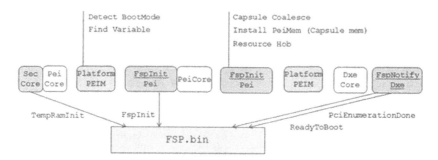

Figure 6-13. *FSP Capsule Update boot flow*

Capsule Update Memory Layout

In Capsule Update boot mode, the difference in memory layout is the temp ram location. In Normal boot mode, the temp ram is at some low DRAM, configured by a PCD, which is used by no one at PEI phase. In Capsule Update boot, usable DRAM is owned by OS, and one can expect this to be reported as ACPI reserved or ACPI NVS. The OS might put the capsule image into any usable DRAM. Specifically, the UpdateCapsule() runtime call from the UEFI runtime service table has a pointer to a scatter gather list of memory allocated by the OS kernel. As such, the firmware, such as the PEI phase and FSP, cannot predict "where" the OS will put the capsule. The PEI phase's responsibility is to discover the capsule and then coalesce or merge the fragments into a continuous run of memory, such that the following DXE phase can ascertain data or code from the Capsule Firmware volume. Additional details on UpdateCapsule can be found in the UEFI Specification at www.uefi.org. Details of the flash and memory during the Capsule flow can be found in Figure 6-14.

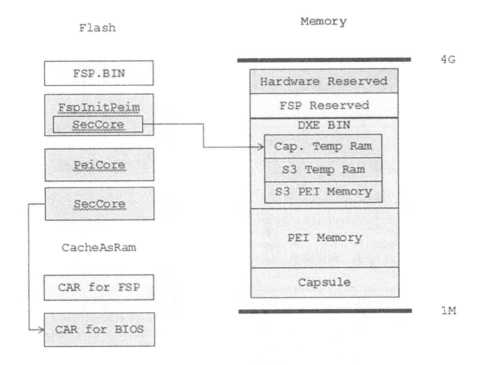

Figure 6-14. *FSP Capsule Update boot memory layout*

In a normal boot DXE phase, a platform driver should allocate capsule temp ram, marking it as reserved to the OS. Then in the Capsule Update phase, the FspInitPei can use it as temp ram for continued functioning.

This section has provided an overview of the Capsule Update boot flow. The flow is very similar to the Normal boot flow, with the exception of additional memory reservation for storing the capsule firmware volume.

Recovery Boot Flow

In Recovery boot, there is only a small difference from the earlier flow: FspInitPei needs to install PEI memory for Recovery Mode. The size might be different with Normal boot mode because the recovery firmware volume will be loaded from some recovery media, such as a USB thumb drive, and put into memory reserved by the PEI phase. This is similar to the Capsule Update in that the PEI phase will pass up a firmware volume not contained in the system board flash: OS-reserved memory for the capsule and on-recovery-media data for recovery. Details of the recovery flow are shown in Figure 6-15.

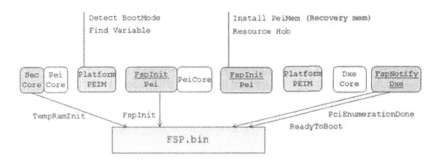

Figure 6-15. *FSP Recovery boot flow*

FSP Recovery Memory Layout

In Recovery boot, the memory layout is the same as Normal boot mode. Details are shown in Figure 6-16.

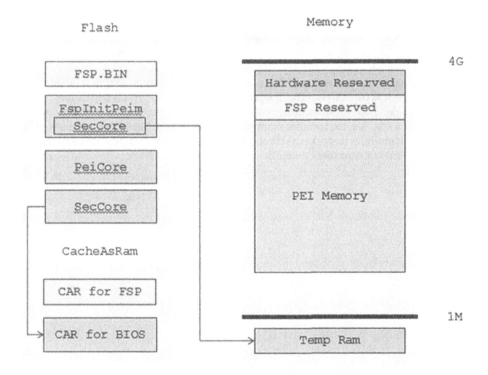

Figure 6-16. *FSP Recovery boot memory layout*

This section has shown how a full set of UEFI PI features can be implemented with the Intel FSP Wrapper Package. These features include Capsule Update, Recovery, and S3. These discussions included the design considerations and memory layout for the different scenarios.

The packages on TianoCOre are prefixed with "Intel" since the FSP EAS is an Intel-published document. This Intel-qualified moniker is very much akin to the Intel Platform Innovation for the Extensible Firmware Interface, or "Framework" specifications, lifecycle. These specifications started viaan Intel self-published matter that Intel subsequently contributed to the UEFI Forum to become the UEFI PI specifications.

coreboot Payload Based upon EDK II

Beyond using EDK II to consume an FSP, a payload for coreboot can be built upon EDK II. Chapter 4 talked about the overall concept of payloads in coreboot. As a quick recap, recall that the coreboot romstage and ramstage do platform initialization, but the set of interfaces exposed to the operating system hand-off can vary. As an old friend once told me, "Compatibility is the software you choose to run," (see http://vzimmer.blogspot.com/2013/02/what-is-compatibility.html), so the payloads vary based upon that criteria, namely the operating system "software" that you wish to run. For example, if you want to launch a PC/AT BIOS–based OS, then Sea BIOS is a choice. Correspondingly, if you want to use coreboot for platform initialization but launch a UEFI-style OS, then the UEFI payload is an option.

There have been many UEFI payloads built in the past, including EDK-based. For this discussion, we build upon earlier EDK II review to show, in addition to EDK II being one means by which to construct an FSP, the generic EDK II code can be used to create a coreboot payload, too. A variant of this payload can be found at http://www.uefidk.com. It consists of a DSC file that includes many generic drivers from TianoCore and a few purpose-built modules that take the coreboot state and adapt it into UEFI. The firmware device (FD) that contains these modules is shown in Figure 6-17.

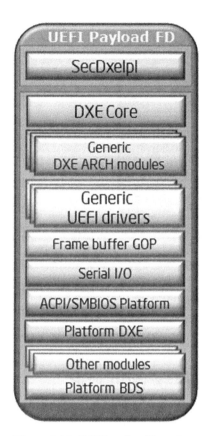

Figure 6-17. *UEFI payload based upon EDK II*

Figure 6-17 shows the spatial view of the code; the UEFI payload in Figure 6-18 describes the temporal flow of the constituent elements. As described in a generic UEFI flow, there is a miniature variant of the same in the payload, namely a SEC module that takes control from coreboot ramstage and passes CBMEM from coreboot into the following payload PEI and DXE phase. One module in the payload is responsible for transforming the CBMEM description of the memory and addressing space topology into UEFI PI HOBs and the UEFI DXE internal tracking elements, like Global Coherency Domain (GCD) entries, for purposes of publishing the resultant descriptions from the UEFI service GetMemoryMap(). The HOBs and GCD can be found in the UEFI PI specifications, and the GetMemoryMap API can be found in the UEFI specification. All of these documents can be found at www.uefi.org.

Execution Flow

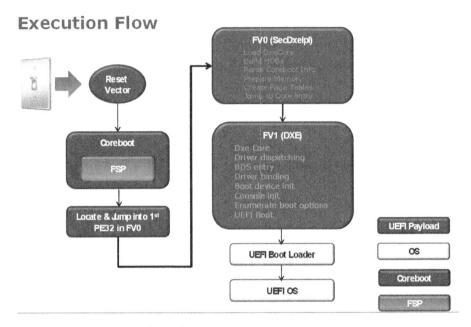

Figure 6-18. *UEFI Payload boot flow*

Building Minnow and MinnowMax with FSP

The preceding discussions talk about infrastructure code, but not a complete platform. Intel FSP provides a simple method to integrate a solution that reduces time-to-market, and it is economical to build. IntelFspWrapperPkg is the FSP consumer in EDK II to support building out a UEFI BIOS. This section describes in detail the work flow and data structure in IntelFspWrapperPkg.

The source trees for Minnow and MinnowMax can be found at http://www.uefidk.com. These distributions include the elements necessary to build a full UEFI-based firmware image, including a build option based upon the Intel FSP. The locations are http://www.uefidk.com/content/minnowboard-uefi-firmware and https://uefidk.com/content/minnowboard-max, respectively.

This section features a simple work flow to adapt an Intel® Firmware Support Package (FSP) (http://www.intel.com/content/www/us/en/intelligent-systems/intel-firmware-support-package/intel-fsp-overview.html.html) –based binary module and an operating system boot loader layer built upon the EFI Development Kit 2 (EDK II) (http://tianocore.Sourceforge.net/wiki/EDK2). The work flow entails retrieving the Intel FSP binary from the Intel website. The FSP binary will be unique for a given CPU, chipset, and memory controller.

The FSP binary can then be adapted to an EDK II style boot environment with the https://svn.code.Sf.net/p/edk2/code/trunk/edk2/IntelFspWrapperPkg/. The FSP binary itself is formatted as a UEFI Platform Initialization (PI) firmware volume and conveys the output results of the FSP initialization in UEFI PI Hand-Off Blocks. These HOBs include details such as the initialized set of main memory, the graphics frame buffer in the case of integrated FSP graphics, and other initialization resources, like TSEG. Beyond the Intel FSP Wrapper, a small complement of EDK II code can be used to provide a minimal set of architectural protocols, DXE core, and a Boot Device Selection (BDS) driver to boot an embedded operating system.

The BDS can provide a standards-based UEFI boot, or alternate BDS implementations can feature direct kernel loads from flash, as in a coreboot payload approach, or direct kernel load from disk, as found in U-Boot.

Three FSP wrapper modules are provided in the Intel FSP Wrapper Package to help EDK II firmware make calls to the FSP binary. FspSecCore will prepare the running environment for FSP binary, search the FSP information header, and then call the two basic FSP APIs (TempRamInit and FspInit). After these two APIs are executed, both the processor and the chipset have been initialized, and memory is also ready for use. At last, FspSecCore will transfer the control to PeiCore. FspWrapperPei will be executed in the PEI phase. It will parse the HOBs produced by FSP and report them to the EDK II BIOS if they are required. Also, it will install memory according to the memory resource information from the FSP. FspWrapperDxe should be run in DXE phase to notify the FSP about the different phases in the boot process. This allows the FSP to take appropriate actions as needed during different initialization phases.

Details on the workflow are as follows.

Before we start the integration, let's first figure out what you need to have.

- *FSP binary*. The binary file that contains the basic CPU and chipset init code; you also get a FSP usage guide.

- *IntelFspWrapperPkg*. The EDK II wrappers we created and put together into a single package; this is available at TianoCore. This package includes the components FspDxeIpl and FspSecCore.

- *Your current EDK II platform code base.*

Now, let's go through following steps to prepare your codebase to incorporate the FSP binary. For the Minnow and MinnowMax projects, these files can be found on http://www.uefidk.com.

1. Change the BIOS flash map file and put the FSP binary at the expected address.

During the build of FSP binary, the base address of FSP binary will be placed at the predefined address; if your flash map layout is different with those predefined addresses, please change them accordingly. Next is the list of the six PCDs used by FSP. For example, in Platform.fdf:

// Base address of bios flash device
SET gEfiFspTokenSpaceGuid.PcdFlashAreaBaseAddress = 0xFFC00000
// Size of bios flash device
SET gEfiFspTokenSpaceGuid.PcdFlashAreaSize = 0x400000
// Base address of cpu microcode
SET gEfiFspTokenSpaceGuid.PcdFlashMicroCodeAddress = 0xFFFB8000
// Size of cpu microcode
SET gEfiFspTokenSpaceGuid.PcdFlashMicroCodeSize = 0x00004000
0x003c0000|0x00020000
gEfiFspTokenSpaceGuid.PcdFlashFvFspBase|gEfiFspTokenSpaceGuid.PcdFlashFvFspSize
FILE = $(WORKSPACE)/MinnowPkg/FspBinary/FvFsp.bin

2. Replace the original SecCore Module with FspPkg's SecCore Module.

In addition, you need to set values for these two PCDs (PcdTemporaryRamBase and PcdTemporaryRamSize). These two PCDs define the base address and size of the temporary memory, which is used in the PEI phase before memory is installed. As in SecCore, FSP has already initialized the memory. You can use any physical memory address, or you can remove any definitions on these two PCDs in platform.dsc and use the default values.

For example, in Platform.dsc:

[PcdsFixedAtBuild]
gEfiCpuTokenSpaceGuid.PcdTemporaryRamBase|0x00080000
gEfiCpuTokenSpaceGuid.PcdTemporaryRamSize|0x00010000
[Components.IA32]
FspPkg/SecCore/SecCore.inf
In Platform.fdf:
// INFIA32FamilyCpuPkg/SecCore/SecCore.inf
INFFspPkg/SecCore/SecCore.inf

3. Add FSP support PEIM and DXE modules from FspPkg.

For example, in Platform.dsc:

[Components.IA32]
FspPkg/FspPei/FspPei.inf
FspPkg/FspDxe/FspDxe.inf
In Platform.fdf:
INF FspPkg/FspPei/FspPei.inf
INF FspPkg/FspDxe/FspDxe.inf

For the open hardware, the website `http://www.uefidk.com/projects` has the landing page (`https://uefidk.com/content/minnowboard-max`) with files to build a full MinnowMax (`http://www.minnowboard.org/meet-minnowboard-max/`) tree.

Presently, these distributions are online as a zip archive. In the future, these sources should evolve to the live open source tree at TianoCore.

This tree supports both a native EDK II build from individual binary and sources, along with the FSP build. The latter is keyed off of MINNOW2_FSP_BUILD in the platform DSC file.

Specifically, as noted in the release notes, you need to open Vlv2TbltDevicePkg\PlatformPkgConfig.dsc.

Modify "DEFINE MINNOW2_FSP_BUILD" macro from "FALSE" to "TRUE". DEFINE MINNOW2_FSP_BUILD = TRUE

The preceding definition tells the build tools to select the modules that work with the Intel FSP Wrapper Package, as opposed to building the firmware wholly from separate .PEI and .EFI files for the PEI and DXE phases of execution, respectively.

Future of the Intel FSP

The Intel FSP is a binary-enabling model that works in tandem with open or closed source IA firmware platform code. The work flow of binaries can include additional tools in the future, such as the Intel® Firmware Engine (http://www.uefidk.com/sites/default/files/resources/SF14_STTS002_100f.pdf). These tools allow for automating the creation of the FSP, or configuring the FSP, such as the PCD-as-VPD for platform adaptation, from a user interface.

In addition to automation tools, the present FSP has the UEFI EDK II platform code SecCore or coreboot rom stage for the hardware reset, but a future evolution of Intel FSP can include moving some of the critical silicon initialization to reset itself. This would entail having a CPU manufacturer code that might even ship with the hardware element with hand-off to platform IA firmware via today's FSP or EFI PI PEI hand-off, such as HOBs.

The work flow, including binary manipulation tools and the migration for the FSP binary to reset, are shown in Figure 6-19.

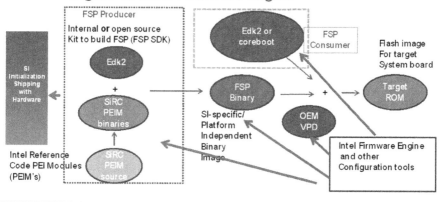

Figure 6-19. *Evolution of Intel FSP*

And as the Intel Framework Specification went to UEFI PI, the Intel FSP EAS could also follow the same pattern and appear in a future UEFI PI specification.

Conclusion

This chapter described several aspects of building firmware using UEFI class technology. The chapter began by building upon the Chapter 4 coreboot section, which is leveraged to compare coreboot phases with UEFI PI flows. This was followed by describing EDK II on FSP via the various boot flows of the Intel FSP Wrapper Package. After this overview, a description of the wrapper enablement of a Normal, Capsule, Recovery, and S3 boot followed. Building upon the Intel FSP Wrapper Package, the construction of EDK II on FSP for Minnow and MinnowMax open hardware platforms followed. After instantiating FSP on these two platforms, a glimpse is provided into possible evolution of the Intel FSP construction workflows with tool assistance and the migration of the Intel FSP binary to the reset vector.

CHAPTER 7

■ ■ ■

Building Firmware for Quark Processors

"Three things cannot be long hidden: the sun, the moon, and the truth."

—The Buddha

The Intel Quark SoC X1000 is Intel's lowest-power SoC, designed to provide performance and reduce development costs for securely managed Internet of Things endpoint devices. It is initially offered as a single-core, single-threaded microprocessor, making it an ideal solution for low-cost, small form factor, fan less and headless designs.

This chapter will discuss the EDK II infrastructure, Quark, and building a minimal Quark tree with the EDK II. The purpose of this review is to touch upon the salient aspects of the EDK II source construction technology and how it relates to the UEFI PI and UEFI standards, respectively.

This Intel implementation of EDK II at TianoCore demonstrates the possibilities available using the scalable architecture of both the code base and the associated underlying industry standards (see `www.uefi.org`). The UEFI firmware size for this Intel Galileo EDK II implementation (`http://uefidk.intel.com/projects/quark`) is 64KB, and given its diminutive size relative to the full Quark EDK II build, it is referred to as "TinyQuark" throughout the rest of this document. TinyQuark boots Yocto Linux (`www.yoctoproject.org`) on the Intel Galileo board using the onboard flash. You can build this solution from the source code available to download using the following URL. Specifically, the TinyQuark code is at `http://uefidk.intel.com/content/get-started-intel-galileo-development-board`.

This chapter presents the internal design of TinyQuark, which can be generalized by developers to make their own small-footprint UEFI firmware.

Overview of UEFI and PI

Before getting into TinyQuark, however, the next sections will describe some of the design intent of the EDK II software infrastructure and the association to the UEFI and PI specifications. These specifications describe interoperability between binary and/or source components. Books like *Beyond BIOS* by Vincent Zimmer, Michael Rothman, and Suresh Marisetty (Intel Press, 2011) describe the specifications, but there hasn't been a single place to describe the implementation. The next section is intended to help with that gap.

History of Implementations and Specifications

Starting with the Extensible Firmware Interface (EFI) 0.92 specification in 1998, there has always been a reference EFI implementation. The sample implementations are intended to help clarify some of the design intent of the specification. As shown in the diagram in Figure 7-1, every corresponding specification has had an associated implementation. Historically, these implementations were of the core components that are portable across a broad set of hardware platforms, but the implementations did not include a full platform source tree.

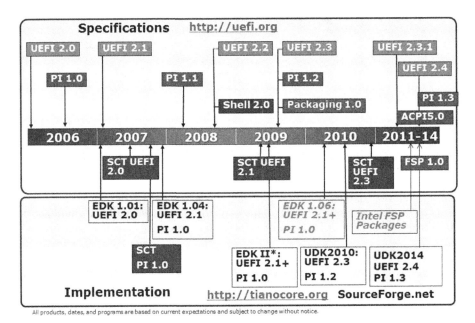

Figure 7-1. Specification and implementation time line

The time line shows the original sample implementation, pre-2006. The original EFI Developer Kit (EDK) had challenges in construction since it was a monolithic tree, and the addition of third-party sources or data was ad hoc, as was library support since EDK didn't codify the set of libraries that were usable by the different phases of execution. The introduction of the packaging concept in EDK II, along with PCDs and the base libraries, provided a way to compose source modules from different entities, have reusable sources across many different architectures, and host development environments. Specifically, EDK only supported the Microsoft tool chain, whereas EDK II supports building under Apple OS X, Microsoft Windows, and various Linux distributions. The clean ANSI-C source files and the Python-based build tools of EDK II help contribute to this portability.

Introduction to EDK II Building Blocks

The EFI Development Kit II (EDK II) is an implementation of the UEFI and PI standards. The EDK II is hosted at www.tianocore.org and features many technologies, including an OS-portable build system, ANSI-C code, and GCC/NASM/MASM–based assembly language sources.

In addition, the source technology is decomposed via "packages." The package concept is covered by the UEFI PI packaging specification and is a means by which to segregate binary and sources. The package boundaries are typically driven by business considerations. The packing concept has many interrelated elements for construction, including the DEC, DSC, FDF, and INF files, along with the Platform Configuration Database. The relationship of these elements, details, and some examples of the same are shown next.

Regarding packages, the most prominent packages are listed next, with brief notes about functionality.

PKG: Packaging

Packaging describes the units of decomposition for various technologies. The packaging boundaries may appear somewhat arbitrary at first but are usually motivated by both technology and business criteria. The former includes aggregating a given type of component in one place, such as the generic bus drivers and core elements in the MDE Module Package. The latter includes things like licensing, wherein the package may contain closed-source binaries and sources for a proprietary technology.

MdePkg

The Module Development Environment (MDE) Package (MdePkg) includes files and libraries for Industry Standard Specifications (i.e., UEFI, PI, PCI, USB, SMBIOS, ACPI, SMBIOS, etc.). You can think of the MdePkg, along with the build tools, as the minimum components to build a PEI Module (PEIM), a DXE driver, or a UEFI driver.

The EDK II code is managed on www.sourceforge.net, but there is also a mirror on GitHub. As such, the source code for this package can be found at https://github.com/tianocore/edk2/tree/master/MdePkg.

The important components are the include and library directories. Within the include directory there are industry standard definitions, protocol and PPIs corresponding to the UEFI and UEFI PI specifications, and architecture-specific files. These files need a corresponding white cover industry standard, a public document, or a published UEFI specification in order to reside in the MdePkg.

The library directory, on the other hand, contains a series of library classes. The directories prefixed by "Base" should be use able in the PEI, DXE, UEFI runtime, and UEFI boot services phases. These are the most generic, portable libraries that do not depend upon underlying interfaces. The other libraries are alternately prefixed by the phase of execution, such as "PEI", "SMM", "DXE", "SEC", or "UEFI." These latter terms designate the phase of execution wherein these libraries apply.

Figure 7-2 describes the various phases of UEFI PI execution.

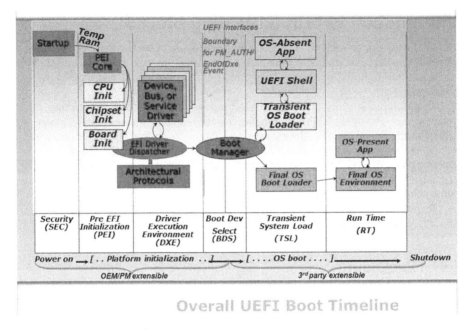

Figure 7-2. *UEFI PI boot flow*

MdeModulePkg

Building upon the MdePkg are implementations of modules, namely the Module Development Environment Modules (MdeModulePkg). These components can be found at https://github.com/tianocore/edk2/tree/master/MdeModulePkg. The PEIMs, DXE drivers, UEFI drivers, and UEFI applications-only definitions from the Industry Standard Specifications are defined in the MdePkg. These components should be portable across a broad class of platforms and CPU bindings, including 32-bit and 64-bit ARM, Intel Itanium, IA32, and X64.

IntelFrameworkPkg

The IntelFrameworkPkg (https://github.com/tianocore/edk2/tree/master/ IntelFrameworkPkg) includes files and libraries for those parts of the Intel Platform Innovation Framework for EFI specifications (a.k.a. "Framework") that were not adopted "as is" by the UEFI or PI specifications. These packages provide a bridge between code written against the Framework Specifications (http://www.intel.com/content/www/us/ en/architecture-and-technology/unified-extensible-firmware-interface/efi-specifications-general-technology.html) and the subsequent UEFI PI specifications. Some of the interfaces changed between Framework and PI, such as the SMM-CIS; whereas other interfaces only exist in the Framework corpus, such as the Compatibility Support Module (CSM).

IntelFrameworkModulePkg

The IntelFrameworkModulePkg (`https://github.com/tianocore/edk2/tree/master/IntelFrameworkModulePkg`) contains modules (PEIMs + DXE drivers+ UEFI drivers) that make reference to one or more definitions in the IntelFrameworkPkg. A diagram of these packages is shown in Figure 7-3.

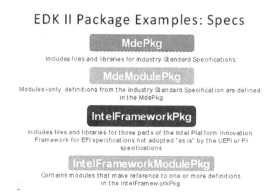

EDK II Package Examples: Specs

MdePkg

Includes files and libraries for Industry Standard Specifications

MdeModulePkg

Modules-only definitions from the Industry Standard Specification are defined in the MdePkg

IntelFrameworkPkg

Includes files and libraries for those parts of the Intel Platform Innovation Framework for EFI specifications not adopted "as is" by the UEFI or PI specifications

IntelFrameworkModulePkg

Contains modules that make reference to one or more definitions in the IntelFrameworkPkg

Figure 7-3. *Important packages for EDK II*

Packages

Packages in the EDK II are groups of modules. A package may support one or more drivers, libraries, or combinations thereof. Example packages, in addition to the ones listed earlier, include drivers and applications related to specific hardware, or drivers and applications related to software components, such as the UEFI specification. The MdeModulePkg is an example of the latter, and the former will be discussed in the context of TinyQuark.

Packages can also leverage definitions and elements of other packages. A hardware package should reference the core UEFI packages, such as the MdePkg, for the definitions of standard UEFI protocols and structure.

Packages have related files, such as XML manifest, DSC, and INF files, in addition to the C and/or assembly-language source files. Figure 7-4 shows the packages' relationship with supporting files.

Distribution Package

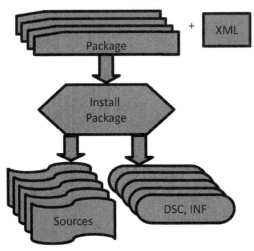

Figure 7-4. *Packages and supporting files*

So the package provides the partitioning of the sources and binaries, but it does not provide for fine-grain control of build options in the actual code artifacts. For that, the PCD comes into play.

PCD: Platform Configuration Database

So what is the platform configuration database goal? First, PCD entries are used for module parameterization; examples include define statements and variables. Among other things, the benefit of PCDs includes reducing the need to edit the source code. Also, there is no need to search for a magic #define statement, like base address registers, for example. These can all be PCD values.

PCDs allow for reusing values across many modules. These fixed-at-build PCDs are very much akin to #defines, but herein they are tied into the build system.

Beyond PCDs, the PCD concept can also be used dynamically, namely to store platform information, like the vital product data serial number. You can use dynamic PCDs for setup options and so forth.

PCDs are related to other build files, such as INF, DEC, and DSC, as shown in Figure 7-5.

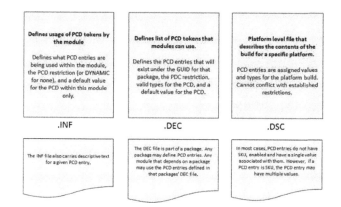

Figure 7-5. *PCD relationship to INF, DEC, and DSC*

There are various types of PCDs, including FeatureFlag, FixedAtBuild, PatchableInModule, and Dynamic.

- *FeatureFlag*: Replaces a switch MACRO to enable/disable a feature (TRUE or FALSE).

- *FixedAtBuild*: Replaces a macro that produced a customizable value. The value of this PCD type is determined at build time and is stored in the code section of a module's PE image.

- *PatchableInModule*: The value is stored in the data section, rather than the code section, of the module's PE image.

- *Dynamic/DyanmicEx/DynamicHii/DynamicVpd*: The value is assigned by one module and is accessed by other modules in execution time.

The PCDs are related to the build process, as follows in Figure 7-6. Specifically, the PCDs are ascertained from the DEC, INF, DSC, and FDF file and included in the autogen. The autogen source files are in turn compiled with the other sources for the resultant driver or PEI module.

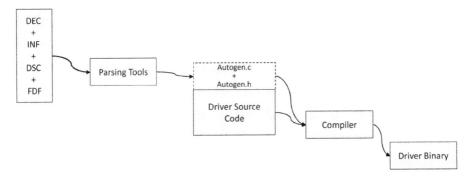

Figure 7-6. PCDs and build flow

In addition to extracting the PCDs from metadata files like INF/DEC/DSC, the PCDs can also be used directly in source files. In this case, the relationship of the source and the build is shown in Figure 7-7.

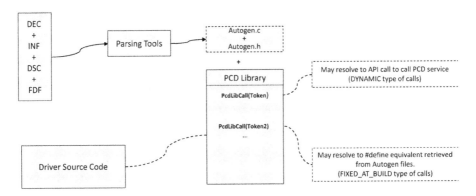

Figure 7-7. PCDs via build and source construction

Syntax

Given the background on the PCDs, the following is an example of the declaration of PCDs for a given module.

```
[PcdsFeatureFlag.common] [PcdsFixedAtBuild.IA32] [PcdsFixedAtBuild.X64]
[PcdsFixedAtBuild.IPF] [PcdsFixedAtBuild.EBC]   [PcdsDynamic.IA32]
[PcdsDynamicEx.X64]
```

```
Example of a PCD during DXE
Defined in ICH X Package DEC
  [PcdsDynamic.common]
  gEfiIchTokenSpaceGuid.PcdIchSataPataConfigs|0|UINT8|0x40000016
The Module INF lists which PCDs get accessed
  [Pcd]
  gEfiIchTokenSpaceGuid.PcdIchSataPataConfigs
The Value to use in New Project Package DSC
  [PcdsDynamicDefault.common.DEFAULT]
  gEfiIchTokenSpaceGuid.PcdIchSataPataConfigs|0
```

Here is an example used in the CODE:

```
DXE - Referenced in the DXE code in NewProjectPkg\ SetupDxe\Platform.c
```

IchSataPataConfigs.Uint8 = PcdGet8(PcdIchSataPataConfigs);
 ● ● ●
 PcdSet8(PcdIchSataPataConfigs, IchSataPataConfigs.Uint8);

Finally, the PCDs can show up in the resultant flash image in many ways, including as a Firmware File System file in the flash image. Figure 7-8 shows one possible layout of the PCDs, along with other binary content, such as the UEFI variable data and the vital product data.

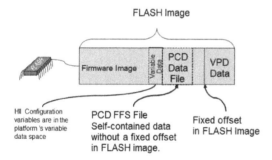

Figure 7-8. *PCDs in a flash image*

Beyond PCDs for parameterizing the build and source files, there is the Platform Declaration File that describes the collection of modules in a build.

DEC: Platform Declaration File

The DEC is the Platform Declaration File (the "D" in DEC is for *declaration*). There is just one DEC file per package. A DEC file is required for EDK II modules using extended INF and extended DSC format files. If you make a new package you must have a DEC file for it.

Syntax

The DEC has a defines section that states what the package is. It gives it a GUID and a name. Every other section described here is optional.

The DEC file may have an includes section stating, "The include directories for this package are as follows:". For example, you might be able to say, "This is my IA64 include and this is my X64 include," and so forth.

In addition, the DEC file also has an optional library class section. It exposes the library classes that are defined in the package.

If you declare any GUIDs in the system, the DEC file has a GUID section. Certain structures have GUIDs defined for them; if that structure is defined in this package, it would be listed here.

The DEC file has a protocol GUID listed for every protocol header file that is in your package. You list the GUID of that protocol in the protocol section. The same is true for PPIs; they are also identified by GUID.

If any module contained in your package defines a new PCD, this is where you look it up.It is possible to reference a PCD from another package, but do not list it here. This location is for new PCDs.

Coincidentally, as soon as you make a new PCD, you must make a new token space GUID, because all the PCDs are defined by a token space GUID, followed by the PCD name. A new token space means you must have a GUID for the token space. So, any new PCDs are also going to have a GUID.

Finally, user extensions are rarely used, but are optionally present. The following is an example DEC file.

```
Example dec
## @file  ShellPkg.dec
##
[Defines]
  DEC_SPECIFICATION     = 0x00010005
  PACKAGE_NAME          = ShellPkg
  PACKAGE_GUID          = 9FB7587C-93F7-40a7-9...
  PACKAGE_VERSION       = 0.40
[Includes.common]
  Include
[LibraryClasses.common]
  ## @libraryclass  Provides most Shell APIs. Only available for Shell applications
  ShellLib|Include/Library/ShellLib.h
  ## @libraryclass  Provides shell internal support Only available for
shell internal commands
  ShellCommandLib|Include/Library/ShellCommandLib.h
  ## @libraryclass  provides EFI_FILE_HANDLE services used by Shell and ShellLib
  FileHandleLib|Include/Library/FileHandleLib.h
  ## @libraryclass   Allows for a shell application to have a C style entry point
  ShellCEntryLib|Include/Library/ShellCEntryLib.h
  ## @libraryclass   Provides sorting functions
  SortLib|Include/Library/SortLib.h
```

```
## @libraryclass    Provides advanced parsing functions
  HandleParsingLib|Include/Library/HandleParsingLib.h
[Guids.common]
  gEfiShellEnvironment2ExtGuid = {0xd2c18636, 0x40e5, 0x4eb5, {0xa3, 0x1b,
0x36, 0x69, 0x5f, 0xd4, 0x2c, 0x87}}
```

This completes the description of the DEC file. Beyond the DEC file, there also needs to be a DSC.

DSC: Platform Description File

A DSC file must define all libraries, components, and/or modules that will be used by one package. DSC files are a list of the following:

- EDK Component or EDK II Module INF files

- EDK libraries (for EDK Components)

- EDK II Library Class Instance Mappings (for EDK II Modules)

- EDK II PCD Entry Settings

The following is an example of a DSC file for the UEFI Shell Package:

```
#/** @file
# Shell Package
#**/
[Defines]
  PLATFORM_NAME          = Shell
  PLATFORM_GUID          = E1DC9BF8-7013-4c99-9437-...
  PLATFORM_VERSION       = 0.4
  DSC_SPECIFICATION      = 0x00010006
  OUTPUT_DIRECTORY       = Build/Shell
  SUPPORTED_ARCHITECTURES = IA32|IPF|X64|EBC
  BUILD_TARGETS          = DEBUG|RELEASE
  SKUID_IDENTIFIER       = DEFAULT
[LibraryClasses.common]
  UefiApplicationEntryPoint|MdePkg/Library/UefiApplicationEntryPoint/
  UefiApplicationEntryPoint.inf
  UefiBootServicesTableLib|MdePkg/Library/UefiBootServicesTableLib/
  UefiBootServicesTableLib.inf
  DevicePathLib|MdePkg/Library/UefiDevicePathLib/UefiDevicePathLib.inf
  DebugLib|MdePkg/Library/BaseDebugLibNull/BaseDebugLibNull.inf
  PcdLib|MdePkg/Library/BasePcdLibNull/BasePcdLibNull.inf
```

FDF: Flash Description File

The FDF file describes information about the flash part. It has rules for combining binaries built from a DSC file. You can create firmware images and optional ROM images for nearly anything you need.

It is possible to have PCD information used in the definition, as well as in some of the PCDs. The patchable ones will be stored at specific places inside the FV file.

Syntax

The FDF file has a header and a FD section, as well as a number of FV sections. It might have a capsule, a VTF, rules, and an optional ROM section if you are trying to build a PCI option on some user extensions. The following is a Backus-Naur Form (BNF) style notation of the FDF file.

```
FDFfile ::= [<Header>]
               [<Defines>]
         <FD>
         <FV>
         [<Capsule>]
               [<VTF>]
               [<Rules>]
               [<OptionRom>]
         [<UserExtensions>]
```

The FD section definitions for flash devices must be in the FDF file. The FV section definitions for firmware volumes must be in the FDF file.

Build: The EDK II Build Command

The EDK II build system is based on Python. This is one way to achieve the cross-OS build environment portability. The build tools directory in the EDK II tree root hosts the source code for the tool. Schematically, the EDK II build process proceeds as shown in Figure 7-9.

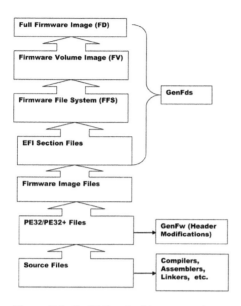

Figure 7-9. *Build flow for binary creation*

Usage of the command is as follows:

```
EDK2 build command
Usage: build.exe [options] [all|fds|genc|genmake|clean|cleanall|cleanlib|
modules|libraries|run]
Options:
  --version        show program's version number and exit
  -h, --help       show this help message and exit
  -a TARGETARCH, --arch=TARGETARCH
                   ARCHS is one of list: IA32, X64, IPF, ARM or EBC,
                   which overrides target.txt's TARGET_ARCH definition
                   To specify more archs, please repeat this option.
  -p PLATFORMFILE, --platform=PLATFORMFILE
                   Build the platform specified by the DSC file name
                   argument, overriding target.txt's ACTIVE_PLATFORM
                   definition.
  -m MODULEFILE, --module=MODULEFILE
                   Build the module specified by the INF file name
argument.
```

To bring all of the metadata and build files together, Figure 7-10 shows the relationship of the source with the FDF, INF, DEC, and DSC files.

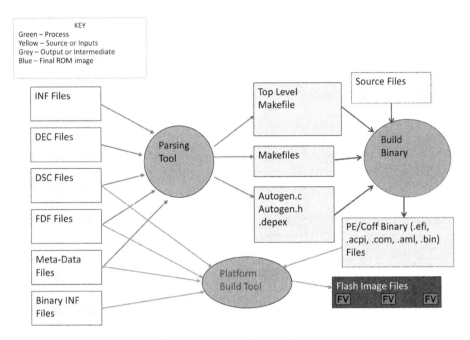

Figure 7-10. *Relationship of all files to the complete build*

INF: INF File

The INF file is updated to define all sources (.c, .h, .uni), libraries, packages, GUIDs, and PCDs used by the module. See the EDK II INF File Specification for more information and examples.

An INF is like a local make-maker file or metadata to inform the build system about which files to use and how to integrate them. The following is an example of an INF file for a serial driver.

```
INF Example SerialDxe
C file
EFI_STATUS
EFIAPI
InitializeSerial (
  IN EFI_HANDLE        ImageHandle,
  IN EFI_SYSTEM_TABLE  *SystemTable
  )
{
  SerialPortInitialize ();
  return
   gBS->InstallMultipleProtocolInterfaces (
        &mSerialIoHandle,
        &gEfiDevicePathProtocolGuid,
```

```
        &mSerialIoDevicePath,
        &gEfiSerialIoProtocolGuid,
        &mSerialIo,
        NULL  );
}

INF file
[Defines]
  INF_VERSION  = 0x00010005
  BASE_NAME    = SerialDxe
  FILE_GUID    = 7507 . . .
MODULE_TYPE   = UEFI_DRIVER
  VERSION_STRING  = 1.0
  ENTRY_POINT  = InitializeSerial
[Sources.common]
  Serial.c
[Packages]
  MdePkg/MdePkg.dec
  MdeModulePkg/MdeModulePkg.dec
[LibraryClasses]
  PcdLib
  UefiBootServicesTableLib

    . . .
[Protocols]
  gEfiSerialIoProtocolGuid
  gEfiDevicePathProtocolGuid

INFfile ::=[<Header>]
<Defines>
          [<BuildOptions>]
          [<Sources>]
          [<Binaries>]
          [<Guids>]
          [<Protocols>]
          [<Ppis>]
          [<Packages>]
          [<LibraryClasses>]
          [<Pcds>]
        [<UserExtensions>]
    [<Depex>]
```

More Information

All of the preceding build specifications can be found at
http://tianocore.sourceforge.net/wiki/EDK_II_Specifications.

Introduction to the EDK II Subset

EDK II is open source implementation for UEFI firmware, which can boot multiple UEFI-aware operating systems. Section 2.6 of the UEFI Specification [UEFI] defines the minimum set of capabilities that UEFI-aware firmware, such as EDK II, must support. We use EDK II BIOS for the Galileo board, which uses the Quark processor.

The Quark build for Galileo is the first fully open-source EDK II–based platform. It leverages the UDK2010 packages, including MdePkg and MdeModulePkg, and adds TinyBootPkg, Ia32FamilyCpuBasePkg, QuarkPlatformPkg, and QuarkSocPkg.

The standard build is 1MB and can be found at
`https://downloadcenter.intel.com/Detail_Desc.aspx?DwnldID=23197`.

This full build includes features described in the UEFI 2.4 and PI1.3 specifications on `www.uefi.org`, and include the capsule update, SMM, S3, PCI, recovery, FAT file system support, and UEFI variables.

Now that the overview of the EDK II build system and associated elements have been discussed, details on the internals of TinyQuark will be used to demonstrate this infrastructure in practice. As such, this section provided an overview of Quark and EDK II. Before we begin on the software, a description of the Quark platform itself is in order.

Introduction to Quark

The Intel Quark System-on-Chip (SoC) X1000 is the first product in a new road map of innovative, small core products targeted at rapidly growing areas, ranging from the industrial IoT to wearables. It brings low-power and Intel compute capabilities for thermally constrained, fanless, and headless applications. With its security and manageability features, this SoC is ideally suited for the Internet of Things and for the next wave of cost-effective, intelligent connected devices. An overview of the Quark hardware platform is shown in Figure 7-11.

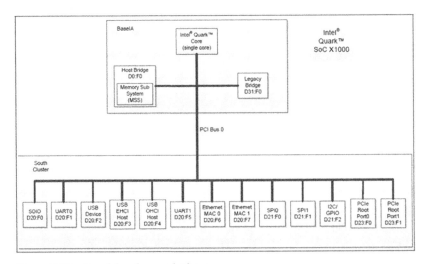

Figure 7-11. *Quark hardware platform*

ROM Flash Image Size Optimization

A set of UEFI/EDK II–related size reduction technologies to make TinyQuark are listed in the following sections. "Write good C code" is *not* mentioned because it is a generic advocacy to have robust, testable code. Instead, this section defines how to apply some logic to provide the minimum feature to the EDK II Quark firmware and still maintain basic UEFI conformance.

In the next several sections, we will discuss the size reduction techniques, one by one. The various techniques used for the EDK II Quark image size reduction are schematically shown in Figure 7-12.

Tech summary

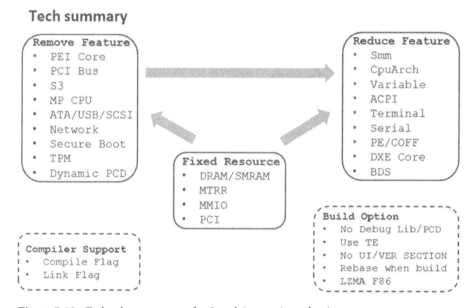

Figure 7-12. Technology summary for Quark image size reduction

Fixed Resource

To begin, the support of fixed system resources is important because it will lead to the direct feature set of the platform.

DRAM/SMRAM

If a platform can have fixed DRAM resource, then we can remove the complicated Memory-Type Range Register (MTRR) calculation algorithm in the CPU driver. The MTRR settings can be a table-driven configuration for this design with a known physical memory map. Refer to QuarkPlatformPkg\Library\QuarkSecLib\SecPlatform.c and http://uefidk.intel.com/projects/quark for more information.

If a platform can have fixed SMRAM, then we can remove the SmmAccess driver that supports the PI SMM interfaces, and just use library to get that value. Refer to QuarkPlatformPkg\Library\SmmPlatformHookLib.

If a platform can have fixed-memory mapped I/O (MMIO) and PCI resources, then we can remove PCI driver. The PCI resource setting can be done by a table-driven configuration. Refer to QuarkPlatformPkg\Pci\PlatformFixedPciResource found in https://uefidk.com/sites/default/files/Intel_Galileo_TinyQuark_64K.zip.

Remove Features

Not all UEFI features are needed in TinyQuark. Some features can be removed directly, like S3 (ACPI), ATA bus (ATA), USB bus (USB), SCSI bus, network (UEFI), HII (UEFI), UEFI secure boot (UEFI), TPM (TCG), or dynamic PCD(UEFI PI Specification).

Removing some features needs fixed resource support. Today, there are complex resource managers in a full EDK II firmware, like the PCI Bus Driver (https://github.com/tianocore/edk2/tree/master/MdeModulePkg/Bus/Pci), which discovers a set of PCI devices and balances the resources. This is an algorithmically complex process that entails significant code logic. For deeply embedded platforms like Quark, wherein the designer elides the ability to add arbitrary devices, a simple driver that declares a fixed set of resources can be used. An example from TinyQuark includes TinyQuark_EDK II\QuarkPlatformPkg\Pci\ PlatformFixedPciResource.

The biggest component removed in TinyQuark is the PEI core. TinyQuark has SEC linked to the DecompressLib, and the code in SEC jumps directly into DxeIpl. DxeIpl links into the memory reference code (MRC), finishes memory initialization, and then jumps into the DxeCore. The DXE core provides the basic UEFI capabilities, such as the boot services.

The detail flow of SEC ➤ DXE is shown in Figure 7-13.

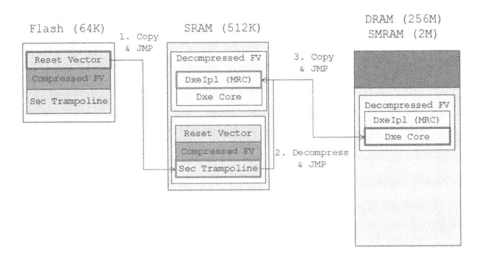

Figure 7-13. *SEC ➤ DXE solution*

Please refer to QuarkPlatformPkg.dsc and QuarkPlatformPkg.fdf for more information on how many of the features are removed:

- For ResetVector module, refer to QuarkPlatformPkg/Cpu/Sec/ResetVector.

- For SecTrampoline module, refer to QuarkPlatformPkg/Cpu/SecTrampoline.

- For DxeIpl module, refer to QuarkPlatformPkg/Cpu/SecCore.

Reduce Features

Even if a component is still needed in TinyQuark, we can make a simplified version. For example:

- *CpuArch*: No SetMemoryAttribute( ) support, because MTRR is fixed and programmed in DxeIpl. Refer to IA32FamilyCpuBasePkg/SimpleCpuArchDxe

- *Variable*: Just expose empty variable driver. Or later we can have some fixed data integrated in this driver. So there is no need to allocate specific Variable FV region. Refer to TinyBootPkg/Universal/Variable/NullVariableRuntimeDxe/NullVariableRuntimeDxe.inf

- *ACPI*: No generic ACPI_TABLE or ACPI_SDT driver. We created AcpiLib to support SetAcpi( ) only in the AcpiPlatform driver. Refer to TinyBootPkg/Library/AcpiTableLib

- *Terminal*: No driver model. Only supportsPcAnsi. Refer to TinyBootPkg/Universal/Console/SimpleCombinedTerminalDxe

- *Serial*: No driver model. Link SerialPortLib directly. Refer to TinyBootPkg/Universal/Console/SimpleCombinedTerminalDxe

- *PE/COFF lib*: Support PE32 only, no PE32+ or TE. Refer to TinyBootPkg/Library/BasePeCoffLibPe32

- *DXE core*: No GUIDED_SECTION, no Decompression, no FVB, no EBC, no HII, no DebugInfo table. Refer to TinyBootPkg/Core/SimpleDxeCore

- *SMM*: SMM is redesigned. We removed SmmCore (see next for more information).

The current EDK II has the SmmIpl, SmmCore, and SmmCpu drivers. SmmIpl will load SmmCore into SMRAM. SmmCore will load all SMM drivers into SMRAM, including the SmmCpu driver, the SmmPch driver, the SmmPlatform driver, and so forth.

After the SmmCpu driver is loaded, SMBASE rebase happens. Then, the next SMI will trigger into the SmmCpu driver. Next, the SmmCpu driver passes control to the SmmCore, and the SmmCore calls each Smm root handler driver, as registered by the SmmPch driver, to dispatch the respective SMI handler. This full SMM topology can be found in Figure 7-14, in which the upper portion of the figures is SMRAM, or memory protected from ring 0 code by hardware, and the lower portion of the boxes designates normal DRAM.

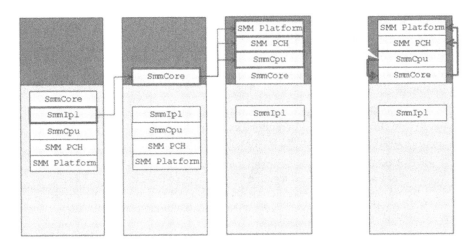

Figure 7-14. *Full SMM core solution*

In this simplified version, we remove the SmmCore. We let the SmmIpl find the SmmCpu driver and load it into SMRAM to do the SMBASE rebase operation. Another activity entails the conversion of all SmmPlatform drivers into a library, and links this library into the SmmCpu drive.

The next SMI will trigger a machine mode switch so that control is passed into the SmmCpu driver, and the SmmCpu driver will call a SmmPlatform library to dispatch the SMI handler. Figure 7-15 provides a diagram of the simplified SMM solution.

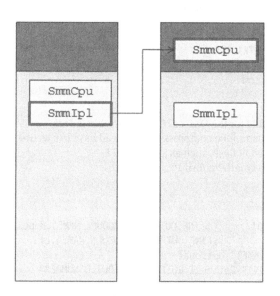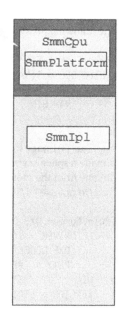

Figure 7-15. *Simplified SMM solution*

Please refer to QuarkPlatformPkg.dsc and QuarkPlatformPkg.fdf for more information on a simplified version driver.

For the SmmIpl/SmmCpu module, refer to IA32FamilyCpuBasePkg/SimplePiSmmCpuDxeSmm.

For SmmPlatform lib, refer to QuarkPlatformPkg/Library/SmmPlatformHookLib.

Compiler Options

In order to support a minimal image size, there are a couple of guiding rules: *do not use the /Zi compiler flag* and *do not use the /DEBUG link flag*. These flags can be added in the debug phase, but do not use them in final release, so that debug information in PE image is removed.

Build Options

Use the NULL Debug lib: DebugLib|MdePkg/Library/BaseDebugLibNull/BaseDebugLibNull.inf. Refer to QuarkPlatformPkg.dsc.

Do not use dynamic PCDs: PcdLib|MdePkg/Library/BasePcdLibNull/BasePcdLibNull.inf. Refer to QuarkPlatformPkg.dsc.

For the Execute-in-Place (XIP) images, use the TE image. Refer to QuarkPlatformPkg.fdf. The following provides an example of the FRF file that provides the TE images.

```
[Rule.Common.SEC]
  FILE SEC = $(NAMED_GUID) RELOCS_STRIPPED {
        TE  TE    Align = 8       $(INF_OUTPUT)/$(MODULE_NAME).efi
        RAW BIN   Align = 16      |.com
}
```

The TE Image format is not applicable for the DXE or UEFI drivers, but it does provide a space savings for images that cannot be compressed by instead have to execute directly from the memory mapping SPI NOR flash, such as SEC and PEI.

Do not use UI/VER section. Refer to QuarkPlatformPkg.fdf.

```
[Rule.Common.DXE_DRIVER]
  FILE DRIVER = $(NAMED_GUID) {
        DXE_DEPEX DXE_DEPEX Optional       $(INF_OUTPUT)/$(MODULE_NAME).depex
        PE32    PE32                       $(INF_OUTPUT)/$(MODULE_NAME).efi
#  UI          STRING="$(MODULE_NAME)" Optional
#  VERSION     STRING="$(INF_VERSION)" Optional BUILD_NUM=$(BUILD_NUMBER)
}
```

Although it doesn't necessarily contribute to the image size reduction, the image must be rebased in order to support Execute-in-Place (XIP). Sometimes the DXE volume can be rebased to the location in the main memory where it will be decompressed. This build-time rebasing omits the time-overhead of the PE/COFF loader to "fix-up" the image during each machine restart. In general, this technique won't work for open platforms because we do not know at firmware build time the size of physical memory or "where" the main DXE firmware volume will be decompressed and copied. Only for deeply embedded platforms with integrated DRAM can such a build-time technique be employed. Additional details from the FDF on how to configure this rebasing follow.

```
[FV.EDK II_BOOT_SLIM]
BlockSize       = 0x1000
FvBaseAddress   = 0x80010000
FvForceRebase   = TRUE
...
```

In order to have compression support, the TinyQuark employs LZMA F86 compression. Refer to QuarkPlatformPkg.fdf.

```
FILE FV_IMAGE = 9E21FD93-9C72-4c15-8C4B-E77F1DB2D791 {
        SECTION GUIDED D42AE6BD-1352-4bfb-909A-CA72A6EAE889 PROCESSING_
REQUIRED = TRUE { # LzmaF86
        SECTION FV_IMAGE = EDK II_BOOT_SLIM
        }
        }
```

Although earlier we mentioned "No GUIDED_SECTION support in the DxeCore", this is a GUIDed section. The reason is that this Guided section will be only supported by DxeIpl to decompress the whole DXE FV. As such, there is no need to have individual drivers in the the DXE FV supported by compression or GUIDed section, thus allowing the DxeCore to remove these support to reduce the size.

Results of the TinyQuark Optimization

After the application of the techniques covered earlier, the TinyQuark ROM demonstrates significant code size savings in the ROM image. Table 7-1 lists some of the metrics.

Table 7-1. *TinyQuark ROM Module Size*

NonCompressed	Size (byt	Category		Compressed	Size (byt	Category
SecTrampoline	8012	Platform		DxeIpl (MRC ~ 17600)	22084	Platform
ResetVector	1208	Platform		SimpleDxeCore	46652	Generic
				SimpleCpuArch	5124	Generic
				Metronome	1252	Generic
				RuntimeDxe	3844	Generic
				PlatformVariableRuntime	1764	Generic
				ResetSystemRuntime	1572	Generic
				SimplePcRtc	3748	Generic
				PlatformInitDxe	5732	Platform
				PlatformFixedPciResource	3140	Platform
				QNCInitDxe	5316	Silicon
				AcpiPlatform	4100	Platform
				AcpiTable	8850	Platform
				SimpleSmmIpl	6164	Generic
				SimplePiSmmCpu	6724	Platform
				IohInitDxe	1268	Silicon
				CombindedTerminalDxe	5332	Generic
				Legacy8259	2020	Generic
				TinyBds	2116	Platform
Summary				Summary		
Generic	0			Generic	77472	
Silicon	0			Silicon	24184	
Platform	9220			Platform	35146	

	Final (b	Percentage	Meaning
Generic	30989	48.46%	UEFI generic API
Silicon	9674	15.13%	Silicon Initialization
Platform	23278	36.41%	Platform Initialization
total	63941		

In addition to the fine-grain metrics in Table 7-1, Figure 7-16 provides a print message from the firmware itself, essentially showing that the entire firmware volume in the flash part occupies less that 64KB, or the smallest region of today's symmetrically blocked SPI NOR flash parts.

```
FV Space Information
EDKII_BOOT_STAGE1_IMAGE1 [99%Full] 65536 total, 65216 used, 320 free
```

Figure 7-16. *Message from the firmware on its size*

This section described how to reduce ROM flash size, especially as larger flash images lead to larger parts, with an impact to the bill of materials (BOM) and ultimate cost of the platform. Beyond cost savings, the other reason to have a smaller image in flash entails performance; copying a smaller binary from flash to DRAM consumes less of the boot time. To reach the smaller binary, the PEI core was omitted and purpose-built PCI Bus drivers and SMM infrastructure were employed. TinyQuark shows an extreme end of the spectrum, but even a generic platform could benefit from a subset of the techniques described.

RAM Footprint Optimization

In the preceding section, we reduced the amount of real estate consumed in the SPI NOR flash, thus allowing more space for the operating system and other data. But the SPI NOR isn't the only factor to impact the BOM. The other factor that impacts a board cost is volatile memory, or RAM usage. RAM is often noted as DRAM, too, for most systems.

As such, we did an analysis on RAM footprint on the 64K TinyQuark, and we realized that the image in Quark firmware is copied four times during boot, which can be avoided in practice.

1. DxeIpl, will prepare Decompressed FV to DxeCore. This is the first copy.

2. Once DxeCore finds a FV, it will copy FV into RAM. The reason is that DxeCore does not know if it is on flash or DRAM. This flash vs. DRAM independence only makes sense if other optimizations are in place, such as setting the MTRRs to ensure that the firmware volume in flash is cached. If not, there is a significant performance penalty in doing direct flash access for each code fetch.

3. Then in the Driver Dispatch phase, the DxeCore constructs a list for all FFS and SECTIONs there. The section stream for FFS is the third copy for each PE/COFF image.

4. Finally, when DxeCore starts loading the UEFI image, it allocates another memory and uses PeCoff library to load and relocate PE image. This is the fourth copy.

The detailed memory layout before optimization is shown in Figure 7-17.

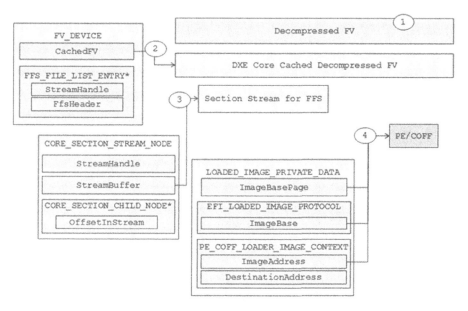

Figure 7-17. *Current DXE core*

Optimization

In order to optimize memory usage, the design technique entails avoiding additional buffer allocations. Instead, the optimization entails reuse of the old buffer as much as possible.

To begin, the Decompressed Fv buffer is the base. This buffer is then reused as the CachedFvcan be a pointer to the original Decompressed Fv buffer. Correspondingly, the section stream for FFS can still point to the original buffer.

Then for the PE/COFF image, we relocate all PE/COFF images at build time. A normal DXE driver or UEFI driver is rebased for its execution address in DRAM so that it can be run directly, without the need for fix-ups. The Dxe Runtime driver is special because it needs to reside in runtime memory (i.e., memory of type EFI_MEMORY_RUNTIME [UEFI]). So the DxeCore just needs to allocate Runtime Paged memory and do the relocation for the runtime driver.

The detailed memory layout after optimization of memory usage can be found in Figure 7-18.

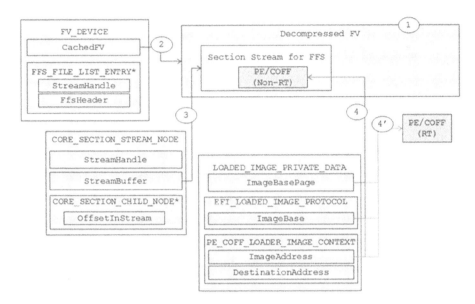

Figure 7-18. *Enhanced simplified DXE core*

Result of Memory Usage Optimization

Before optimization, the memory size used is 760K (624K allocated during boot + 136K decompressed FV). After optimization, the memory size used is 340K (204K allocated during boot + 136K for the decompressed FV).

In addition to the overall metric, a finer-grain accounting of memory usage can be found in Table 7-2.

Table 7-2. *TinyQuark Component RAM Size*

Component (MemType)	Size (K)	Page
1) Decompressed FV	136	34
ACPI Reclaim (9)	48	12
ACPI NVS (0xA)	8	2
Runtime Code (5)	16	4
Runtime Data (6)	12	3
Boot Code (3)	0	0
Boot Data (4)	120	30
-- Stack	32	8
2) Total allocated during boot	204	51
Total memory Used	340	85

This section describes the how to reduce the RAM footprint size. Historically, memory usage in the pre-OS has been considered "free" since the operating system will reclaim most of the resources, but for resource-constrained embedded systems, the DRAM size can be strictly limited. As such, optimizing the boot-time drivers to reuse buffers instead of allocating additional pages allows for an optimum memory footprint during the early phase of execution.

Conclusion

This Intel implementation of the EDK II is a demonstration showing the possibilities available using the scalable architecture of EDK II source code technology and the flexibility of the UEFI Specification. The 64K "TinyQuark" demonstrates the scalability of the EDK II architecture and how to create a UEFI-conformant firmware solution that has a very small flash size and can minimize DRAM usage. This allows for a slim boot load environment for a subsequent UEFI OS, or a slim execution environment for bare-metal execution that can suffice just using UEFI services.

CHAPTER 8

■ ■ ■

Putting It All Together

"The future depends on what you do today."

—Mahatma Gandhi

Embedded firmware has a lot of facets beyond the topics we could cover in this book. Our goals have been to provide enough knowledge and tools to get you started quickly when you deal with an embedded design based on Intel Architecture. The contents in this book may not have anticipated all the changes in the specifications and APIs that were under development when we were writing this book, but the framework of the book can represent the essence of the ideas and examples shown in the book. Regardless of whether you have read all the chapters in this book, you should have learned about the key ingredients mentioned in it: Intel FSP, coreboot, EDK II, Chromebook firmware, and the unique firmware features that embedded industries are looking for.

If we include automotive, industrial, medical, retail, smart home and building, avionics, military, print imaging, gaming, and other broad market sectors in the picture, there are many versatile design requirements—ranging from using completely open standards to using only proprietary closed specifications; and from performing multiple general-purpose functions to possessing only a single dedicated function; and from having a long life cycle that spans a couple of decades to a short life cycle that lasts just long enough until the next coolest thing comes out. Some sectors require a rigorous certification process to examine every line of code shipped in the unit to ensure safety and security, and it is costly if any line of the code needs to be updated from both a time and a monetary perspective. That explains why some crucial components, such as the recording technology embedded in the black box of an airplane, do not seem to evolve as quickly as other sectors are experiencing. Each vertical sector has to develop its own methodology to optimize its own firmware development approach to maximize its value.

From the perspective of firmware development methodology in these vertical sectors, developers can choose a high-touch design model using an army of developers to write every line of code, or choose to use a low-touch turnkey model with only a handful of staff to turn control knobs provided by a software utility that cranks out a firmware binary at the other end. It is the decision of the business development managers, not only based on the customers they are targeting, but also on a long-term view of the business.

From the ecosystem perspective, some vertical sectors have a large well-established ecosystem; some have only a small ecosystem with only a few players in it. The availability of the either high-touch or low-touch solutions may not be consistently available at the same time.

Therefore, the spectrum of supporting all these vertical sectors is wide open and full of variables. The thing we need to keep in mind is that there is no one-size-fits-all solution out there. Even within the same company selling the same source code to their customers, some customize the common source code and turn them into two or more products to serve different market sectors. For example, it is a very typical process for a RTOS vendor to provide one RTOS product for avionic customers to satisfy safety-related certification, and yet another RTOS product for military customers to use for security-specific certification. Safety standards—such as ARINC 653, ISO 26262, and IEC 61508—define critical requirements that are very different from security-focused standards that regulate data integrity and protection. The most important standard, MILS (Multiple Independent Levels of Security) architecture, defines four conceptual layers of separation in separation kernel and hardware, middleware services, trusted applications, and distributed communications. The RTOS or firmware vendors in these spaces frequently provide several products to serve the customers that need certain certification done. It is very costly and tedious to run through the line-by-line source code certification process; some said that it can be $50 or more per line to cover the certification. That is why sometimes a smaller code size is critical to some market sectors.

RTOS and Intel FSP

As discussed in Chapter 2, there were more than 120 active RTOS projects being developed for various applications and vertical markets at the time this book was written. Intel FSP can be a useful ingredient if these RTOS vendors are looking for a reliable way to support Intel Architecture.

Traditionally, RTOS products have been mainly designed for microcontrollers and low-end microprocessors rather than feature-rich microprocessors; therefore, there has not been a lot of demand to support Intel's Atom and Core products until recently, as IoT devices are becoming important and Intel pushes Quark SoC and other low-power products to the market. As Moore's Law continues to affect microprocessors' size and power reduction, it is more and more feasible to use high-performance Intel processors in IoT and embedded devices. Intel has put in a considerable amount of effort to make embedded-friendly products. As a result, more and more developers are looking for RTOS solutions to support Intel microprocessors; this is especially true since Quark SoC was introduced to the market in 2014.

There are currently two ways for a RTOS to work with a microprocessor that requires some silicon-level programming:

- An RTOS vendor can choose to put a firmware stack or bootloader underneath. Just like a PC, the target system can first boot a firmware stack, such as BIOS, and then boot the RTOS kernel using a GRUB or similar OS bootloader. This is a viable solution as long as boot speed and code size are not the critical design requirements. A size- and speed-optimized firmware stack can make the option more appealing too.

- RTOS can also have a native silicon initialization code built inside the RTOS stack. With Intel FSP, RTOS vendors can choose to boot natively by integrating Intel FSP into the RTOS boot code.

In 2012, Wind River Systems did a demo at the Intel Developer Forum to boot to a VxWorks kernel on an Intel platform in 350 milliseconds using native Intel silicon initialization code. Obviously, the demo was done without graphics and PCI devices. RTOS vendors often deal with a system without graphics and PCI devices; therefore, it is a viable solution for RTOS vendors to integrate a small silicon initialization code, such as Intel FSP, and add other components on top of it, if necessary.

Intel FSP and Open Source Philosophy

When the Intel® Quark™ SoC X1000 Series was announced, its EDK II source code was fully released as an open source project on Intel's web site. It is actually a source code without the involvement of Intel FSP. If an open source code base has all the source code available, do we still need Intel FSP? This is a good question, and the answer is: it depends. As we discussed in this chapter, many embedded firmware developers do not have the time or the expertise to look for components inside an open source codebase, and they are frequently looking for a way to quickly enable their own firmware stack to boot to their value-added features. Giving them all the source code that contains the silicon initialization code is useful, but it does not help if they need to quickly find the components inside the source code and port it over to another firmware stack. The EDK II source code uses a diver model for device initialization, and the documentation provided has comprehensive data to guide a developer to extract the source, if needed. Therefore, it is very feasible for a seasoned firmware engineer to find all the necessary source code to port it over to a different codebase.

Even though many hard-core open source advocates always love fully opened source code, as a compromise, many open source developers don't mind picking up some code that other people have written, tested, and verified, and then wrapped in a binary file. Because these developers don't have too much value to add to the code (serving a very specific hardware enablement mission), the code can be treated as part of the "hardware" as necessary. For example, a chip needing rigid and sensitive hardware initialization may not have too much room for innovation. Obviously, this is debatable; many developers can still add value by optimizing and reducing the code size if they want to. Silicon vendors may not have done the best job in optimizing the code to initialize their chips.

That said, the majority of the developers do not have as much time to look for firmware code in the open source repository to construct a firmware stack, or simply do not have the expertise to experiment open source projects.

Even though Intel FSP is far from a turnkey solution, it encapsulates enough silicon initialization code to provide the flexibility that people need to pick and choose a different firmware stack to work with. One day, Intel may decide to make all the components inside Intel FSP open source; but even if that happens, the concept of having all the silicon code in one place, such as Intel FSP, should still be the best option for people who do not want to invest time in figuring out how to initialize Intel's silicon.

Since the goal of Intel (and potentially other silicon vendors as well) is to simplify the silicon initialization work inside a firmware stack, it is predictable that there will be many types of firmware solutions available to the market from Intel to help developers—from completely open source to completely turnkey. Some solutions may require more work than the others; and some may be no work at all beyond turning a few knobs on a utility-based GUI user interface. Intel FSP will be a key component of all. As shown in Figure 8-1, the options can be an integration of FSP inside a host firmware, or a turnkey Boot ROM that allows customization by an OEM and ODM, or to the solution where the designers can pick and choose components from a set of prebuilt initialization modules.

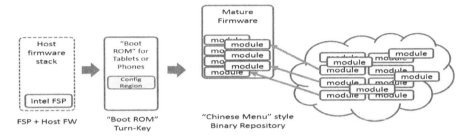

Figure 8-1. *Prebuilt silicon and hardware module options*

For example, in some markets that involve standardized platforms with limited hardware selections, "Boot ROM"-type turnkey solutions can be made available to simplify the development work. In some mature markets with many known hardware components, bus topology, and standards, there can even be a binary repository for constructing a complete ROM by using "Chinese Menu"-style of configuration tool recently introduced at the 2014 Intel Developer Forum.

Customization and Production of Intel FSP

Some advanced developers might have gone beyond just consuming Intel FSP in their firmware projects; they may be thinking about customizing and producing FSP for themselves or their downstream customers. For example, some IBVs and ISVs are in the business of creating firmware solutions—such as Board Support Package (BSP), services, and tools, and they might already have an intimate knowledge of Intel silicon. These vendors can consider producing a customized FSP to a special market that they want to serve. The other possibilities are when an OEM or ODM customizes Intel FSP for a particular family of their products, or when an OEM/ODM wants to distribute a FSP to its own vendors after customization. All these scenarios can be made possible in the future.

It Is a Community Effort After All

Regardless of whether you have read the book thoroughly, or picked and chose the chapters you were interested in, this book is written to help you develop a firmware stack for Intel Architecture quickly and effectively. During the process of developing Intel FSP, and while writing this book, we received a lot of good feedback and suggestions on how to make Intel FSP better, and how to make this book more useful. We are in an era of openness; as part of the process in embracing openness, we encourage you to contribute your constructive ideas as well.

The four authors and countless reviewers of this book are coming from different companies (Intel, Google, Sage, and Huawei). We are extremely proud that we are able to pull this book together to introduce to you the firmware solutions for different embedded and IoT devices. We know that there are still many stones unturned and many interesting topics not yet discussed related to this topic, but this is hopefully a good starting point to get everyone excited and involved.

Together, we can make embedded firmware easier and better, so that we can have more intelligent and reliable products; this is why we wrote this book. Regardless of whether the source code is UEFI-based or coreboot, or U-Boot, or RTOS, we hope that everyone can benefit from this book.

Now, go write some firmware.

APPENDIX A

Sample Boot Setting File (BSF)

```
/** @file

    Boot Setting File for Platform Configuration.

    This file contains an 'Intel Peripheral Driver' and is
    licensed for Intel CPUs and chipsets under the terms of your
    license agreement with Intel or your vendor.  This file must not
    be modified by end users or could render the generated boot loader
    inoperable.

    Copyright (c) 2014 Intel Corporation. All rights reserved
    This software and associated documentation (if any) is furnished
    under a license and may only be used or copied in accordance
    with the terms of the license. Except as permitted by such
    license, no part of this software or documentation may be
    reproduced, stored in a retrieval system, or transmitted in any
    form or by any means without the express written consent of
    Intel Corporation.

    This file is automatically generated. Please do NOT modify !!!

**/

GlobalDataDef
    SKUID = 0, "DEFAULT"
EndGlobalData
```

StructDef

```
    Find "VLV2UPDR"
        Skip 24 bytes
        $gPlatformFspPkgTokenSpaceGuid_PcdMrcInitTsegSize          2 bytes
        $_DEFAULT_ = 0x0001
        $gPlatformFspPkgTokenSpaceGuid_PcdMrcInitMmioSize          2 bytes
        $_DEFAULT_ = 0x0800
        $gPlatformFspPkgTokenSpaceGuid_PcdMrcInitSPDAddr1          1 bytes
        $_DEFAULT_ = 0xA0
        $gPlatformFspPkgTokenSpaceGuid_PcdMrcInitSPDAddr2          1 bytes
        $_DEFAULT_ = 0xA2
        $gPlatformFspPkgTokenSpaceGuid_PcdeMMCBootMode             1 bytes
        $_DEFAULT_ = 2
        $gPlatformFspPkgTokenSpaceGuid_PcdEnableSdio               1 bytes
        $_DEFAULT_ = 1
        $gPlatformFspPkgTokenSpaceGuid_PcdEnableSdcard             1 bytes
        $_DEFAULT_ = 1
        $gPlatformFspPkgTokenSpaceGuid_PcdEnableHsuart0            1 bytes
        $_DEFAULT_ = 0
        $gPlatformFspPkgTokenSpaceGuid_PcdEnableHsuart1            1 bytes
        $_DEFAULT_ = 1
        $gPlatformFspPkgTokenSpaceGuid_PcdEnableSpi                1 bytes
        $_DEFAULT_ = 1
        Skip 1 bytes
        $gPlatformFspPkgTokenSpaceGuid_PcdEnableSata               1 bytes
        $_DEFAULT_ = 1
        $gPlatformFspPkgTokenSpaceGuid_PcdSataMode                 1 bytes
        $_DEFAULT_ = 1
        $gPlatformFspPkgTokenSpaceGuid_PcdEnableAzalia             1 bytes
        $_DEFAULT_ = 0
        $gPlatformFspPkgTokenSpaceGuid_AzaliaConfigPtr             4 bytes
        $_DEFAULT_ = 0
        $gPlatformFspPkgTokenSpaceGuid_PcdEnableXhci               1 bytes
        $_DEFAULT_ = 1
        $gPlatformFspPkgTokenSpaceGuid_PcdEnableLpe                1 bytes
        $_DEFAULT_ = 1
        $gPlatformFspPkgTokenSpaceGuid_PcdLpssSioEnablePciMode     1 bytes
        $_DEFAULT_ = 1
        $gPlatformFspPkgTokenSpaceGuid_PcdEnableDma0               1 bytes
        $_DEFAULT_ = 1
        $gPlatformFspPkgTokenSpaceGuid_PcdEnableDma1               1 bytes
        $_DEFAULT_ = 1
        $gPlatformFspPkgTokenSpaceGuid_PcdEnableI2C0               1 bytes
        $_DEFAULT_ = 1
        $gPlatformFspPkgTokenSpaceGuid_PcdEnableI2C1               1 bytes
        $_DEFAULT_ = 1
```

```
$gPlatformFspPkgTokenSpaceGuid_PcdEnableI2C2              1 bytes
$_DEFAULT_ = 1
$gPlatformFspPkgTokenSpaceGuid_PcdEnableI2C3              1 bytes
$_DEFAULT_ = 1
$gPlatformFspPkgTokenSpaceGuid_PcdEnableI2C4              1 bytes
$_DEFAULT_ = 1
$gPlatformFspPkgTokenSpaceGuid_PcdEnableI2C5              1 bytes
$_DEFAULT_ = 1
$gPlatformFspPkgTokenSpaceGuid_PcdEnableI2C6              1 bytes
$_DEFAULT_ = 1
$gPlatformFspPkgTokenSpaceGuid_PcdEnablePwm0             1 bytes
$_DEFAULT_ = 1
$gPlatformFspPkgTokenSpaceGuid_PcdEnablePwm1             1 bytes
$_DEFAULT_ = 1
$gPlatformFspPkgTokenSpaceGuid_PcdEnableHsi               1 bytes
$_DEFAULT_ = 0
$gPlatformFspPkgTokenSpaceGuid_PcdIgdDvmt50PreAlloc       1 bytes
$_DEFAULT_ = 2
$gPlatformFspPkgTokenSpaceGuid_PcdApertureSize           1 bytes
$_DEFAULT_ = 2
$gPlatformFspPkgTokenSpaceGuid_PcdGttSize                1 bytes
$_DEFAULT_ = 2
Skip 5 bytes
$gPlatformFspPkgTokenSpaceGuid_PcdMrcDebugMsg            1 bytes
$_DEFAULT_ = 0
$gPlatformFspPkgTokenSpaceGuid_ISPEnable                 1 bytes
$_DEFAULT_ = 0
$gPlatformFspPkgTokenSpaceGuid_PcdSccEnablePciMode       1 bytes
$_DEFAULT_ = 1
$gPlatformFspPkgTokenSpaceGuid_IgdRenderStandby          1 bytes
$_DEFAULT_ = 0
$gPlatformFspPkgTokenSpaceGuid_TxeUmaEnable              1 bytes
$_DEFAULT_ = 0
$gPlatformFspPkgTokenSpaceGuid_PcdOsSelection            1 bytes
$_DEFAULT_ = 0x4
$gPlatformFspPkgTokenSpaceGuid_eMMC45DDR50Enabled        1 bytes
$_DEFAULT_ = 1
$gPlatformFspPkgTokenSpaceGuid_eMMC45HS200Enabled        1 bytes
$_DEFAULT_ = 0
$gPlatformFspPkgTokenSpaceGuid_eMMC45RetuneTimerValue    1 bytes
$_DEFAULT_ = 8
Skip 156 bytes
$gPlatformFspPkgTokenSpaceGuid_PcdEnableMemoryDown       1 bytes
$_DEFAULT_ = 0x00
$gPlatformFspPkgTokenSpaceGuid_PcdDRAMSpeed              1 bytes
$_DEFAULT_ = 0x02
```

```
            $gPlatformFspPkgTokenSpaceGuid_PcdDRAMType              1 bytes
            $_DEFAULT_ = 0x01
            $gPlatformFspPkgTokenSpaceGuid_PcdDIMM0Enable           1 bytes
            $_DEFAULT_ = 0x01
            $gPlatformFspPkgTokenSpaceGuid_PcdDIMM1Enable           1 bytes
            $_DEFAULT_ = 0x00
            $gPlatformFspPkgTokenSpaceGuid_PcdDIMMDWidth            1 bytes
            $_DEFAULT_ = 0x00
            $gPlatformFspPkgTokenSpaceGuid_PcdDIMMDensity           1 bytes
            $_DEFAULT_ = 0x01
            $gPlatformFspPkgTokenSpaceGuid_PcdDIMMBusWidth          1 bytes
            $_DEFAULT_ = 0x03
            $gPlatformFspPkgTokenSpaceGuid_PcdDIMMSides             1 bytes
            $_DEFAULT_ = 0x00
            $gPlatformFspPkgTokenSpaceGuid_PcdDIMMtCL               1 bytes
            $_DEFAULT_ = 0x09
            $gPlatformFspPkgTokenSpaceGuid_PcdDIMMtRPtRCD           1 bytes
            $_DEFAULT_ = 0x09
            $gPlatformFspPkgTokenSpaceGuid_PcdDIMMtWR               1 bytes
            $_DEFAULT_ = 0x0A
            $gPlatformFspPkgTokenSpaceGuid_PcdDIMMtWTR              1 bytes
            $_DEFAULT_ = 0x05
            $gPlatformFspPkgTokenSpaceGuid_PcdDIMMtRRD              1 bytes
            $_DEFAULT_ = 0x04
            $gPlatformFspPkgTokenSpaceGuid_PcdDIMMtRTP              1 bytes
            $_DEFAULT_ = 0x05
            $gPlatformFspPkgTokenSpaceGuid_PcdDIMMtFAW              1 bytes
            $_DEFAULT_ = 0x14

    Find "VLYVIEW1"
            $gPlatformFspPkgTokenSpaceGuid_PcdImageRevision               4
            bytes     $_DEFAULT_ = 0x00000303
            Skip 24 bytes
            $gPlatformFspPkgTokenSpaceGuid_PcdPlatformType                1
            bytes     $_DEFAULT_ = 2
            $gPlatformFspPkgTokenSpaceGuid_PcdEnableSecureBoot            1
            bytes     $_DEFAULT_ = 2

EndStruct

List &EN_DIS
    Selection 0x1 , "Enabled"
    Selection 0x0 , "Disabled"
EndList
```

```
List &gPlatformFspPkgTokenSpaceGuid_PcdDIMMSides
    Selection 0x0 , "1 Ranks"
    Selection 0x1 , "2 Ranks"
EndList

List &gPlatformFspPkgTokenSpaceGuid_PcdIgdDvmt50PreAlloc
    Selection 0x01 , "32 MB"
    Selection 0x02 , "64 MB"
    Selection 0x03 , "96 MB"
    Selection 0x04 , "128 MB"
    Selection 0x05 , "160 MB"
    Selection 0x06 , "192 MB"
    Selection 0x07 , "224 MB"
    Selection 0x08 , "256 MB"
    Selection 0x09 , "288 MB"
    Selection 0x0A , "320 MB"
    Selection 0x0B , "352 MB"
    Selection 0x0C , "384 MB"
    Selection 0x0D , "416 MB"
    Selection 0x0E , "448 MB"
    Selection 0x0F , "480 MB"
    Selection 0x10 , "512 MB"
EndList

List &gPlatformFspPkgTokenSpaceGuid_PcdOsSelection
    Selection 0x1 , "Android"
    Selection 0x4 , "Linux OS"
EndList

List &gPlatformFspPkgTokenSpaceGuid_PcdDIMMDensity
    Selection 0x0 , "1 Gbit"
    Selection 0x1 , "2 Gbit"
    Selection 0x2 , "4 Gbit"
    Selection 0x3 , "8 Gbit"
EndList

List &gPlatformFspPkgTokenSpaceGuid_PcdEnableLpe
    Selection 0x2 , "ACPI Mode"
    Selection 0x1 , "PCI Mode"
    Selection 0x0 , "Disabled"
EndList

List &gPlatformFspPkgTokenSpaceGuid_PcdDRAMType
    Selection 0x0 , "DDR3"
    Selection 0x1 , "DDR3L"
    Selection 0x2 , "DDR3ECC"
    Selection 0x4 , "LPDDR2"
```

```
    Selection 0x5 , "LPDDR3"
    Selection 0x6 , "DDR4"
EndList

List &gPlatformFspPkgTokenSpaceGuid_PcdMrcInitTsegSize
    Selection 0x01 , "1 MB"
    Selection 0x02 , "2 MB"
    Selection 0x04 , "4 MB"
    Selection 0x08 , "8 MB"
EndList

List &gPlatformFspPkgTokenSpaceGuid_PcdPlatformType
    Selection 0x2 , "BayleyBay Platform Type"
    Selection 0x3 , "BakerSport Platform (ECC) Type"
EndList

List &gPlatformFspPkgTokenSpaceGuid_PcdMrcInitMmioSize
    Selection 0x400 , "1.0 GB"
    Selection 0x600 , "1.5 GB"
    Selection 0x800 , "2.0 GB"
EndList

List &gPlatformFspPkgTokenSpaceGuid_PcdGttSize
    Selection 0x1 , "1 MB"
    Selection 0x2 , "2 MB"
EndList

List &gPlatformFspPkgTokenSpaceGuid_PcdSataMode
    Selection 1 , "AHCI"
    Selection 0 , "IDE"
EndList

List &gPlatformFspPkgTokenSpaceGuid_PcdDIMMBusWidth
    Selection 0x0 , "8 bits"
    Selection 0x1 , "16 bits"
    Selection 0x2 , "32 bits"
    Selection 0x3 , "64 bits"
EndList

List &gPlatformFspPkgTokenSpaceGuid_PcdEnableSecureBoot
    Selection 0 , "Disabled"
    Selection 1 , "Enabled"
    Selection 2 , "Auto"
EndList
```

```
List &gPlatformFspPkgTokenSpaceGuid_PcdApertureSize
    Selection 0x1 , "128 MB"
    Selection 0x2 , "256 MB"
    Selection 0x3 , "512 MB"
EndList

List &gPlatformFspPkgTokenSpaceGuid_PcdDRAMSpeed
    Selection 0x0 , "800 MT/s"
    Selection 0x1 , "1066 MT/s"
    Selection 0x2 , "1333 MT/s"
    Selection 0x3 , "1600 MT/s"
EndList

List &gPlatformFspPkgTokenSpaceGuid_PcdDIMMDWidth
    Selection 0x0 , "x8"
    Selection 0x1 , "x16"
    Selection 0x2 , "x32"
EndList

List &gPlatformFspPkgTokenSpaceGuid_PcdeMMCBootMode
    Selection 0x0 , "Disabled"
    Selection 0x1 , "Auto"
    Selection 0x2 , "eMMC 4.1"
    Selection 0x3 , "eMMC 4.5"
EndList

BeginInfoBlock
    PPVer       "1.0"
    Description "BayTrail platform"
EndInfoBlock

Page "Platform"
    Combo $gPlatformFspPkgTokenSpaceGuid_PcdPlatformType, "Platform Type",
    &gPlatformFspPkgTokenSpaceGuid_PcdPlatformType,
        Help "Select Platform Type."
    Combo $gPlatformFspPkgTokenSpaceGuid_PcdEnableSecureBoot, "Enable Secure
    Boot", &gPlatformFspPkgTokenSpaceGuid_PcdEnableSecureBoot,
        Help "Enable/disable secure boot. Auto by default."
    Combo $gPlatformFspPkgTokenSpaceGuid_PcdOsSelection, "OS Selection",
    &gPlatformFspPkgTokenSpaceGuid_PcdOsSelection,
        Help "Select Operating System"
EndPage

Page "Memory Down"
    Combo $gPlatformFspPkgTokenSpaceGuid_PcdEnableMemoryDown, "Enable Memory
    Down", &EN_DIS,
        Help "Enable = Memory Down, Disable = DIMM"
```

```
    Combo $gPlatformFspPkgTokenSpaceGuid_PcdDRAMSpeed, "DRAM Speed",
    &gPlatformFspPkgTokenSpaceGuid_PcdDRAMSpeed,
        Help "DRAM Speed"
    Combo $gPlatformFspPkgTokenSpaceGuid_PcdDRAMType, "DRAM Type",
    &gPlatformFspPkgTokenSpaceGuid_PcdDRAMType,
        Help "DRAM Type"
    Combo $gPlatformFspPkgTokenSpaceGuid_PcdDIMM0Enable, "DIMM 0 Enable",
    &EN_DIS,
        Help "Please populate DIMM slot 0 if only one DIMM is supported."
    Combo $gPlatformFspPkgTokenSpaceGuid_PcdDIMM1Enable, "DIMM 1 Enable",
    &EN_DIS,
        Help "Please populate DIMM slot 1 if only one DIMM is supported."
    Combo $gPlatformFspPkgTokenSpaceGuid_PcdDIMMDWidth, "DIMM_DWidth",
    &gPlatformFspPkgTokenSpaceGuid_PcdDIMMDWidth,
        Help "DRAM device data width."
    Combo $gPlatformFspPkgTokenSpaceGuid_PcdDIMMDensity, "DIMM_Density",
    &gPlatformFspPkgTokenSpaceGuid_PcdDIMMDensity,
        Help "DRAM device data density."
    Combo $gPlatformFspPkgTokenSpaceGuid_PcdDIMMBusWidth, "DIMM_BusWidth",
    &gPlatformFspPkgTokenSpaceGuid_PcdDIMMBusWidth,
        Help "DIMM Bus Width."
    Combo $gPlatformFspPkgTokenSpaceGuid_PcdDIMMSides, "DIMM_Sides",
    &gPlatformFspPkgTokenSpaceGuid_PcdDIMMSides,
        Help "Ranks Per DIMM. "
    EditNum $gPlatformFspPkgTokenSpaceGuid_PcdDIMMtCL, "tCL", DEC,
        Help "tCL"
            "Valid range: 1 ~ 255"
    EditNum $gPlatformFspPkgTokenSpaceGuid_PcdDIMMtRPtRCD, "tRP_tRCD", DEC,
        Help "tRP and tRCD in DRAM clk - 5:12.5ns, 6:15ns, etc."
            "Valid range: 1 ~ 255"
    EditNum $gPlatformFspPkgTokenSpaceGuid_PcdDIMMtWR, "tWR", DEC,
        Help "tWR in DRAM clk"
            "Valid range: 1 ~ 255"
    EditNum $gPlatformFspPkgTokenSpaceGuid_PcdDIMMtWTR, "tWTR", DEC,
        Help "tWTR in DRAM clk"
            "Valid range: 1 ~ 255"
    EditNum $gPlatformFspPkgTokenSpaceGuid_PcdDIMMtRRD, "tRRD", DEC,
        Help "tRRD in DRAM clk"
            "Valid range: 1 ~ 255"
    EditNum $gPlatformFspPkgTokenSpaceGuid_PcdDIMMtRTP, "tRTP", DEC,
        Help "tRTP in DRAM clk"
            "Valid range: 1 ~ 255"
    EditNum $gPlatformFspPkgTokenSpaceGuid_PcdDIMMtFAW, "tFAW", DEC,
        Help "tFAW in DRAM clk"
            "Valid range: 1 ~ 255"
EndPage
```

```
Page "South Complex"
    Combo $gPlatformFspPkgTokenSpaceGuid_PcdeMMCBootMode, "eMMC Boot Mode",
    &gPlatformFspPkgTokenSpaceGuid_PcdeMMCBootMode,
        Help "Select EMMC Mode."
    Combo $gPlatformFspPkgTokenSpaceGuid_PcdEnableSdio, "Enable SDIO",
    &EN_DIS,
        Help "Enable/disable SDIO."
    Combo $gPlatformFspPkgTokenSpaceGuid_PcdEnableSdcard, "Enable SD Card",
    &EN_DIS,
        Help "Enable/disable SD Card."
    Combo $gPlatformFspPkgTokenSpaceGuid_PcdEnableHsuart0, "Enable HSUART0",
    &EN_DIS,
        Help "Enable/disable HSUART0."
    Combo $gPlatformFspPkgTokenSpaceGuid_PcdEnableHsuart1, "Enable HSUART1",
    &EN_DIS,
        Help "Enable/disable HSUART1."
    Combo $gPlatformFspPkgTokenSpaceGuid_PcdEnableSpi, "Enable SPI",
    &EN_DIS,
        Help "Enable/disable SPI."
    Combo $gPlatformFspPkgTokenSpaceGuid_PcdEnableSata, "Enable SATA",
    &EN_DIS,
        Help "Enable/disable SATA controller."
    Combo $gPlatformFspPkgTokenSpaceGuid_PcdSataMode, "SATA Mode",
    &gPlatformFspPkgTokenSpaceGuid_PcdSataMode,
        Help "Select SATA controller working mode."
    Combo $gPlatformFspPkgTokenSpaceGuid_PcdEnableAzalia, "Enable Azalia",
    &EN_DIS,
        Help "Enable/disable Azalia controller."
    EditNum $gPlatformFspPkgTokenSpaceGuid_AzaliaConfigPtr, "Azalia
    Configuration Pointer", HEX,
        Help "Address of the Azalia Configuration Data."
            "Valid range: 0x00 ~ 0xFFFFFFFF"
    Combo $gPlatformFspPkgTokenSpaceGuid_PcdEnableXhci, "Enable XHCI",
    &EN_DIS,
        Help "Enable/disable XHCI controller."
    Combo $gPlatformFspPkgTokenSpaceGuid_PcdEnableLpe, "Enable LPE",
    &gPlatformFspPkgTokenSpaceGuid_PcdEnableLpe,
        Help "Choose LPE Mode."
    Combo $gPlatformFspPkgTokenSpaceGuid_PcdLpssSioEnablePciMode, "Enable
    PCI mode for LPSS SIO devices", &EN_DIS,
        Help "Enable PCI Mode for LPSS SIO devices. If disabled, LPSS SIO
        devices will run in ACPI mode."
    Combo $gPlatformFspPkgTokenSpaceGuid_PcdEnableDma0, "Enable DMA0",
    &EN_DIS,
        Help "Enable/disable DMA0."
    Combo $gPlatformFspPkgTokenSpaceGuid_PcdEnableDma1, "Enable DMA1",
    &EN_DIS,
        Help "Enable/disable DMA1."
```

187

```
    Combo $gPlatformFspPkgTokenSpaceGuid_PcdEnableI2C0, "Enable I2C0",
    &EN_DIS,
        Help "Enable/disable I2C0."
    Combo $gPlatformFspPkgTokenSpaceGuid_PcdEnableI2C1, "Enable I2C1",
    &EN_DIS,
        Help "Enable/disable I2C1."
    Combo $gPlatformFspPkgTokenSpaceGuid_PcdEnableI2C2, "Enable I2C2",
    &EN_DIS,
        Help "Enable/disable I2C2."
    Combo $gPlatformFspPkgTokenSpaceGuid_PcdEnableI2C3, "Enable I2C3",
    &EN_DIS,
        Help "Enable/disable I2C3."
    Combo $gPlatformFspPkgTokenSpaceGuid_PcdEnableI2C4, "Enable I2C4", &EN_DIS,
        Help "Enable/disable I2C4."
    Combo $gPlatformFspPkgTokenSpaceGuid_PcdEnableI2C5, "Enable I2C5",
    &EN_DIS,
        Help "Enable/disable I2C5."
    Combo $gPlatformFspPkgTokenSpaceGuid_PcdEnableI2C6, "Enable I2C6",
    &EN_DIS,
        Help "Enable/disable I2C6."
    Combo $gPlatformFspPkgTokenSpaceGuid_PcdEnablePwm0, "Enable PWM0",
    &EN_DIS,
        Help "Enable/disable PWM0."
    Combo $gPlatformFspPkgTokenSpaceGuid_PcdEnablePwm1, "Enable PWM1", &EN_DIS,
        Help "Enable/disable PWM1."
    Combo $gPlatformFspPkgTokenSpaceGuid_PcdEnableHsi, "Enable HSI", &EN_DIS,
        Help "Enable/disable HSI."
    Combo $gPlatformFspPkgTokenSpaceGuid_ISPEnable, "Enable ISP", &EN_DIS,
        Help "Enable/disable ISP."
    Combo $gPlatformFspPkgTokenSpaceGuid_PcdSccEnablePciMode, "Enable PCI
    mode for SCC devices", &EN_DIS,
        Help "Enable PCI Mode for SCC devices. If disabled, SCC devices will
        run in ACPI mode."
    Combo $gPlatformFspPkgTokenSpaceGuid_eMMC45DDR50Enabled, "eMMC45 DDR50",
    &EN_DIS,
        Help "Enable eMMC45 DDR50"
    Combo $gPlatformFspPkgTokenSpaceGuid_eMMC45HS200Enabled, "eMMC45 HS200",
    &EN_DIS,
        Help "Enable eMMC45 HS200"
    EditNum $gPlatformFspPkgTokenSpaceGuid_eMMC45RetuneTimerValue, "eMMC45
    Retune Timer Value", DEC,
        Help "Select Timer Value"
            "Valid range: 0 ~ 15"
EndPage
```

```
Page "North Complex"
    Combo $gPlatformFspPkgTokenSpaceGuid_PcdMrcInitTsegSize, "Tseg Size",
    &gPlatformFspPkgTokenSpaceGuid_PcdMrcInitTsegSize,
        Help "Size of SMRAM memory reserved."
    Combo $gPlatformFspPkgTokenSpaceGuid_PcdMrcInitMmioSize, "MMIO Size",
    &gPlatformFspPkgTokenSpaceGuid_PcdMrcInitMmioSize,
        Help "Size of memory address space reserved for MMIO (Memory
        Mapped I/O)."
    EditNum $gPlatformFspPkgTokenSpaceGuid_PcdMrcInitSPDAddr1, "DIMM 0 SPD
    SMBus Address", HEX,
        Help "SPD Address of DIMM."
            "Valid range: 0x00 ~ 0xFF"
    EditNum $gPlatformFspPkgTokenSpaceGuid_PcdMrcInitSPDAddr2, "DIMM 1 SPD
    SMBus Address", HEX,
        Help "SPD Address of DIMM."
            "Valid range: 0x00 ~ 0xFF"
    Combo $gPlatformFspPkgTokenSpaceGuid_TxeUmaEnable, "Enable TXE UMA",
    &EN_DIS,
        Help "Enable/disable Unified Memory Reservation for TXE engine."
    Combo $gPlatformFspPkgTokenSpaceGuid_PcdMrcDebugMsg, "MRC RMT Message
    Display", &EN_DIS,
        Help "Enable/disable MRC RMT Message Display."
    Combo $gPlatformFspPkgTokenSpaceGuid_PcdIgdDvmt50PreAlloc, "Internal
    Graphics Pre-allocated Memory", &gPlatformFspPkgTokenSpaceGuid_
    PcdIgdDvmt50PreAlloc,
        Help "Size of memory preallocated for internal graphics"
    Combo $gPlatformFspPkgTokenSpaceGuid_PcdApertureSize, "Aperture Size",
    &gPlatformFspPkgTokenSpaceGuid_PcdApertureSize,
        Help "Select the Aperture Size."
    Combo $gPlatformFspPkgTokenSpaceGuid_PcdGttSize, "GTT Size",
    &gPlatformFspPkgTokenSpaceGuid_PcdGttSize,
        Help "Select the GTT Size."
    Combo $gPlatformFspPkgTokenSpaceGuid_IgdRenderStandby, "Enable Render
    Standby", &EN_DIS,
        Help "Enable/disable Integrated Graphics Render Standby."
EndPage
```

Index

■ F

■ G

■ H

Printed in the United States
By Bookmasters